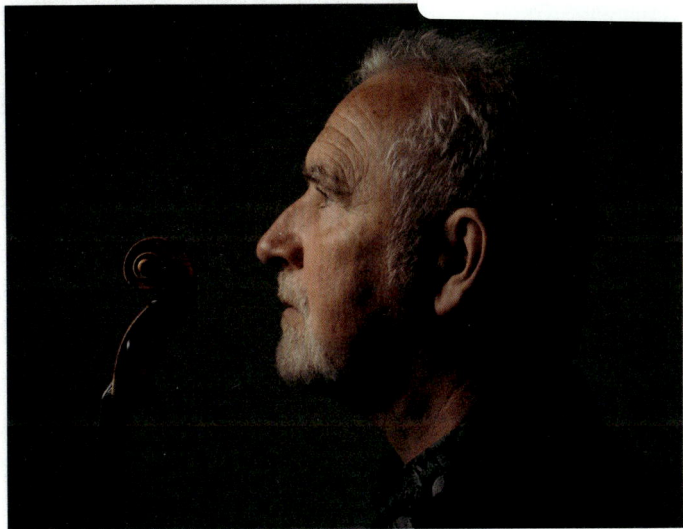

Paul Cassidy was born in Derry in 1959. He has spent his entire working life with the Brodsky Quartet. Together they have played over 3000 concerts in more than 60 countries and made in excess of 70 recordings. Paul is a prolific arranger. In addition to his countless works for strings, he has collaborated with Elvis Costello, Björk, Sting and many other eminent composers. Examples of these can be found on Brodsky albums such as Petits Fours, Moodswings, Rocking Horse Road, The Juliet Letters and Björk's Family Tree.

Got Beethoven is Paul's second book and follows on from *"Get Beethoven!"* – the rip-roaring story of his life before Brodsky. *Got Beethoven* was written to celebrate the quartet's 50th anniversary in 2022.

He lives in London with his wife, Jacqueline (cellist and founder member of the Brodsky Quartet) and their two daughters, Holly and Celia.

For further information, including a selection of photographs to accompany both books, please visit:

www.paulcassidy.org

Reactions to "Get Beethoven!"

Did music save Paul Cassidy's life? Possibly. His memoir is hilarious, sometimes tragic, and occasionally terrifying. It's a miracle he lived to tell the tales, and also surprising that the impetuous youth who so vividly leaps out of these pages should have turned out to be a musician of rare wisdom and poise.

Andrew Ford, ABC Music Show

Paul Cassidy invites us into the early experiences that shaped his life as a world-class musician. A wildly funny, searingly honest, and beautifully told memoir.

Sara Mohr-Pietsch (BBC)

This memoir is astonishing! Heartfelt and absolutely hilarious. Get This!

L. Tunney

A real page-turner. My wife and I were fighting over it... neither of us wanting to put it down. It reads more like a gripping novel than a memoir. It's laugh-out-loud funny whilst being informative, sad and inspiring.

Bill Drewe

Had me gripped from the very beginning.
Had me in tears one minute and laughing out loud the next.

J Cook

COULD NOT PUT THIS BOOK DOWN!! It's like a juicier, more complex Billy Elliot!

Hally Brown

Derry Girls meets *Composer of the Week* in this candid, funny, inspiring story. Give Netflix and Prime a rest for a few hours - you'll not regret the investment.

Dermot McCauley

This book got me hooked because of its passion, openness and clarity. It shows so clearly what a little soul needs for escape. It should be read at every school in Northern Ireland as it is a history book kids won't reject. Hope you will find time to read the book in public. The public should hear your words!

K. Kobermann

Got Beethoven

My first 40 years in the Brodsky Quartet

Paul Cassidy

Matador
Unit E2 Airfield Business Park,
Harrison Road, Market Harborough,
Leicestershire. LE16 7WB
Tel: 0116 2792299
Email: books@troubador.co.uk
Web: www.troubador.co.uk/matador
Twitter: @matadorbooks

ISBN 978 1803130 590

British Library Cataloguing in Publication Data.
A catalogue record for this book is available from the British Library.

Printed and bound in Great Britain by 4edge Limited
Typeset in 11pt Sabon by Troubador Publishing Ltd, Leicester, UK

Matador is an imprint of Troubador Publishing Ltd

*I would like to dedicate this book to my remarkable
colleagues – Jacqueline Thomas and Ian Belton.*

*To think about starting a string quartet at the age of ten,
is extraordinary – to have retained that resolve, that passion,
those feverishly high standards for fifty years and still be looking
to improve, is humbling.I salute you both and thank you for the
ride which, now together with Krysia, we're still happily taking.*

*It's also for my precious girls, Holly and Celia –
a small memento of the crazy life they were born into.*

Contents

'Went abroad,
came back a Brod.'

"Middlesbrough – where even is Middlesbrough?"

Seemingly content with my geographical ignorance, this was a question I often asked myself during my time at the Royal College of Music. In truth, it wasn't so much a case of *where* this place was, more a question of why so many of my fellow musicians came from there.

The conundrum was solved in my final term at 'the college' when, in May 1982, I received a dream phone call from the Brodsky Quartet asking me if I would be interested in auditioning for the recently vacated viola position. Though I'd only ever heard them play once, at a Lutoslawski Symposium up in Aldeburgh, I had become increasingly aware of their growing reputation and was hugely excited at the prospect of playing with them. Where I had fallen in love with classical music aged fourteen, developed a passion for chamber music at college – and from the moment I first played in a string quartet, aged seventeen, had become totally smitten with that form of music-making – these youthful veterans had all been bitten by the classical bug in infancy and had already been playing in *this* quartet since they were ten years old.

It transpired that Michael Thomas, Ian Belton, Alexander Robertson and Jacqueline Thomas, the original four members of the quartet, all hailed from this aforementioned formidable stable. It has since become apparent that these kids were unwittingly a part of an exceptional moment in musical education in the north-east of England, something akin to the modern day El Sistema, the extraordinary results of which were plain to see. (Some other examples among my immediate peers were

William Bruce, the Dales (Caroline, Miranda and Susan), John Kane, the Kaznovskis (Jan and Michal), Cathy Lord, Susan Monks, Tony Robson, Ursula Smith, Alison Wells... I could go on, but you get the picture. It wasn't simply that they were numerous, either; these were all high-class, impressively capable musicians.)

When the local youth orchestra's Friday evening rehearsal was over, these four youngsters, still hungry for more playing, would retire to the Thomas family home (Mike and Jacky are brother and sister) and play quartets late into the night, often in the garage out of respect for their long-suffering siblings.

It's tough enough working so intensely as supposed adults; one can barely imagine what madness must have been unleashed in those teenage scrums. Fisticuffs; people forcibly made to stay when things had become too much to bear; brutal nicknames employed without a care for fragile dispositions; all weaknesses tracked down, exposed and highlighted by the bloodthirsty mob. With no guidance whatsoever, these children endured the full impact of pubescent nastiness at unnaturally close quarters.

Alongside these undeniable personal challenges, however, it must have been exhilarating to be a part of that impenetrable block of energy. Legendary stories abound of those early days... A rehearsal of Bartok's 5th Quartet, when Ian reached for the score only to find that Jacky's precious four-legged 'best friend', Conkey, had eaten it.

They had no concept of what might be appropriate repertoire for their formative years. Janacek, Bartok, late Beethoven and Schubert Quartets were ever present on those bent wire stands. If things got too challenging, rather than admit defeat, they would stick on a recording of the offending work and feverishly play along.

There's that wonderful account of how, being so taken with a performance of Shostakovich's 11th Quartet on the radio but unable to get the music, they set about writing out the parts by ear. I've seen those parts and I can tell you, they aren't far from the original.

My audition consisted of two contrasting but equally intense weekends; an orgy of playing together up in Manchester, followed by a highly structured set of rehearsals in London on two carefully selected works none of us knew. Truth be known, I immediately loved this group and they seemed to instantly take to me. We suited each other on almost every level. However, foolhardy we were not. We all knew what a momentous decision lay before us. But that said, it's also important in such situations not to underplay the chemistry and lose the momentum vital for any relationship. Having allowed the dust to settle and got some requisite formalities out of the way, we embraced the inevitable and joined forces against the world. Strange terminology, I know, but that's how it felt then and still feels today. Though we lived and breathed classical music with every fibre of our young bodies, the classical music profession was never an easy fit for us Northern types. Nevertheless, one way or another, these square pegs would have to find a way of surviving in a world full of round holes.

This was the band I was joining. I was edging into a complex, four-way relationship, forged like Teesside steel in the wilds of anarchic immaturity. When most youngsters their age were reenacting cowboys and indians, these four were rehearsing chords and intonation; while their peers were busy playing marbles, they were playing Mozart. They were a force to be reckoned with from the outset, single-minded and ruthless. They entered college as a foursome, leaving Jacky no choice but to leave school prematurely, gain early entry to the college herself, and take her A levels from a distance, on her own.

Notwithstanding these not inconsiderable pressures, she took all these things in her determined stride and, unsurprisingly if you know the girl, got straight As.

These prodigious young adults had already been playing in this group for five years before I had even heard of a string quartet, fully ten years by the time we first met, but I had packed a lifetime's study into five short years. They had exceptional experience for a student group taking their first steps in the big bad world, but I had unparalleled energy devoid of cynicism. They had not found it easy filling Alex's shoes – the snag list was lengthy – but I was equally demanding. I did not suffer fools and would never have settled for anything less than absolute brilliance and indefatigable commitment. Life is so random, such a jigsaw of coincidences. It's a hackneyed analogy that a quartet is like a marriage; for two people to find each other is remarkable, but four...!

The quartet started out as the Cleveland Quartet, their home town of Middlesbrough being, at that time, in the county of Cleveland. But a chance meeting with the already firmly established Cleveland Quartet of Ohio during a study period at the Dartington Festival left them in no doubt that a new name had to be found. Pondering this dilemma at a meeting in Eleanor Warren's office (she was the then-Head of Strings at the Royal Northern College of Music-where they were studying), she drew their attention to the imposing portrait hanging on the wall above her desk. It was in the likeness of a certain Adolph Brodsky. He had been a particularly impressive musical figure. Having fled Russia during the Revolution he had settled in Manchester, where Barbirolli had invited him to become concertmaster of the Hallé Orchestra. He went on to become the first principal of the RNCM and even had his own quartet, called the Brodsky Quartet. He had a successful career as a soloist, becoming the dedicatee of the Tchaikovsky Concerto, a composer he counted among his closest friends, along with the likes of Grieg, Brahms and Elgar. Not only did he premiere the Tchaikovsky Concerto, but the Brodsky Quartet premiered Tchaikovsky's three quartets. Elgar dedicated his solitary work in the medium to the Brodsky Quartet.

This guy seemed to be tailor-made for the fledgling group's needs. What a pedigree. A household name in the north of England but with an international career. A quartet member who was also a high-flying soloist. A hugely respected personage steeped in the traditions of string playing, but out there, befriending composers at the very forefront of contemporary music. Add to this the powerful brevity of the name and the tantalising fact that it was foreign, a plus point not to be underestimated in the warped world of classical music, and there was no decision to be made. Cleveland became Brodsky there and then. The rest, as they say, is history.

The '80s

'Competitions'

Three of us had come to the end of our studies but because Jacky was effectively a year behind, the decision to continue basing ourselves in Manchester was therefore an easy one – at least until she had completed her course. We came to an arrangement with the college whereby, in return for a couple of concerts and some teaching, we would get a room to work in. A workspace is a tremendously valuable commodity for any group and the stunning Hermitage Room in Hartley Hall afforded us a great start in our working lives.

I say 'our working lives', but when I joined this impressive ensemble, life was already beginning to place a heavy burden on its young shoulders. Alex's departure had not gone unnoticed by promoters, many of whom were reluctant to book the new line-up till they were sure of what they were getting. This resulted in their hitherto impressive diary becoming alarmingly empty. Despite this worrying fact, or perhaps because of it, we worked morning, noon and night, and then some. Though sensitive to my newcomer status, I naturally became very proactive and my fresh-faced enthusiasm seemed to inspire a collective drive to address this lamentable situation. The approach was simple but effective: play well! Well, it's true, we did try to play well, but we also wrote a personal letter to every single promoter the quartet had ever played for, enclosing our nice new publicity shots and updated biography, and as a result, by the end of our first year together we had played forty concerts instead of three.

We started our concert career, quite fittingly, in Middlesbrough and Derry, but in that first season also played in Newcastle, Manchester, Liverpool, Bristol and London, to name but a few. These outings were all in the UK however, and we had our sights on global domination. Realising the need for something to affect a change, something dramatic that would get our name out there on the international stage, we reluctantly took the decision to return to the cut-throat world of competitions. Though they had done reasonably well in earlier forays, taking the Menuhin Prize at the first Portsmouth Competition (despite their naive and extraordinary decision in the wardrobe department – to wear matching brown shirts in front of a largely Jewish jury) and both the Janacek Medal and Audience Prize in Evian, there had been a long hiatus in this area. We agreed to have a final go at winning one of these things.

No sooner had we turned our minds to this than we got an enquiry from the Independent Broadcasting Association asking if we would represent them at the upcoming European Broadcasting Union String Quartet Competition, to be held in Cambridge the following spring. Whilst this appeared heaven-sent at that moment, nothing ever seemed to be straightforward for us. We soon found out that the BBC would be hosting the event and now we would be showing up representing their national rivals. Whereas the IBA broadcasted virtually no classical music, the BBC had a whole station devoted to it. We hoped not to make too many enemies.

Our IBA journey turned out to be a colourful one. We visited practically every independent radio station in the country, meeting people not wholly immersed in the classical world. We would be bringing our music to an audience that may never even have heard of a string quartet.

Jacky made her parents promise not to come to Cambridge; neither Ian's nor mine entered the equation. Our preparation had been like a military exercise and we wanted no distractions if we were to be successful in our mission. Moments before our opening performance, we were lining up in the foyer of the West Road Concert Hall when Jacky decided she needed a quick visit to the loo. On entering the facility, she noticed an oddly familiar stranger furtively messing with her oversized scarf and then spending an inordinately long time at the hand dryer.

"I do not believe it… Mam! I thought you promised to leave us alone. We asked you specifically to stay away. This is important for us, you know!" cried Jacky, genuinely perturbed.

"I'm sorry, Jack, we just couldn't do it. We won't bother you, honestly," rallied Mam, pathetically.

It was inevitable that Tom and Francine would ignore our pleas and invade our precious retreat. They were both huge music lovers and having witnessed its birth, quite literally in part, had come to view the quartet as their very own baby. They did bother us, in fact. Through nothing more than well-meaning generosity on their part, we found ourselves endlessly eating and socialising with them when we would rather have been quiet and solitary; leaking precious energy, minds wandering instead of focusing. Despite these distractions, the week went well and we ended up winning not only first prize, but every prize available. The final concert was broadcast live across Europe on the EBU network, excellent exposure for ones so young.

Having done well at the EBU, we thought it prudent to maximise potential and do two more competitions whilst in that frame of mind. Immediately after Cambridge we headed for the first ever Banff Competition, in the Canadian Rockies. We arrived on top of the world feeling on top of the world, buoyed by our recent success.

Participating groups were given their own room in which to work, which was wonderful; and their own room in which to live together... not so wonderful. Whilst it was hardly ideal for us lads to have to share a cramped space under such circumstances, it must have been downright hellish for Jacky.

I had selected Jack London's *Call of the Wild* as some appropriate light reading for the trip, getting well into it on the flight there. That night at 'lights out' we were collectively trying to deal with the dreaded jet lag but enjoying little or no success. I imagine it was out of a mild sense of delirium that I decided a bedtime story could be the remedy for our ails. There on our bunk beds, huddled up against the cold, I began – gingerly at first, unsure of my audience.

"Bonzo [craftily changing details to conceal my source] was like no other dog. His brawn came from his husky dad; his brains, from his sheepdog mum."

Palpable silence filled the room. *Surely they can't be asleep already?*

"And?" begged Jacky.

"Go on, go on!" barked the lads.

And so, on I went. With extended toilet breaks during the day, I managed to arm myself with enough material for the next night's instalment. Giving away my inspiration would have ruined the fantasy of a scene which betrayed the tenderness of our years.

I realise now that these bedtime tales must have influenced what happened next. Often, one of the rounds in these competitions involves learning and performing a specially commissioned piece. This is actually a good idea and one that we would normally have taken seriously, but the heady mix of the altitude and our high spirits unleashed a more frivolous approach in an attempt to liven up what was in truth a fairly torrid work. We agreed that what this piece needed was some sort of narrative to save it from itself. We dreamt up a comedy that starred our esteemed colleagues and dear friends, the Hagen Quartet. Having performed it for them after an evening spent playing five-a-side footy, table tennis and shove halfpenny, word got out of the existence of our little joke and the next day, during an interview for CBC, I was cajoled into telling the story. Though I have no doubt it was the inadequacies of our playing that led to our eventual dismissal at the semi-final stage, this inconsequential sideshow probably didn't endear us to the organisers of the competition. Attending the final was not an uplifting experience but we could at least take heart from the number of audience members who made a point of saying how much they had enjoyed our performances.

In those days, Banff was home to Zoltan Szekely, the former first violin of the old Hungarian Quartet, and we managed to secure some days of study with him in the aftermath of the competition. Our plan was to study the Bartok Quartets since he had known Bartok personally and had even played some of those great masterpieces to the man himself. Not only that, he was the dedicatee of the Second Rhapsody, and one story going around which unnerved us slightly was that, when he returned to re-record that piece thirty years after the initial rendition, his performance clocked in at exactly the same overall duration. To us, this somehow showed a terrifying lack of musical growth, and our fears were exacerbated when a group who had been studying with him for months gave a recital of two Bartok Quartets. Pretty much everything they did was alien to our approach to these pieces, and when we spoke to them backstage they only confirmed our fears; they were doing everything they'd been told, to the letter.

Our first class was at 9am the next day. What to do? We decided comprehensively against playing Bartok and instead agreed upon late Beethoven, something else for which the Hungarians had a name. We arrived at Mr Szekely's apartment promptly, made our excuses for the change of repertoire and set about Op.127. Having persevered with our early morning rendition of the first movement, Mr Szekely silently got to his feet, made his way over to the turntable in a corner of the room and fished out a 1950s' LP of himself and his colleagues playing the same movement. Without so much as a word, he dropped the needle onto the vinyl with a hair-raising screech and returned to his comfy chair. When that decidedly dodgy reading came to an end, he unceremoniously turned off the power, turned to us and announced without a hint of embarrassment, "Now you know what we're aiming for."

Four hours later, we had not got past those glorious opening chords, had not played one note of that sunny, embraceable Allegro. That life-affirming opening gesture had become a depressing pit of fear and self-doubt. Job done!

Meanwhile, we had convinced ourselves that the imposing Banff Springs Hotel was in fact the Overlook from Kubrick's chiller *The Shining*, and decided a visit was in order. After a dip in the hot pools and a particularly decadent hot chocolate, we had a moment of enlightenment ourselves; we changed our plans and caught the next available flight out of there. Banff had extended us a warm welcome and we thoroughly enjoyed our time there, but we had enough subversive types within our ranks, each one expert at denting confidence and exposing weakness. We needed guidance, inspiration and positivity. Sadly we never did find them. One inspiring and extraordinary fact we heard about Szekely was that he had won Wimbledon back in the '20s, when it was still an amateur tournament. Wish I'd asked him for a tip on how to keep those uptight forehands from ballooning out of court – opportunity missed.

The next stop on the competition merry-go-round was Tokyo, home of the Min-On Competition. Though a certain amount of financial assistance was available for these sorties, by no means would all our expenses have been covered, and so it was that we reluctantly boarded an Aeroflot flight via Moscow.

It was as though we had stepped onto the set of a Monty Python sketch. A high percentage of the seats were actually broken in one way or another and it took a more courageous person than me to push that seductive recline button. We were already taxiing when, under the seat in front of me, I was unfortunate enough to spy a small collection of discarded engine bits. It's one thing fudging it with your Meccano set, quite another with the workings of a 737. We did somehow get airborne and in time, refreshments arrived. A flimsy, misshapen, grey tray was unceremoniously thrust upon one… in one's lap, had the drop-down table not been employed in time. Looking down in horror, we could see that the sum total of our repast at this stage was *pan con burro ransido*. This butter had obviously been commandeered from some random equatorial land that, after many years, had finally relented and concurred that it's acquisition in the first place had been a misplaced extravagance. The ball of crumbling bread had been prepared specially by a badelynge of spiteful ducks, hell-bent on revenge for all those years of being fed stale crusts and heels. This miserable accompanist was about to be joined by our soloist for the day, that most colourful of violin virtuosi, *Entrée Griu*. A grey – like the tray – lump of unrecognisable meat, unsettlingly reminiscent of a prehistoric beast's defunct internal organ, complete with designer gristle, was forked out of a nasty great pot and deposited straight onto the tray itself by a charming stewardess who hadn't quite made the cut in the 1968 Olympics due, in no small part, to her having taken the weightlifter's medication instead of the gymnast's. It came as no surprise that the in-flight entertainment amounted to endless reruns of last year's news, barely visible through the permanent fuzz presented to us by the hopelessly inadequate screen. At one stage, by way of a diversion as much as anything, I threw caution to the wind and headed off in search of a toilet. I ended up at the rear of the aircraft and, to my amazement, found that one could simply unhook a camouflaged mesh curtain and walk into the hold containing all the luggage. Imagine such a scene in this day and age. I decided to take advantage of the farcical situation. I got my viola and sneaked off to practise in the hold, where I got a solid hour's work done completely unnoticed.

We were put up in what seemed like a toy hotel overlooking Tokyo's Shinjuku Station. It wasn't quite one of those creepy pod places where worker bees go to snatch a few hours' sleep, but my word, the rooms were tiny. The bathroom was a portable plastic affair in the corner of the room, itself a portable plastic unit accessed from an inflatable corridor. Everything from breakfast to dinner came pre-packed and sealed from vending machines. The whole place made you feel as though you had crossed a line and were now in a game of Playmobil. This in itself was disturbing enough but from the 38th floor, it was downright terrifying. I got woken up by screams on that first night. Poor Jacky, who was in the next room, had surfaced to find she was sharing her cramped cubicle with a sizable rodent, which was not multicoloured and definitely not plastic. Next morning, the ant-like display of the commuters going about their business on the pavements far below brought one's insignificance sharply into focus.

We'd been issued individual welcome packs upon arrival with itineraries, the detailed nature of which had to be seen to be believed:

Hotel pick-up: 08.33

    Upon arrival at Suntory Hall, Practise Rm 7 will be at your disposal from 09.25 – 10.43.

    Your 1st Round performance will start at 11.01 and finish at 11.13. You will play two movements from Beethoven's Op.18 No.6.

    After twelve minutes the lights will be dimmed. This will signal the end of your performance.

And so it went on, with every detail carried out to the letter. It was a surreal experience walking out onto such a huge stage, spying who we were led to believe was Sandor Vegh sitting halfway back in the giant, cavernous auditorium, taking our seats in silence and beginning to play. As we got to a particularly poignant moment in the slow movement, the lights began to fade as planned. We took no notice, continuing to unfold the ravishing music in the dark. As you can imagine, this caused pandemonium, not for Mr Vegh, who remained unfazed in the glow of his personal lamp, but for the backstage helpers who got hopelessly flustered by the unimaginable eventuality that the next group might miss their 11.19 slot. Soon a white-gloved helper scurried onstage and insisted we stop. We must have come across as precocious brats but in truth, we just could not countenance that we might have come all this way to play one and a half movements of Beethoven. Also, to stop in the middle of a short but glorious movement like that one, seemed inhuman. Thankfully, we did live to fight another day and on this, the occasion of our last competitive outing, we would go on to win five of the six prizes on offer, only missing out on the actual first prize. This went to one of the sixty or so Asian groups that had entered. Fair enough.

'Italy'

Being able to drive is a basic requirement for any group member and Jacky took it upon herself to show me the ropes in this respect. How I loved those lessons. They provided me with a legitimate reason for being alone with Jacky, the woman, as opposed to seated next to Jacky, the cellist. Having suppressed my inherent driving skills as long as seemed even vaguely plausible, and notwithstanding the bizarre manoeuvre I performed – not to be found in any recess of The Highway Code – so as to fail my test the first time around, my driving lessons with Jacky sadly had to come to an end. Jacky took my failure as a personal affront, a slight on her impeccable teaching credentials, and firmly maintained that I had not been paying sufficient attention during lessons. Whilst this is an accusation I cannot, with all due conscience, refute, I fear a more practical and less romantic version of events is that the government, faced with the mouthwatering prospect of doubling its money on a popular everyday occurrence, has a decision to make; pass or fail.

Having passed at the second attempt, I closed in on buying my first car, a tasty black Renault 18 GTX. This baby was way too powerful for a kid who thought he was Paddy Hopkirk and that roads were circuits to be navigated at speed. It was a nasty winter's evening as I made my way to pick up a friend from Woking Station. That country road was windy, it had been raining hard and I was going too fast. Before I knew it, I had hit an enormous, invisible puddle, aquaplaned 100m across the road, off the other side and smashed head-on into a tree. I awoke to the sight and sound of the boys in blue cutting through the roof above my head with chainsaws. I remember feeling mortified, apologising profusely, and fumbling with the keys.

"I'm so sorry, chaps, won't be a moment. Just get this thing started again and I'll be out of your way."

The paramedics eventually eased me out through the newly improvised cabriolet into the waiting ambulance and off to hospital. I was lucky to survive the impact; the car had concertinaed to half its size yet I came away virtually unscathed. We did have to postpone a concert in Luton the next day but we continued with the Italian tour later that week.

One of the things that had come out of our trip to Banff was meeting and befriending Piero Farulli, the violist from the Quartetto Italiano. He had been impressed with us and immediately offered us a tour of his native country. The good old British Council got involved and we subsequently arrived in Rome the night before the first concert to meet with our guide for the trip, Jack Buckley – or Uncle Dunque, as he became known. Jack had spent half his life in Italy and spoke Italian fluently but with a thick Lancashire accent; where Les Dawson would say 'right then', he would say 'dunque'. Whether or not it was archaic we couldn't tell, but for us it came straight out of a first-year Latin class and it tickled us no end. We ribbed him mercilessly.

Our first trip to Italy was always going to be exciting, but with Jack at the helm it became something truly special. On arrival, pink champagne at his place was followed by a delicious Romanesque dinner *al limone* in a gorgeous little *taverna rustica*. The next night's aftershow bash was an altogether more grand affair. As guests of the British ambassador we stayed in the palatial Villa Wolkonsky, where the quality of the food more than matched the opulence of the residence. For kids like us, coming back to your room to find your underwear and socks from the day before all washed and ironed could be a puzzling, if not worrying, experience.

Jack was a gourmand, and every concert on our ten-day tour was planned around a particular restaurant or dining experience. I remember asking him why the concert in Palermo, which was on his birthday, had to be in the morning.

"Because we simply have to eat at La Botte and they only do lunch on a Sunday."

He was right, of course. It was funny to see him nervously consulting his watch with mounting agitation as the Mafia families filed into the Green Room after the concert to congratulate us and introduce us to their daughters. This was hardly a chore for us, but we were clearly being way too gracious and spending much too much time grinning inanely at the *bellas signorinas*. Imagine my embarrassment, standing there amongst these impeccably turned out Sicilians with my left ear hanging off and the left side of my face horribly swollen and dripping stitches. Jack eventually prised us away and ferried us to an unforgettable birthday lunch, complete with surprise cake, candles, songs, the lot.

In Naples a crazy thing happened. I woke up in the middle of the night, soaked in sweat and shaking like a leaf. I made my way to the bathroom and, already in a bit of a state, nearly flipped when I saw myself in the mirror. I was covered in purple bruising. My arms, upper legs and left shoulder were particularly spectacular, and the seatbelt had presented me with a vibrant sash worthy of any 12th July parade – all this a week after the crash. It was what you might term a 'wake-up call'. There should be cars for young drivers that can only go up to 40mph. (Oddly, exactly one year to the day after this first accident, and once again on my way to see the same friend, I would have another, although not my fault this time and not as serious. I escaped unscathed but my wonderfully characterful, hot-orange Beetle was written off.)

The final concert of the tour in Italy was to be in Firenze and, given the diversity of the repasts Jack had choreographed for us on our travels, we were most curious to see what he had lined up for us on our last night. The concert went well and we got an opportunity to thank Signor Farulli for his invaluable assistance in making the tour happen.

With customary diplomacy, Jack extricated us from the post-concert formalities and soon we were walking along an ancient cobbled street near to that most evocative of all pharmacies, Santa Maria di Novella. Stumbling upon this treasure for the first time, as I had the day before, was an uplifting experience. I recall just standing there in the entrance, entranced by the beauty of the place and seduced by the incomparable aroma emanating from within. I still have a little bottle of heavenly liquid, purchased that day nearly forty years ago. Now it was late evening, however, and everywhere was closed or closing, which rendered Jack's next move all the more strange. He turned into the entrance to a bank. *What can he be doing?* we wondered. Next to the formidable double-fronted security door there was a hidden stone staircase that led to an understated hostelry on the first floor. We were not impressed. Why had our food guru taken us to this glorified wine bar for our big celebratory meal together?

We tried to remain upbeat as we were shown to our table but when Jack ordered only wine and cheese, our good natures were sorely tested.

"What's going on, Jack? Is this some sort of joke? A halfway house before we hit the real restaurant, perhaps?"

When it arrived, he explained that the wine, bread and cheese had all come from the same farm and that that farm was called Sassicaia. Nowadays, as with most things, you can go and buy a bottle of this most delicious nectar of the gods at any half-decent wine store, but back then this was something exceptional and distinctly Italian. Furthermore, experiencing a wine like this is one thing, but the heartwarming knowledge that the accompanying bread and cheese were produced on the very same land turned it into a spiritual event. Yet again, Jack had outdone himself and educated us. Though our bellies may have been sold short that evening, our souls were well and truly nourished.

'Sutton Place'

In 1983 we were approached and offered a post as Quartet in Residence for South East Arts. The timing could not have been better. Our collective studies had come to an end and there was a general feeling of wanting to vacate Manchester and embrace the world we were eager to conquer. Sutton Place was to be the unlikely base for this residency. Built in 1521 by Henry VIII for Richard Weston, it is one of the most beautiful houses you could possibly imagine. A breathtaking arrangement of warm brick and seductive leaded windows, it was originally a four-sided structure around a central courtyard until one of the wings was destroyed by fire in 1782, leaving the more open and welcoming three-sided building we arrived at in 1984. For a time, the house had been the home of J P Getty, the undisputed wealthiest man in the world at the time, and had thus come under close scrutiny from the world press. Getty, being a notoriously private man, gave them little to talk about, save for one silly tidbit – that the owner had installed a payphone for the use of his guests. Though suspect, this action was not without precedent; the Courtaulds, for example, had had payphones at Eltham Palace.

Upon Getty's death in 1976 the house went up for sale and was bought by a similarly wealthy American by the name of Stanley Seeger. Stanley was even more of a recluse than Getty and though we met him once or twice during the three years we shared his space, we spoke to staff who had been in his employ for fifteen years or more and had never laid eyes on him. Where Getty had let the gardens go mostly to grass and paid little attention to the house itself, Mr Seeger transformed the place and maximised its considerable potential. Rumour had it that he had bought it for £8m and then spent an additional £5m on renovations before moving in.

Sir Geoffrey Jellicoe was enticed out of retirement to design the gardens, which would boast such features as a black outdoor swimming pool with added bits, which, when seen from the air, would reflect a particular Miro painting, and a magnificent marble wall sculpture by Ben Nicholson, unveiled by Charles and Diana, no less. Sir Hugh Casson was given the job of updating the interior, though Stanley had some ideas of his own. Every bedroom had a specific theme – Swedish, French, Italian and so on. Monet's kitchen at Giverny was painstakingly recreated and the vast main rooms saw no expense spared. Stanley had a world-renowned art collection and these opulent rooms provided the perfect space to show it off. Unusually for someone in his position, Stanley was a gifted musician. He had studied composition with Dallapiccola and, together with a collaborator, Francis James Brown, wrote some film scores, including *The Priest of Love* (1981) under the pseudonym Joseph James.

Our residency guaranteed a number of concerts over the next three seasons and an affiliation to the University of Surrey, but without too much teaching. It also meant we were given the use of a cottage on the Sutton Place estate. Whilst the cottage was undeniably idyllic, size-wise it was totally inadequate for a quartet plus partners. We came up with an arrangement whereby Ian and I, both single at the time, would share the house, and the quartet would share the costs of the other two's accommodation elsewhere. Mike rented a flat in London and Jacky got her foot on the property ladder by buying a modest but charming terraced cottage in nearby Woking.

This appointment coincided with us signing our first recording contract and, consequently, one of the first things we did there was make our inaugural LP for ASV. We chose the Elgar Quartet in homage to our namesakes, for whom the work had been written, and coupled it with the sadly neglected quartet by Delius.

Making a recording of anything is a stressful business but making a recording that would effectively announce our arrival in the music world at large was nerve-wracking. The venue could hardly have been more appropriate; the glorious main sitting room of Sutton Place was as quintessentially English as it's possible to be, albeit on a grand scale. It was other matters, unforeseen and beyond our control, that would serve to make our already inhumanly tight schedule of two days a very tense affair indeed. Firstly, the open plan nature of the great house meant that the engine room for the recording would have to be all the way up the stairs in the library, what seemed like a mile from where we were set up. Hence, we lost a lot of time in the dreaded initial process of trying to get the sound right, with us having to race up and down in order to listen and the engineer having to do the same in reverse to make any adjustments to the mics. To add to our woes, the staging they had thoughtfully provided for the occasion was rickety and made a noise every time we moved, and we were on the Heathrow flightpath. We vacated the stage and, hoping air traffic control would be kind to us, banked on our second and final day being a bit more straightforward, with fewer takes rendered useless by extraneous noises. We arrived the next morning to find that some kind person had decided to light a roaring fire to make the environment more cosy. How we managed to salvage that situation and even make an award-winning CD is beyond me.

Sotheby's have built their reputation on satisfying the often-unreasonable demands of the super-rich, but when it came to Mr Seeger they really outdid themselves. Quite apart from adding to his ever-increasing collection, it was here that he would find not only his future partner Christopher Cone, but the man who was to run Sutton Place, Roger Chubb. It was Roger whom we would liaise with when we came to undertake our next challenge at the house: the curation of a concert series.

One of the great characteristics of Sutton Place was its effortless juxtaposition of old and new, something we tried to reflect in what would become our annual series of six concerts there. Traditional meets cutting-edge was the order of the day. The artists were of international standing and the audience would have valet parking, champagne on arrival and a sit-down dinner afterwards in the enormous dining room that occupied the entire upstairs of the west wing, above the gallery. Whereas upstairs was all oak panels and magnificent tapestries, the downstairs was ultra-modern – white walls, glass and steel. While the art in the main house remained mostly the same, this extensive exhibition space would change biannually.

George Crumb's 'Black Angels' for electric string quartet is a piece we have quite a history with and one that will appear again and again throughout this book. It's an iconic work, unique in so many ways and brimming with imagination and invention. There are three highly evocative techniques within its pages that I have not come across anywhere else in music – imagine that! Written in response to the Vietnam War, and completed on Friday 13th July 1970, it is a deeply personal piece that relies heavily on numerology and the occult. Its thirteen movements carry such striking titles as 'Sarabanda de la Muerte Oscura', 'Devil Music' and 'Sounds of Bones and Flutes'.

Our first performance was in Sutton Place on Friday 13th July 1984, when we presented a programme of Smetana's first quartet 'From my Life', coupled with 'Black Angels'. You have to remember that the vast majority of the audience at these concerts was made up of upper middle-class suburban types able to fork out £90 each to spend an evening in this majestic stately home. Contrary to his fanatically reclusive personality, the owner of this historic house had a wicked sense of humour, and as we took to the stage that evening we found that between the rehearsal and concert, he had replaced the understated collection of paintings that normally hung behind the performers with a vast canvas depicting the Lone Ranger and Tonto, the masked one holding in his hand not a Colt 45 but an enormous penis. The well-heeled throng was already unnerved and we had to try to remain focused on pulling off a moving account of this great Romantic masterpiece overlooked by Tom, Dick and Harry.

How Stanley must have giggled to himself. He never came to any events but everything was secretly filmed and relayed to his private screen where he could watch proceedings without feeling threatened.

We were constantly talking about introducing more theatre to our performances, not as some sort of cheap gimmick but as a way of showing certain works in a new light, exploring their inherent storylines, and also freeing up our approach to performance. With this in mind, we entered into a relationship with the director Di Trevis working on a performance of Shostakovich's 11th Quartet. The work was enlightening in many ways and had all the potential we had imagined, but incorporating something like this into your everyday schedule presents enormous difficulties. Most of our venues do not have theatrical facilities, and without proper back-up – in terms of lighting and so on – such efforts can end up looking amateurish. Not the desired result.

Our plan for this evening began to unfold during the interval, which was an extended affair as we had to reset the stage. Instead of the customary glass of claret or chablis accompanied by warmed blinis, dripping cream cheese and caviar, the increasingly bemused public were served Bull's Blood in stout goblets and darling little bat-shaped toasts adorned with sumptuous roasted red peppers, by waiters in full regalia complete with vampire teeth. Upon their return to the hall, the audience were confronted by the same quartet who had played the first half but this time already in position, stony-faced and, with the exception of Jacky, shirtless. Our stage design included the use of UV lights, so our white shirts had had to go. We decided against the employment of a simple black T-shirt in favour of the more confrontational topless look. So, black tailcoats and trousers for the lads, long black gown for the lady; we all four had big white bow ties. I had a foot pedal that when hit simultaneously illuminated the pencil-thin UV lights on our stands and plunged the rest of the auditorium into complete darkness. All the audience could then see were our four bow ties and the hair of our bows painting firefly images as we went along. Though I say so myself, it was an amazing effect, and yet not one we ever repeated. At the conclusion of the piece, I once again hit the pedal and the audience found us exactly as they had last seen us, sitting formally and emotionless. We took no notice of their applause and they gradually, self-consciously, vacated the space, many trying to make jokes with us as they passed. We remained statuesque.

Life at Sutton Place was never dull; it always seemed to be on the cusp of a drama. Early one morning, Roger Chubb phoned in a terrible panic. The American pianist Aldo Ciccolini had cancelled his sold-out recital planned for the following evening. We couldn't very well step in as we were already doing two concerts in the relatively short season, but someone of comparable standing had to be found, and quickly. I tried to calm Roger's frazzled nerves and explained that if anyone could get us out of this mess, it would be our trusty manager, David Sigall. My instinct proved right and, with his renowned, unflappable brilliance, David phoned me back not an hour later to say that none other than Teresa Berganza happened to be in town, was free that night, and had agreed in principle to doing the date. The angel spoke! This wasn't just a solution to the problem; for many, this was probably an unexpected extra thrill. Roger set about informing the paying guests, David went in search of a pianist and began ironing out the details, I went off to rehearse at the big house, all pleased with myself.

Whereas to us this seemed like a crisis averted, to Stanley it opened a can of worms, and another much more complicated problem raised its ugly head. Apparently, all the art in the house was completely wrong for Ms Berganza. Not only the semi-permanent fixtures, the Picassos, the Bacons, the Kandinskys and so on, but the entire exhibition currently on display in the gallery had to go. Mayhem engulfed the building just before lunch on the day before her recital. A veritable army of white-coated people arrived in various types of van to begin the massive reorganisation process. Enormous removal lorries arrived, one to take away the current exhibition, another to deliver the new one. In typical Stanley fashion, this was to be no ordinary replacement. He had chosen to present for Teresa a full-blown collection of African art complete with drawings, paintings, sculptures and installations. The scene was further enhanced by ponds and streams full of tropical fish, these in turn flanked by trees and plants; birds flew freely throughout the landscape. We watched open-mouthed as this astonishing transformation unfolded before us with consummate efficiency. As the first members of the audience arrived at one door, the final licks of paint were being administered here and there and the last bits of detritus swept up and disposed of out another. This operation was made all the more impressive by the fact that Stanley had masterminded the whole thing from his yacht on Lake Geneva. That evening after the show, when the last of the guests had gone home, Roger, Ian and I took a seat among the six wives of Henry VIII. The man himself and his six unfortunate brides had been painstakingly depicted on lavish cushions upon the grand sofa that faced the baronial open fireplace. Roger unearthed a Hine Cognac and some Cuban Cigars, the likes of which we had never experienced before and will likely never experience again. This was what Sutton Place was all about; a brief glimpse of life on another scale, a canvas on which pretty much all conceivable imaginings could be realised. This is something the jobbing musician has to deal with on a day-to-day basis: seeing how the other half lives at close quarters from a vantage point of extreme normality. We would spend three years in this rarefied environment before moving on to the set of another soap – Cambridge University.

In the summer of 1984 we made the first of fourteen consecutive visits to the great Dartington Festival and had our first encounter with the inspirational composer Peter Maxwell Davies. We were keen to make an impact and were particularly excited at the prospect of presenting the 'Angels' in a late-night slot. Though all the necessary technical equipment – microphones, cables, lines of tuned glasses, gongs and whatnot – did look a tad incongruous in the glorious medieval hall, preparations for the performance went remarkably smoothly. We spent a lot of time trying to get the sound just right but couldn't have made allowances for the fact that the guy with the power, i.e. the volume control, was a teensy-weensy bit unhinged. It is undeniable that the direction at the opening of the first movement 'Night of the Electric Insects' is marked ffff and should shock the listener, but our new fifth member really let it all hang out and, ignoring our previous travails, pushed the fader to the max. Such was the intensity of the noise that Sir Peter – or Max, as he was affectionately known – sprang from his seat, ran out of the hall and, legend has it, was physically sick. Many followed suit and did not return. Those who stuck around, ourselves included, were privy to a particularly wild account of the work.

This could hardly have been more different to an incident in that hall a few years later when, at the end of a performance of Lutoslawski's quartet, the composer jumped to his feet, ran onto the stage and embraced us all with fond, tearful hugs and kisses, shouting all the while, "It's theirs, it's theirs!" We tried many times over the years to get him to write another quartet but he always refused, saying that if you've written something that successful, you shouldn't try to follow it up. Just as well Ludwig didn't think like that.

The Crumb is unquestionably a masterpiece, a work in which new and old techniques sit naturally side by side. If these techniques are well executed and carried out to the letter, the piece stands a chance of success, but ultimately, you're in the hands of the sound person.

'Miyake'

Simon Morris arrived as a postgraduate student from Durham University while I was in my third year at the RCM. We quickly became friends and even formed a quartet together with the violinists Jacqueline Shave and Sarah Whelan. But alongside our musical activities, I think we recognised a mutual entrepreneurial streak, a desire to branch out, to add another string to our bows. Aside from being a seriously good cellist, Simon, with the help of his two brothers, was already building up a bit of a property portfolio. Here was someone who effortlessly waltzed into a top cello-playing job with the Academy of St Martins yet still found the time and energy to diversify. While my friends and I were squatting in the back end of Harlesden, Simon and his brothers were buying and renting houses in Durham. I remember being thoroughly disappointed when he later went off to teach at Winchester School, only to be fully reassured by finding out that he and his brother David had bought an old property there that they were busy renovating and turning into the all-new Winchester Violin Shop. Ah, that's ma boy!

Soon, Simon and David would hook up with a like-minded soul in Steven Smith, buy an extensive warehouse space near Waterloo and establish the Morris and Smith Violin Shop. Simon had found his *raison d'être*. Next, he and Steve would take over the world-famous violin empire of Beare's from Charles himself and eventually gain complete domination by purchasing the historic and iconic W E Hill and Sons.

In the early '80s Simon got headhunted to be the stunt double for David Bowie, a cello-playing alien in the film *The Hunger*. One perk of this super cool assignment was a visit to an extremely posh hairdresser in Mayfair. Simon was arguably fortunate that the image required was closer to The Duke than to Ziggy, and he came out (so to speak) looking spiffing. I remember that haircut costing £120 – I'd hate to pay that even now but back then, it really was showbiz.

When the filming was over, Simon threw a small dinner party to celebrate and since I was on my own at the time, his girlfriend, Junri, decided to invite a friend of hers to make up the numbers. That chance meeting turned out to be an enormously fruitful one. This girl was the PA to none other than the legendary designer Issey Miyake. We in the quartet had never been ones for those impossibly heavy and inflexible tailcoats, complete with ludicrous starched collars, bow ties etc., and had already been experimenting with other garb. An irate letter from Dorking Music Club accusing us of not taking our concert there seriously because we had turned up in suits (the preferred dress of the Amadeus Quartet at the time) only served to reinforce the depressing reality of the world we were operating in. The strength of our convictions, however, meant that we would not give up easily, and I could hardly contain my excitement at the prospect of what doors my new friend could potentially open for us.

The first was the one leading to the Miyake Studio in South Kensington. I spent the whole of the next day there, getting to know the people engaged in bringing these groundbreaking designs to the streets of London and to my amazement, left that same evening with a huge cardboard box stuffed with thousands of pounds' worth of clothes. I had put forward the suggestion that alongside the tremendous innovation, there was a side to Miyake that was undeniably classic yet equally recognisable as uniquely him (this would eventually result in his 'Permanente' line). 'What better vehicle for showcasing this to the world than a young, cutting-edge string quartet?' was my line. Issey loved the idea.

Naturally, that initial rehearsal was awkward. Understandably, not all my colleagues were completely convinced as I fished out yet another gaudy, indecipherable item of clothing from my box of tricks. A little patience, however, and soon we found ourselves able to see past the balaclava with chain or the lopsided, oversized top in parachute silk, pieces designed with the catwalk in mind, to the more workable yet no less revolutionary formal gear, designed for more normal wear and heaven-sent for our purposes. These breathtaking, quality garments would release us from the shackles of the horribly cramping servant's uniform and allow us to express ourselves freely on the world stage. Predictably, we had the usual knee-jerk reaction from the dark, stuffy corners to this – as they saw it – attention-seeking and risque departure. But soon, when people like Mitsuko Uchida and Mischa Maisky followed suit, the cobwebs got blown away and the floodgates opened. Soon we were all rejoicing in this new-found liberalism. Classical musicians were not only feeling more comfortable on stage but actually forming their own identities.

Armed with our new look, we went to do a photoshoot for the cover of an album called *Brodsky Unlimited*. These situations are invariably tense affairs. Endless waiting around, everyone with their own idea of how we should be looking, swinging wildly from the bog-standard – pretty girl with cello seated at the front, bunch of dodgy-looking lads lined up to the rear – to the ridiculous – spread-eagled on the floor with violins between your legs and the cello spike up your nose. In fairness, this had been one of the more agreeable days spent in front of the lens and we all seemed confident that we'd got the shot. It was as we were leaving the studio that we noticed the photographer's brand spanking new Harley Davidson parked in the corner. It was a beautiful example of this iconic machine and we couldn't help ourselves taking a closer look. Tim (Richmond) sensed the moment and before long had the four of us on board, posing for all the world like a rock group. This was just a bit of fun at the end of a long day, of course... sure thing, man! All the other footage that we'd spent so long on went to the bottom of the pile when the record company saw these shots. The usually hyper-conservative employees at Teldec couldn't see past this image and so the 'bike shot' found its way onto the cover of a classical quartet's CD of favourite encore pieces and our public perception was edged further in a certain direction. The press had a field day, but at least it was the international press who were noticing and not some fuddy-duddy from Dorking.

Our relationship with Issey blossomed and in 1986 he asked us if we would do the music for his Paris show. After much discussion, we decided that the best way of doing this might be the ultra-spontaneous route. It was nerve-racking but we arrived in Paris the day before the actual show with a gargantuan pile of music and parked ourselves in the thick of things backstage. The level of activity was feverish and the buzz of energy intoxicating. It was a vast, white, open warehouse space only nominally cordoned off into various sections. The whole place was mirrored; piles of garments, some discarded, some waiting to be altered, littered the floor.

Rail upon rail of every conceivable type of clothing crisscrossed the vista. A veritable army of makeup artists, pressers, dressers, seamstresses and stylists calmly and expertly went about their business in the midst of this chaotic scene. Models of all shapes and sizes scooted around in various states of nakedness, oblivious. In the midst of this well-oiled machine, we must have seemed like four dishevelled flies in the ointment. Issey and his team explained to us the idea of the show and the various sections within the overall concept. We chatted amongst ourselves, separated our scores into what we felt were potentially relevant piles, and the rehearsal began. The models would appear in various creations and we would react accordingly. A riot of shapes and colours and we would reach for Janacek. Clean, formal lines inevitably brought Mozart to the stands. An ingenious, contemporary twist on some ancient Japanese attire, complete with wacky glasses and space-age backpack, would send us the way of Ichiyanagi, Webern or Dutilleux. By no means were all of our initial ideas met with positive reactions. Quite often, in fact, Issey would recoil, wave his arms around and call us to a halt. We would then try to decipher where we had gone wrong before trying another excerpt or a different piece altogether. In this way, though it took all night, we achieved our goal and everyone involved was happy and excited by the outcome. It was then our job to mould the very different styles so that the end product was like one seamless, flowing musical work.

For the show itself, we were positioned behind an opaque gauze curtain, only to be revealed at the climax of proceedings, when Issey unveiled us and led us down the catwalk sporting the funky black boiler suits he had designed for the occasion. At the aftershow party, Issey quizzed me about the collection. Notwithstanding that this era saw the birth of such radical innovations as 'Pleats and those amazing crumpled materials, I answered as best I could from my ill-informed perspective, touching upon this and that, but in the end I singled out a particular jacket that had been modelled by Mikhail Baryshnikov as being the most beautiful piece of all. He found it curious how I had picked out this item, explaining that it had also been one of his favourites and yet no one, either here in London or in New York, had ordered it. This meant that that jacket was an absolute one-off, never to be repeated. About a month later, a 'special delivery' package arrived at my home. It was the jacket.

Later that year we met up with him again, this time in Tokyo. Our trip happily coincided with Lucy Rie's first ever Japanese exhibition, which Issey had organised, and we gave a private concert to open the event. At dinner he nonchalantly enquired as to how we were going to spend the next day, our one free day during the tour. Having not really given it much thought, we awkwardly made out that we would probably get some rest and maybe wander around Tokyo a bit.

"Have you ever been to Kyoto?" he enquired.

When we told him that we hadn't, he turned to Heather, his PA in Japan, who happened to be the American ambassador's daughter, and whispered a brief message in her ear. She immediately arose from the table and excused herself. In the blink of an eye she returned, handing each one of us an envelope containing a detailed itinerary of what we would now be doing tomorrow.

We caught an early Hokkaido Shinkansen, Tokyo-Kyoto, and were met on the platform by a wonderfully smiley gentleman in a smart uniform, holding a sign that read 'MR PAUL'. Shinju was to be our guide and driver for the day. He took us to this temple and that museum. In those days, Westerners were quite a novelty, even in Tokyo, but in Kyoto we were viewed like pop stars. Being the historic and cultural capital of the country, the place was packed with students of all ages and each and every one of them wanted to have their photo taken with us. He took us for coffee – nice, lunch – delicious, green tea – yuck! Yes, the spectacle is enchanting, but the stuff itself... times must have been hard when that sludge was dreamt up. Several nasty, sweet, sticky balls of gue were needed to even begin to negate the horrid aftertaste of my one tiny sip.

Dinner was quite another matter. We had our own private room in what was widely considered to be the best restaurant in Kyoto. Everything was picture-book perfect and extremely formal. It took us about twenty minutes to persuade them to let our lovely chauffeur join us. Even when they finally gave in to our shameful request, they were not one bit happy. Nor was he, by the way; he was terribly embarrassed by our actions and remained ill at ease throughout. But we couldn't accept the fact that our friend would be left to sit in the car while we tucked into some top-notch nosh. I like to think that even at that stage of our lives we had reasonably eclectic palates. We'd been around a bit and sampled some quirky cuisine, but this banquet was on a whole other level, throwing our delightful Shinju into a semi-permanent state of simultaneous shock and hysteria. Wide-eyed, he carried an inane grin and a slightly troublesome dribble that he was struggling to control; this was high-class authenticity of an almost historic nature, the sort of food he'd only ever seen in books. For us, tired and hungry after a long day travelling and sightseeing, the sight of another lone grasshopper – presented as it was, *au naturel* on an oversized, highly decorated dish – was managing to feed only our visual senses. As tiny course after tiny course was brought forth, it was difficult to know how to pace oneself – that is, if one was consuming anything – and I was surprised to learn in retrospect that the 'fillet of bamboo' had been the entrée. I remember poor Ian not enjoying two hours in the lotus position, though the copious amounts of sake went some way to relieving that situation. It was an extraordinary dining experience and an altogether memorable evening, but while Shinju went home replete with food and stories with which to regale his family and friends, shamefully, I have to admit that we had to visit a fast food joint at the station before boarding the train home. Though we would return to Kyoto many times, we could never begin to repeat that special day when, with the right word in the right ear, Issey had presented us with a privileged experience, a kind of Thomas Cook day trip for the elite.

'From Yehudi to Terry via the Caribbean'

One of the first things on my 'to do' list when I arrived in London back in '76 was to witness Menuhin in concert. Sadly, by this time, Yehudi was tortured and severely hampered by that horrible twitch that plagued his later performances. They say that it was when he started questioning how he did what he did that arguably the most sublime violinist of all developed a stammer about halfway along every down-bow. Though he continued playing for decades it was something he was never able to rectify. Tragically, he was eventually confined to the upper half of the bow.

Though I was lucky enough to meet him several times during various concert situations over the years, I only once got to speak to him properly, at his 70th birthday concert. When asked what he would like to hear at this event, he replied, "The Brodsky Quartet playing Mendelssohn's A minor Quartet."

The quartet had won his very own prize for the most outstanding young quartet at the first Portsmouth Competition ten years earlier, and he clearly hadn't forgotten them. It's also worth remembering that he had studied with Adolf Busch for a time so would almost certainly have been aware of the quartet repertoire. It was a huge honour but goodness me, it was scary, attempting to play with this 'string god' sat on the front row only a few feet away. We got through it somehow and he was openly effusive afterwards, inviting us back to his home for a glass of champagne.

The concert took place in St. Michael's Church, Highgate, opposite Yehudi's extraordinarily beautiful home on The Grove. It was humbling

being in the presence of this gentle man, so softly spoken, charming and
self-effacing, bewildering to anyone who knew the passion and bravura
of, particularly, his early recordings of the Bruch, Elgar and Brahms
Concertos – those and so many others remain potentially unsurpassed.
Not to mention his humanitarian efforts and his pioneering work in
breaking down musical barriers through collaborations with the likes of
Ravi Shankar and Stephane Grappelli. I found him an exemplary being.

At a loss for words, I latched on to a story my sister Joan had told me,
and asked Yehudi if he remembered visiting Glenveagh Castle in Donegal.

"Oh yes, very well," he lied. "Frightfully impressive place, with
stunning grounds, I seem to recall."

Maybe he did remember. My confidence grew and off I went.

"My sister once did the tour of Glenveagh and the guide got to the
point where he listed some of the many dignitaries and celebrities who had
stayed there over the years. Such and such an actor, this Prime Minister, that
President. 'Oh, and Shughie McMenamin slept in that bedroom there,' he
said. 'Shughie McMenamin?' asked Joan involuntarily. 'Aye, ye know Shughie
McMenamin, yer man that plays the fiddle,' came the indignant response.
After some puzzling, the penny dropped. 'You mean Yehudi Menuhin!' said
Joan. 'The very boy,' he concluded, with not a flicker of recognition."

This is a bit of an Irish trait. There's a pub in Derry that's been
there for about forty years now, called Da Vinci's. The locals still call it
McGlinchey's.

Yehudi seemed to like the story; his face lit up and he let out that
wonderfully mischievous laugh of his. What stories this man must have
had on the tip of his tongue. He didn't even bother telling me, as I found
out later, that during his brief visit to my home county, he'd taken the time
to go and play in the local pubs. This was totally normal for him; none
of that stuffy nonsense. He had no time for elitism; on the contrary, he
encouraged us all to enjoy his exceptional gift and openness to all music.

Coincidentally, Yehudi's home was a house I would get to know rather
well in years to come. When Jacky and I first moved to Crouch End in
1992, we became best friends with our next-door neighbours, David and
Anita. David was an IT guru, a brilliant musician and a fantastic cook;
Anita, a high-flyer in the world of publishing. We must have known them
for about eighteen months when, one day, I noticed a black-and-white
photo on display in their hallway.

"Anita, that photo of you in the hall... the guy with you seems so familiar. Who is that?" I asked.

"Oh, that's Sting," she said nonchalantly.

"Ah, of course it is. How did you meet him, then?" I asked.

"Well, he's my brother," she replied.

Which brings me to this terrific story that I heard – not from Anita, I hasten to add, but from someone in the classical world. The story goes that when the Menuhins were selling their magnificent Highgate home, it came to the attention of Mr Sumner, who was actively looking for just such a property at the time. Well aware that his turning up at a house for sale might well affect the price unfavourably, but not being prepared to buy a house he hadn't seen, left Sting with a bit of a dilemma. In the end, using an alias, he made an appointment to view the house, arrived by motorcycle and conducted the entire operation in full leathers, his helmet firmly in place. Whether it's true or not I find somehow irrelevant. The idea of Sting, all biked up like Bruce Wayne of an evening, being shown around her very traditional, oak-panelled home by Lady Menuhin, is priceless. What is certainly true is that Mr Sumner did buy the house and when David and Anita were having their house renovated, they spent some months up there. It wasn't next door but was always well worth the trip.

After the collapse of Laker in '82, one of my sisters, who'd been working for them for years, took up employment with Caribbean Airways, and I didn't complain, not once. This was back in the good old days when airline employees were able to get free travel for their family members, and Barbados was an undeniably attractive destination for a young man craving a break from the often-depressing British winters. I hitched a ride south more often than I care to admit on those old but lovable DC10s.

Barbados back then was paradisiacal. Sure, you had the old money up on the west coast, those veterans who never liked to stray too far from the sanctuary of Sandy Lane, but with the exception of a couple of stand-out oases, like Sam Lord's Castle and the magnificent Crane Hotel, the rest of the island was delightfully sleepy and slightly rundown. The Bajan people are amongst the friendliest I have encountered anywhere and I soon found myself hanging out with an adorable set of people made up of locals and some blow-ins, all of whom would remain friends for life.

At the centre of this party was a unique gentleman by the name of John Chandler. John owned the oldest hotel on the island, a great big knickerbocker glory of a place; it was the incomparable pink dream of the south coast, the Ocean View. If John Cleese had but known of its existence, he could have swapped the delights of Torquay for this ready-made set, complete with more characters than he would have needed, overlooking the Caribbean Sea. The Ocean View was a jewel of a place. Some insufferable corruption, which I never fully understood, would see it eventually razed to the ground. The site still lies empty instead of treasured as a priceless landmark. It was steeped in a history that now *is* history. It embodied an era of romance, charm and class that is unachievable in this day and age. All manner of people mingled there – the walls of its breathtaking Crystal Room knew more scandalous secrets than is wise – but those who loved and cherished it were the eccentrics, the dreamers.

John and the Ocean View were a match made in heaven. Both were a potent mix of beauty, old values, humour and extreme naughtiness. John's parties were legendary. The hotel staff would file across that treacherous main drag to his home to serve us all dinner before the rum punches did their job and the guests were introduced to the dressing-up cupboard, whereupon all bets were off. One unforgettable memory of those evenings was of Ginny and Marion (a chic Manhattan couple who had retired next door) saying their goodbyes on the terrace. As the aptly named Ginny turned to perform her royal wave, she lost her balance and, falling backwards, disappeared from view over the balcony. It was a shocking thing to witness and we all screamed loudly as we ran to her aid. We needn't have worried, however, because by the time we reached her, she was lighting a cigarette and gaily commenting, "Now why hadn't I thought of that before? Saves taking the stairs."

Ginny had fallen fifteen feet into a strategically placed plant pot, the palm and the rum cushioning her fall.

On other occasions we would bomb up the east coast for a picnic, but a picnic John-style. There were no manky sandwiches or warm beer here. John would always make sure there was a table and chairs; flying fish salad was presented on silver platters and washed down with chilled champagne from cut glass flutes. John is the most natural host I have ever met and a first-class raconteur. Though no longer at his beloved Ocean View, he and his wife Rain run the breathtaking Lancaster Great House in St. James, a must-do item on every visitor's itinerary.

My other great friend on the island is also one of John's oldest friends, the sensual bundle of womanliness that is Sue Walcott. Sue is the owner of the Waterfront Cafe, an infamous Bajan hotspot. Apart from being an infectiously fun and lovable person, Sue has great vision and a formidable business brain. She single-handedly transformed the Careenage area of Bridgetown from a derelict, rat-infested wharf into what it is today: the thriving, bustling centre of town.

Over the years, the quartet played in Barbados many times. We often played in the Ocean View itself and, in fact, played at the opening of Sue's cafe. I rue the fact that the group's love affair with the Caribbean hasn't flourished in the way it might have. Travel and accommodation costs are a significant obstacle. On more than one occasion, our plans to tour there with Wayne Marshall or, in later years, Willard White have been scuppered for one reason or another. Dear George Martin was determined to invite us to Montserrat but ill health thwarted his efforts.

One place we did visit, however, was Trinidad. I recall a performance of the Mozart Clarinet Quintet with Keith Puddy in which the glorious slow movement was completely obliterated by a tropical downpour bouncing off the corrugated iron roof. During our short stay there the weather was hellishly humid, and the school where we were giving lessons was without air conditioning. The charming man responsible for inviting us was a blind amateur viola player called Patrick. He was keen to have a lesson and I, happy to oblige. Not wanting to take up any of the precious practise rooms, we went off in search of a quiet corner to have our tête-à-tête. We settled on a remote fire escape at the foot of a long staircase and Patrick started grappling with the first Bach Cello Suite. Though his playing left a lot to be desired, I was humbled by his intrepid nature and commitment. The more I got into the lesson, the hotter I got. With the sun beating down on the glass doors, this stairwell was becoming like a furnace. I was deeply uncomfortable and perspiring like a comic book character. In my desperation, I suddenly realised the blindingly obvious... Patrick couldn't see me! Inviting him to continue with the Courante, I quietly peeled off my sticky clothes, stopping short at my scanty briefs. It took a minute or two to get used to this bizarre scene but I was feeling cooler and soon forgot about the weirdness of it all as the lesson intensified once again. It wasn't until the lesson was over and I went to retrieve my clothes from the banister where I had hung them to dry that I realised, to my horror, that all the students and the rest of my quartet had finished their studies and, hearing the racket coming from the back staircase, had come to investigate. What a sight must have greeted them. How they kept their composure I'll never know. I hope Patrick didn't think it was a reflection on his playing when the gathered mass finally erupted in a fit of giggles.

Towards the end of our time at Sutton Place, our mentor of old, Terence Weil, announced that he was going to call it a day. He would vacate his teaching position at the RNCM and though he would honour the few playing commitments he had left in his diary, he would not be accepting any more. Terry's illustrious career came to a fitting close with a performance of the great Schubert Quintet, alongside us, broadcast from the BBC Pebble Mill Studio in Birmingham.

In these latter years, Terry had become enchanted by the undeniably enchanting seaside village of Cadaques on the Costa Brava. In spite of its nightmarish approach road, a seemingly endless succession of corkscrew bends cascading in from on high, this one-time home of Salvador Dali was a bustling place with reasonable beaches, great swimming and a plethora of eating and drinking establishments. It also had a successful festival in which we often performed, affording us welcome opportunities to visit our old friend. Gradually, Terry graduated from various rented apartments to actually buying a place of his own. He became a bit of a local celebrity. El Capitano, as he was known, spent his days in one or other of these cafes, crabbitly upping sticks as the shadows forced him on to the next terrace in his pursuit of the sun. You remember those halcyon days in Spain, when you would order a gin and tonic and the waiter would put on a show, engaging in conversation with a local seated nearby while flatly refusing to look at your glass as he poured and poured. Mind you, having said that, this endearing habit has not been wholly consigned to the history books. Albeit on a slightly different tack, we just recently, in the Tierra Astur Restaurant in Oviedo, experienced the highly erotic result of accepting a glass of their speciality local cider. The waitress (for ladies, read waiter) approaches your table and, holding the glass somewhere just below her midriff, fully extends her other arm high above her head. Then, without so much as a glance upwards – instead catching your eye in a fixed stare – she proceeds to tilt the bottle until the golden liquid has filled your glass. All this is performed with barely a drop spilt. I'll have another one of those, please! This intoxicating nonchalance in the alcohol department was only one of the reasons that resulted in Terry's choice of destination. Though he could speak not a word of Spanish, he did fully embrace the culture and undoubtedly brought a dash of eccentricity and colour to that already gaudy place.

We used to love visiting him there. Breakfast would consist of a baguette or some croissants, winched up to his seafront apartment in a basket from the cafe below. Lunch was perhaps an asparagus salad or something hastily thrown together with whatever was fresh in the market, and then for dinner, we would visit a different place each evening with the proviso that we finished the day on the terrace of his favourite cafe playing Backgammon, Scrabble or Cribbage and indulging in one or two of that rather deadly late-night tipple, *café cremat.*

Though spending more and more time in Spain, Terry's main residence was a basement flat in Hampstead, which he had bought off the council. Part and parcel of his retirement plan was to get rid of this place and upgrade his place in Cadaques. This coincided rather fortuitously with the exact moment that I was beginning to think about trying to find a place to buy, inspired by Jacky's lead. A flat in one of London's premier addresses however, wasn't exactly on the cards for me at that time. (Chamber music is not renowned for its financial rewards, as the following anecdote spells out: During a film session at Abbey Road Studios, the viola section was called upon to cope with a difficult bit of ensemble writing. We nailed it on the first take and both the composer and the conductor openly congratulated us on such competence. Pete Lale, the *numero uno* session violist turned to us and said with a broad grin, "Ha, didn't spend twelve years in a quartet for nothing." Quick as a flash, his desk partner for the day, Rachel Bolt, turned to him and replied, "Oh yes, you did!")

One day, Terry was lamenting the fact that he couldn't make his move work cleanly. Certain rules to do with council properties meant that he had to wait another two years before he could sell. For me, this was intriguing. Though I could never have afforded his flat then, perhaps given two years to save and work towards it, I could be better placed to realise my dream and get my foot on that all-important property ladder. Together, we came up with the following plan.

We would immediately get three estimates and agree on a fair sale price for the flat. I would then rent the flat for the two years till Terry was legally able to sell, at which time I would purchase the property minus the rent I'd already paid. It was a deal made in heaven. Hey presto, I had my own place and Terry got to move to where he wanted to be, there and then. Furthermore, he didn't have to go through the tiresome business of putting his flat on the market, dealing with estate agents and so on.

Even though I knew Terry's place and we were both hugely excited by these hitherto unforeseen circumstances, this was still a massive decision for me and I felt I needed to see the place again in order to consolidate my thoughts. My visit the next day did nothing to deter my eagerness.

It was undeniably basic and its walls were covered in a thick, brown film of nicotine, but its location more than made up for it. Before signing on the dotted line, however, I decided to take a stroll to clear my head and take in the immediate neighbourhood. As I climbed the steps to the pavement, the sun came out and I found myself heading towards the surrounding Heath. I hadn't taken so much as ten paces when I noticed, on the opposite side of the street, a fairytale path all covered in dripping clematis and jasmine, falling away towards the unknown. Unable to resist, I crossed over and took the path. In the twinkling of an eye, it took a turn to the left and transported one into an impossibly gorgeous country scene with lakes left and right, huge swaying trees and lush open meadows as far as the eye could see. This was literally a hop, skip and a jump from my potential new front door. Any worries I may have had were allayed by this heavenly vista before me. I raced back to the flat and told Terry that as long as he was happy, I would very much like to go ahead with our ingenious plan. He was thrilled and we shook on it there and then.

"Just out of interest, Paul, how come you returned so quickly from your walk? What convinced you so readily?" asked Terence as I left.

"Oh, it was that stunning little path onto the Heath over there. It's unreal. Like a dream, you know?" said I.

"What path's that, then?" said Terry through a cloud of Weighty smoke.

He'd only lived there for twenty-two years.

Inevitably, Terry's punishing lifestyle began to catch up with him. He was never very mobile and had for many years relied on a bottle of Kaolin and Morph to get him through the day. But now things got serious. We watched in horror as, bit by bit, our old pal lost his legs. First toes would go, then feet, lower limbs, on and on until finally both legs had been taken away. For what it's worth, it was the cigarettes that caused this horrible sequence, a habit he never managed to kick, right up to the end.

We were asked to do a concert marking the tenth anniversary of Britten's death, not six months after we'd played at Sir Peter Pears' memorial. In those days I played on the 'Britten' viola, which Peter had given me after a performance I gave of Britten's 'Lachrymae' in the Maltings in the spring of 1982. This was December '86. We had just vacated the stage of a packed Wigmore Hall; one could still hear the final few heartfelt handclaps of what had been a rapturous reaction to Britten's magnificent 2nd Quartet. I had not even had a chance to put away the famous instrument when I felt a tap on my shoulder. Heart still pounding, adrenaline racing, I wheeled round to address the insensitive being who had violated that precious moment and was confronted by a stern stranger in a gangster-style belted raincoat and matching Trilby.

Ignoring any protocol the occasion might have demanded, he waded straight in with, "My name is Isador Caplan from ze Britten-Pears Foundation. You have something belonging to us and ve vant it baack."

To be made to feel like a criminal is disturbing at the best of times, but under these circumstances it was deeply hurtful and not a little shocking. Our confrontation ended there. I stood in stunned silence, viola in hand, as my hitman slipped away like quicksilver through the advancing well-wishers who were by now pouring into the Green Room. I felt sick to my core, any relief or excitement at the success of the event we had just pulled off – in the name of Mr Caplan's precious BPF – extinguished.

Personal hurts and injustices aside, I was now faced with a harsh reality. I had no money and was about to have my only means of getting any unceremoniously taken away from me. Let there be no doubt, Sir Peter gave that instrument to me. His words to me in the Red House were, "Dear boy, that thing has lain there, under that piano, for the last thirty years. If it's of any use to you, I'd like you to have it."

The problem was that even though Peter and Ben had spent much of their lives living together as a married couple, in those days Peter had no legal right to give anyone anything that had belonged to Ben. Regardless, it wasn't the ownership of the thing that bothered me – I had never once

laid claim to it – it was simply the thought of not being able to use it.
Forthwith, I received a formal letter from the Foundation demanding the
return of the viola. The impending absence of an instrument superseded
the cavernous pit where my stomach once was and, salvaging a tiny
vestige of self-esteem, I composed a begging letter that I sent to Hugh
Maguire, Colin Matthews and Oliver Knussen. These three gentlemen
were heavyweights in the world of Britten and I counted them as friends.
Having your heart in the right place doesn't always mean a whole lot in
the murky waters of finance and law, however, so I awaited their response
with an impending sense of doom.

I am pleased to report that the tale had a happy ending. My three
musketeers were suitably outraged by the events I had detailed in my letter
and managed to persuade the powers that be that: a) It had never been my
intention to steal anything. Indeed, I had paid for the initial and rather
costly restoration of the said instrument out of my own pocket; and, b)
What better life could Ben's viola possibly have than that of a travelling
musician, singing out across the world from the heart of a string quartet
the intimate sounds that he himself had wrestled from the depths of his
own being?

I subsequently received a second piece of correspondence from the BPF,
not a summons nor an apology, but a contract stating that the instrument
was to remain in my possession for as long as I continued to play in the
Brodsky Quartet. This distasteful incident behind us, Ben's Guissani and
I embarked on the second leg of our twenty-five-year journey together.

'Romania'

The British Council was invaluable to us in those early days. Their invitations often coloured in depressingly white sections of our diary and invariably added some exotic stamps to our passport pages. One such invitation was to Romania, that impossibly romantic place steeped in legends from Enescu to Dracula to Ceaușescu. We were about to glimpse the dark and terrifying world of one, Nicolai Ceaușescu.

We found them a trifle over-dramatic, the BC meetings prior to our trip, during which they warned us about bugged hotel rooms and basically made us swear on oath that we would not engage in political conversation whilst there. We'd already been to Poland and Czechoslovakia, armed to the teeth with cigarettes and ladies' tights when really all those poor people wanted was toilet roll. I know from bitter experience that the Derry Journal is no substitute for Nouvelle Super Soft, and we all four made it our business to raid the hotel housekeeping trolleys every day, handing over bagfuls of these precious commodities to passers-by. However, our visits to these other countries had been short and we had spent most of our time in Warsaw and Prague. The upcoming Romanian trip was a proper tour lasting ten days.

We were met at the airport by a BC representative and a dark, handsome stranger by the name of Daniel Ionescu. Daniel was to be our translator and guide for the entire trip. Dion, a highly respected cartoonist in his own right, spoke our language fluently.

The BC had insisted we arrived a day before our first concert so that they could formally welcome us with a little drinks party, which in reality turned out to be yet another security briefing. The ambassador's *amuse-bouches* were strictly *amusantes* and we returned to our hotel in need of dinner. It's always been one of our unspoken rules never to eat in the hotel but to venture out in search of adventure, both culinary and cultural, so we were disappointed when Daniel gently insisted upon staying in to eat. Too hungry to protest, we reluctantly followed him into the restaurant. Unusually, the BC had booked us into one of the premier hotels in all of Bucharest and the restaurant was, like the building itself, palatial. Often referred to as the 'Little Paris of the East', Bucharest is a magical place full of wide boulevards and stunning buildings. The low-level lighting of the communist era only served to enhance the feeling of intrigue. It has to be said, at least from this evening's experience, that the comparison with Paris ended with the architecture.

Upon entering the grand eatery we were eagerly escorted to one of the prime tables, which was laid out with linens, silver and crystal. Here we were left to peruse the over-sized, gold-embossed menus. There were more waiters in full uniform than actual diners in this pretentious room, all of them feverishly busy, yet we were quite unable to gain their attention. When the situation had lost any comedic value and we were on the point of screaming, leaving, or both, Daniel asked if any of us smoked. Ian, being the only guilty party, was then asked if he had any foreign cigarettes about his person. Presently, a brand new pack of full-strength Marlboro was strategically placed on the table, whereupon a veritable squadron of betailed, hitherto deaf and blind people encircled our table. The ornate menus soon proved to be completely worthless as the maitre d', employing his well-rehearsed routine, expertly managed to persuade us all to have the same thing, a speciality of the house. Daniel explained to us later that this would almost certainly have been the only choice available to us. We did, however, finally get something to eat, which is more than can be said for many of the city's inhabitants that evening. Ian's duty-free purchase was looking increasingly like a good deal.

Daniel flatly refused to engage in any kind of political conversation, blatantly changing the subject any time that banned topic came up. We were desperate to find out more of what life was really like there but our constant questions were left unanswered. I was already burdened with a feeling of hopelessness after just one evening in this surreal game but when, in the lobby of the hotel after our meal, I clumsily tried to give Daniel a few measly dollars in a pathetic attempt to assuage my choking guilt, his terrified reaction seemed so exaggerated as to be farcical. With only minimal eye contact, he signalled for me to follow him outside into the street. We walked a short distance from the hotel to a place where he obviously felt safer before he rammed home, in hushed tones, what I had already been told a hundred times – that during our time in Romania, we would be closely monitored, spies were everywhere, and no one was to be trusted. Though I managed to furtively pass him the few crumpled dead presidents in our goodnight handshake, I was careful not to compromise him again during the days ahead.

I could never understand how these dictators worked. From my distant, safe cocoon, I would naively dismiss the whole predicament as idiotic. Why, in heaven's name, didn't enough like-minded people just get together and overthrow the bully and his cronies? A short time up close and exposed to the reality of such a hideous regime would open my eyes and educate me in that respect.

The next afternoon we left the hotel for our rehearsal. As we made our way along a bustling main street, all of a sudden there was a piercing whistle. In a flash, one in three of my fellow pedestrians produced whistles and morphed eerily into drill sergeants, organising us all away from the street and up against the walls, where we were to remain motionless. The majestic boulevard had come to a halt and been cleared in a matter of moments, just in time for the colossal cavalcade of cars, motorcycles, military vehicles and Limousines to sweep by at a pace, uninterrupted. I doubt old Nick was on his way to our rehearsal, somehow; perhaps he had an important matter of state to attend to, or maybe it was Elena, off on an urgent shopping trip to the big Paris of the West.

Yes, it's true, I've witnessed this sort of thing right here on our streets. When ER has to get from a thoughtlessly scheduled appointment to Ascot for the Coronation Cup they will indeed clear the M4, but poor old Lizzie is in her nineties and visibly adores all things equine. Besides, monarchs have been attending that shindig since her long-lost second aunt once removed, Anne, started it all back in 1711. But there was something much more sinister about this manoeuvre. The way in which so many seemingly ordinary citizens reacted as one, turned into automatons at the sound of a whistle and then, just as seamlessly, transformed themselves back into Joe Bloggs, the person next to you… seeing those whistles made the experience all the more chilling for me. I'd spent long evenings back in Shantallow with a similar whistle in my pocket – a whistle that, if I'd been caught in possession of it, would have seen me spend seven years in jail, no questions asked. It scared the hell out of me to think that, at the tender age of twelve, I had been coerced into such a dangerous situation as that, one I knew little or nothing about. I was no different to these people. Fear, peer pressure and distorted information had led us, like Nicolai's abusive dad's few sheep, to a lowly state of 'follow the leader'.

In a glorious twist of fate that afternoon, we would be transported from the nadir to the zenith of human behaviour. As we left that vile street scene and entered the hallowed interior of Bucharest's stunning concert hall, we were enveloped by the celestial sounds of a choir. Our entrance did not escape the notice of the choirmaster, who immediately silenced the assembled vocalists, saying, "Ladies and gentlemen of the choir, it's the Brodsky Quartet." With broad, infectious grins, the whole group burst into spontaneous applause. The conductor turned to us and said, "We are honoured to have you here and would like to sing something for you by way of welcoming you to our city."

With barely a word of preparation, these beautiful people sang some haunting Penderecki just for us. Their open display of unconditional camaraderie was almost unbearably moving. For us, a bunch of kids in our early twenties, to be addressed in such an intimate way was deeply touching.

At our sold-out concert that evening we received one of the warmest receptions I think we've ever had. I'll never forget coming out after Beethoven's Op.18 No.6, with which we opened the programme, to a standing ovation and a shower of flowers that flooded the stage from every corner of the auditorium. These people were being treated abominably, they were being starved of food, resources and love, and yet, in the face of such horror, they had not lost their dignity or their resolve. Music is arguably the most powerful tool we possess to fan the flames of hope that can all too easily be dampened and buried within us. To witness its release is perhaps the most valuable privilege afforded the working musician.

The next day's concert was a flight away, in a place called Satu Mare. As a performing artist, this is the life you sign up for: up too early after the inevitable late night, bit of a dodgy breakfast you don't really want, enter the confined space of a car or van and embark on what is often a lengthy journey with other people when the very last thing you feel like doing is interacting with other people. Then check into the next second-rate hotel, do a rehearsal, go through your own warm-up routine, do the show, finally head out for something hopefully nice to eat and drink before retiring later than you had planned and getting not quite enough sleep before the next day's Groundhog Day itinerary. For the most part, these days pass with only your average helping of spice. Romania, however, was determined to liven up the *menu du jour*. Each day was to be more memorable than the last.

The transport from the airport into the city of Satu Mare was an ancient, ridiculously oversized bus. As we clattered along the single-lane country roads, we passed hordes of schoolchildren just walking along together in the middle of nowhere.

"Where can they be going?" we asked.

It turned out they were simply doing what they did every day – walking the several miles home from school. We implored our driver to stop. Health and Safety was a thing of the future and suddenly we had a bus full of kids, standing, sitting, lying across one another; they scrambled on that jalopy in any way they could. These children were living through one of the most notoriously brutal regimes of modern times. They were clearly malnourished and yet they entertained us royally, making a mockery of our glum expressions with their infectious bonhomie. They were so excited when they found out we were musicians coming to play in their very own town.

"Can we please come to the concert?" they chorused.

"Of course you can," we replied.

Not believing for a moment that any of them would turn up, we told them that they had to pick up their tickets thirty minutes before the show, otherwise they would have to be sold. We stepped out onto the stage and were greeted by a veritable sea of those, by then familiar, grins. After the concert they all came to see us. All wanted photos, including their parents, who had brought us gifts of chocolate, flowers and homemade grappa in ornate bottles. We have those bottles to this day, though they've been empty for some time. What a sacrifice that must have been for them. What a gesture, giving when they had absolutely nothing to give. We stood around for ages, hugging and laughing, gesticulating madly in the absence of even a single common word. Eventually the gathering dispersed, they went home – no doubt to prepare for tomorrow's trek to school – and we repaired to the only restaurant still open for business. It was an interesting place, dimly lit and on several different levels. It was buzzing, presumably made up of audience members because when we entered they all stood up, applauding and cheering. Here, again, we were handed impressive menus full of mouthwatering dishes, but Daniel whispered conspiratorially that, once again, there was only one thing on offer – a kind of goulash. It wasn't till our food arrived and we began to tuck in that we realised with horror that no one else in the restaurant was eating. Our vantage point up there on the top table made it all the more difficult to swallow. At the same time, we couldn't exactly hand it round and if we left some, that would surely show even more ignorance. This damned country was playing havoc with our emotions.

As luck would have it, we were able to offer the kids one last tiny gesture of goodwill. The next morning, we once again passed them on the road and gave them a lift, this time back to school.

We were going back to Bucharest for a private concert at the British ambassador's home. The day after that, we did some teaching during the day and got invited round to Daniel's apartment for dinner in the evening. We were painfully aware of the austere conditions these people were putting up with in their daily lives. There were snaking queues where folk spent many hours gradually pushing their cars towards a solitary petrol pump, not knowing if the petrol might run out just as they finally reached it. Even if they were successful, they were only allowed a few litres each. It was the same sorry scene at bread shops and grocery stores. That day, when we arrived at Daniel's place, there was pandemonium because a small truck pulled up in the empty market square outside his soulless, concrete apartment block with a couple of crates of over-ripe tomatoes in the back.

Daniel's mother, Pamela, and some of his closest friends joined us that evening. We all crammed into his tiny room and somehow cobbled together a meal. It was a wonderful evening but, inevitably, one punctuated with horror stories graphically detailing the grim realities of life under Ceaușescu. With the record player turned up and everyone whispering, the locals were cautiously opening up. One young woman there was facing the terrifying prospect of performing an abortion on herself, and not for the first time. Living in a society where there was no contraception outside of the all-too-perilous natural methods, and with the brutally enforced anti-abortion law of 1966, women found themselves cornered into an unenviable position devoid of sympathy or understanding. The harrowing tales of woe were so disturbing that we were lining up to marry these poor unfortunates in an effort to release even just one soul from this tortuous fate.

A couple of days later we were boarding our flight from Iasc to Brashov when, out of nowhere, a convoy of official cars sped across the tarmac, screeching to a halt just in front of us, by the steps to our small twin-engine jet.

Without so much as a word or a sideways glance, the passengers of these cars pushed past us and onto the waiting aircraft. We were informed matter-of-factly by the stewardess that our seats had been commandeered and that we would have to find alternative means of travel. Daniel's immediate acceptance of this bewildering situation only served to infuriate us all the more. Our vociferous protestations about having an important concert that night fell on very deaf ears and proved to be short-lived as the steps were taken away, the door closed and the aircraft began to taxi towards the nearby runway. They at least had the decency to offload our bags, but that's where their concern ended. Incredulous at what had just happened, we re-entered the terminal building and started looking for the next flight to Brashov. The only other flight that day would have got us there too late for the concert and was, in any case, already overbooked. Once again, Daniel's defeatist attitude had us incensed. Yes, he looked crestfallen and was upset about the fact that we would not play in Brashov that night, but equally he was accepting of what had just happened and totally resigned to the new day that lay before us. He would contact the BC who would in turn relay the news to the people in Brashov. Meanwhile, he hoped that the hotel we had just left in Iasc had some rooms available for that night.

We, on the other hand, had other ideas. Having ruled out planes and trains, we turned our attention to automobiles. Car hire was anathema. Even if you somehow found a car, there was no petrol. For the same reason, taxis were a non-starter; this was a seven-hour drive. Unperturbed, we stood around making one improbable suggestion after another as to how we might accomplish our goal. I felt like Georgie Best in that infamous game for San Jose when a blatant 'no goal' was given against his team and his prolonged, angry diatribe towards the referee only resulted in him receiving a yellow card. He was heard to say upon the restart, "Just give me the fuckin' ball!" His colleague duly obliged and George went on one of his legendary mazy runs goalward. Defenders were left either on their arses or swinging at thin air till, finding himself with only the keeper left to beat, the Belfast Boy stuck it in the bottom right-hand corner. It was voted the Budweiser Goal of the Year that season and was arguably one of the greatest goals of all time.

It was a moment of sublime retribution born out of anger and frustration, not unlike that glorious moment when, out of the corner of my eye, I spotted a curious vehicle, complete with uniformed driver, parked in a leafy corner of the airport forecourt. Reluctantly, Daniel followed me over to this gentleman and helped me quiz him. To this day, I have no idea what that guy and his bus were doing there at that exact moment in time, but there they were. It was an enormous, bright yellow, 64-seater bus in the style of those old American school buses – and, bafflingly, full of gas. We struck a deal with this guy there and then, to drive us seven hours across the Transylvanian Alps. With nothing to eat or drink, and only one short toilet break deep in some wood or other, we rocked and rolled our way to Brashov, shimmying past enormous potholes and various types of wild animal. We came to rest in front of our hall a mere forty-five minutes late for the concert. News of our escapade had reached our public and in a show of solidarity, they had all stoically remained, chatting and smoking and generally clogging up the pavement outside. They cheered and clapped as we descended from our battle bus and ran into our dressing rooms, determined to get the show on the road as soon as possible. I'd like to say that our ensuing performance was a worthy candidate for some award or other, but I fear that we were still moving from the journey and our shaking limbs were not ideally suited to the various bowing techniques demanded of us. Never mind; the feeling of beating the system was reward enough and besides, I can't stand bloomin' Bud. There was an undeniably convivial atmosphere about the place, though, and we finished with an extended encore section where we could all forget the trials and tribulations of the day that had been.

I would be lying if I said that during the concert, our minds and tummies weren't collectively wandering in the direction of the much-advertised post-concert reception. We hadn't eaten since the frugal hotel breakfast in Iasc a full fourteen hours earlier and the fortissimo rumblings were interfering with the pianissimo dynamics of Debussy's

'Beau Soir'. At the end of the concert, a couple came into our dressing room and announced that they would escort us to the reception. We did not need a second invitation and followed these two at a pace. She was very glamorous and obviously quite well-to-do; he, the second clarinet in the local orchestra, was equally dapper in his sharply pressed black pants and leather jacket. Orchestras, like all institutions, had several party members within their ranks and this one had been delegated the job of entertaining us for the evening. They led us to a dimly lit section of the foyer, where they studiously unwrapped one baguette-style sandwich of ham and cheese for each of us, washed down by a communal bottle of local vodka. It took much persuasion on our part for Daniel to be invited, and this couple, even when language constraints rendered us silent for long periods, resolutely ignored him for the duration of the meal. Once again, Romania had served up a day to remember.

Daniel's work inevitably brought him to the attention of the wrong people and within months of our first meeting, though not directly related to that meeting, I'm sure, the authorities began to close in on him. Stop searches and idle threats quickly turned into beatings and days in a cell. Through an extraordinary series of coincidences, Daniel finally managed to pull off the unthinkable; despite the heartache of leaving his mother home alone, and the potential consequences of that, he escaped.

I had just come off a long European tour when I received the crackly phone call from an exhausted but overjoyed Daniel. He had wangled permission to attend an exhibition of his work in Bulgaria and from there had made it across the border into Greece and was now in Athens. Unsure of his next move, I told him that I was on my way and took a flight that very night. We met up in the dingy, sweaty arrivals hall of Athens Airport and boarded a bus into the town centre. Luckily, given that Daniel was currently of no fixed abode, Athens in summer time is the proverbial 'city that doesn't sleep', but the first thing to do next morning was to rectify that situation. We found a room not a stone's throw from the Plaka. It was a room best suited to the hours of darkness. I shudder to think how many other life forms we shared that space with, but it was all I could afford and it served its purpose for now. Next stop was the British Embassy. It seemed obvious to try to get him into the UK but after several days of queueing, filling in forms and conducting interview after interview, it became clear that this was not going to happen. With considerably less hope, we repeated this lengthy and tiresome process at the US Embassy, only to find that, to our amazement, they eventually conceded and agreed to let Daniel in. The enormous relief and feeling of euphoria made those ten long days well worth the effort. Daniel had to remain in Greece until such time as his paperwork was made ready and then off he went into the unknown.

A totally new life unfolded for him in the Big Apple. He would go on to live in Queens and work for many prestigious publications including the NY Times, the New Yorker and Time Magazine. I managed to get him a couple of exhibitions here in London and we got to meet up on our visits to the US. Pamela thankfully survived any fallout from Daniel's escape and eventually joined him in New York after many Romanians enjoyed a bumper Christmas in 1989. Santa brought Nick and Elena a few surprise packages that day – not all of them, I would suggest, entirely welcome. On that December day, revenge was indeed served up cold. Too quick, too good for them, I hear you cry. The footage was impossible to take in. Was this really happening right there on the screen, just beyond our steamy pudding? How do you ensure retribution for such evil? The financial and social aftermath of a tyranny is also challenging to deal with. Ironically, many would say life had actually been better under this mad dictator. Everyone had a job; everyone had a place to live. What a price to pay, though. The human spirit has to be more precious than these securities, and our freedom to travel and speak our minds worth almost any hardship.

Regardless, Romania entered a new era that day and is surely now a better place in which to live. In time, Daniel and his mother returned to Bucharest, where he continues to enrich the artistic life of that community.

'Amati'

The concert had probably been as average as many we had given that year, but the overall weekend experience was memorable. I'm struggling to remember what we played but the venue was a magnificent orangerie-style building perched high up, overlooking Lulworth Cove; the champagne was chilled and the *hors d'oeuvres*, copious and delectable. The audience members seemed to have stumbled off an Edwardian film set and conversed in an exaggerated plummy tongue, which only served to accentuate my horribly out of place Donegal lilt. Being just along the coast from the set of a more recent show, *Fawlty Towers*, I decided to take a leaf out of old Basil's book and not mention the war. Keep the conversation on music and not the great conflict and all should be well. As the post-concert bash came to a close, a gentleman purposefully approached me and began quizzing me intently on my life as a violist.

Had I always played the viola? Why did I change from violin? Where had I studied and with whom? Did I have my own instrument?

It was my negative response to this final question that prompted him to ask if I would be interested in trying a viola that he had just inherited from his father. The instrument hadn't been played for many years and he knew very little about it, but it was a family heirloom and he was most keen to have it used. This was a Saturday night and we were due to stay locally before making our way to Dartington on the Monday. As luck would have it, this chap lived only a short detour off the A303 so I agreed to call on him on my way through.

That night, as was often the case back in those days, we were staying in private hospitality – or hostility, as it's affectionately known. This always proved to be a sickening game of chance. One night you might find yourself in a warm, cosy environment among people who could easily become friends; the next, in a cold, austere scene, opposite folk with whom you had no empathy whatsoever. On this occasion it was our good fortune to follow a Bentley back through the country lanes and up the meandering driveway to Minterne, the family home of Lady Digby.

Minterne had been in the Digby/Churchill families since 1620 and its majestic countenance oozed history. We were welcomed in by Lady Digby herself, who trotted around in a wonderfully nonchalant manner, introducing us and giving instructions to family, staff and pets alike. We were offered supper and various nightcap possibilities and encouraged to sleep as late as we wanted. This was not a hotel and breakfast could be had at any time of the day, especially on a Sunday. Armagnac in a cut glass, in front of a roaring fire with a friendly spaniel, is not something I can easily resist so I embraced a moment of nostalgic repose before retiring to my appointed room.

The next day remains like a dream in my mind. Though still only mid-morning, the day was already warm as the sun illuminated the near-perfect rural picture that greeted my sleepy eyes as I pushed open the heavy sprung door to the kitchen. Rays of sunlight poured in from the adjoining conservatory, creating a magical glow in the throbbing hub of the house. People moved around, some at work, some at leisure, exchanging pleasantries as they went about their day. The cats, who had predictably cornered the warmest spots on the cushioned window seats or woollen throws, barely forced open an eye to acknowledge my entrance. The dogs, on the other hand, scurried excitedly over and back, round and round, picking up random bits of paraphernalia and dropping them by my feet, wagging their entire bodies, their tails so far between their legs as to be tickling their chins. Breakfast was a mouthwatering, help-yourself set-up. Freshly squeezed orange juice; a bowl of the granola you yourself can never find, drenched in an exotic fruit salad with yoghurt and honey from the farm; big doorsteps of homemade, wholemeal bread hacked from a rustic shape, Aga-toasted to perfection and laden with cold chunks of very creamy, very salty butter; a bit too much proper, crumbly cheddar and thick-cut, whiskey-infused marmalade, all washed down with some first flush darjeeling that Aunt Harriet had sent over from West Bengal.

Into this aristocratic snapshot wafted three achingly gorgeous girls, probably touching base between sojourns on a Greek island and in the

South of France, their laissez-faire attitude encouraged by the presence of old money. That tired, tousled, sun-kissed look – last night's perfume gaining in intensity in tandem with their gossip. Shot through Vaseline, their carefully thrown on, ripped T-shirt or oversized boyfriend's shirt, offered a perfectly judged glimpse of another world.

Too good to be true... enter boyfriends. All flailing limbs, puppy-dog eyes and teeth, rugger shirts and signet rings. This harsh new perspective was starting to play havoc with my digestion, so I skulked off unnoticed for a brief constitutional.

After we'd rehearsed, we reconvened down by the pool where we spent a glorious afternoon swimming, playing croquet and, best of all, tennis on a proper lawn tennis court. These blissful activities were accompanied by homemade lemonade and subsequently a sumptuous cream tea, all served upon request, in situ. We dined at the local pub so as not to over-impose and next morning were up early and on our way westward, this divine idyll consigned to the memory bank.

It wasn't long till I was pulling into the drive of the man with the viola. My expectations were low and I was perfecting the oft-repeated summing-up speech, which goes something like, "Oh yes, it's very nice. Such a lovely patina. One piece back, which is unusual. Impressively even tone throughout, yet with a distinct character."... Now, where's the door?

In point of fact, nothing could have prepared me for the vision that lay before me. This doctor from Dorset had unsuspectingly inherited the most beautiful viola I had ever seen. The label read Nicolo Amati and after an intimate hour spent with this beauty, I had no reason to doubt its authenticity. The excited owner explained to me in no uncertain terms that his plan was to have the viola certified forthwith so that he could get it properly insured in readiness for its new guardian, me, to pick it up on my way back from Dartington. I left that house in a state of euphoria. I arrived at Dartington in a bubble of happiness, literally jumping for joy as I told my colleagues and friends about my new-found love. But we were going to be here for two whole weeks; the anticipation, the wait, would be unbearable. Maybe I could pick it up sooner. Surely these piffling formalities could be sorted in a matter of hours and we could be reunited immediately thereafter. Why postpone the heavenly moment?

Next day I phoned the good doctor to relay my thoughts, only to find that he, in his excitement, had phoned the dealer Peter Biddulph, who, upon hearing the name Amati, had suggested they meet that very same day. It was inevitable that from this moment on, I would fade from the picture. Mr Biddulph, ironically an old friend, quite naturally saw only dollar signs and strongly advised the good doctor not to lend out such an important instrument but to instead allow him to organise a frantic bidding war that could result in the two men pocketing some serious lolly. I doubt even Peter could have imagined that my short-lived best friend would soon go on to become the first £1m plus viola ever sold. I never saw it again.

'Mr Fahey takes a punt'

Our residency at Cambridge University – the first in its 800 year history – was initially funded by Citibank, under the guidance of the wonderful Catherine Graham-Harrison. Without her vision, that insitution might have passed another century without a resident string quartet. Not that that would have mattered a jot to that old-boy network. As long as this high-class section of the British farming community, shamelessly funded by starstruck, overseas students, continues to provide the right stock to oil the corrupt wheels of power, frankly, who needs the distraction of a few entertainers? Our arrival there, at an age barely exceeding that of the students, was entirely at the whim of the eccentric and wickedly frivolous head of music Alexander Goehr. Things seemed to be tootling along swimmingly for a year or two but then Citibank appeared to lose interest and we had to find someone to take their place else the long-awaited residency might be painfully short-lived. Enter Patrick Fahey.

One doesn't always remember the precise moment a friendship begins; often, even the best of pals achieve closeness gradually. Neither of these scenarios fit myself and Pat. I had circuitously ended up at a party in Mayfair where I knew only the hostess. Upon arriving I could see I was way out of my depth. Everyone was considerably older than me and oozed confidence and sophistication; I was a penniless greenhorn dolled up in my Sunday best. Such was my discomfort that I quickly employed a survival strategy that would hopefully see me through the next half hour till I could excuse myself without seeming rude. I decided to be always on the move, whether it be in search of a drink, in need of the loo or trying to catch the attention of someone who was always just vacating the room I was in. During one of my farcical forays across the hallway, the front doorbell went and I, being next to it, thought it only polite to open the door. Who should enter proceedings but… Lulu. Just as gorgeous in real life as in the image etched in my mind's eye, her presence, far from making me wanna shout, rendered me dumbstruck.

Things were really ramping up and it was at this juncture, as I was plotting my escape, that I first heard his dulcet tones. A familiar ballad came drifting across the airwaves, immediately easing the tension in my contorted body. I checked my stride and gingerly followed the sounds till I located the vocalist, a full-blown male Paddy savouring the attention of a flock of enthralled females. Gradually my confidence returned, along with my voice, and before you could say 'cockatoo', we were belting out songs I hadn't heard for ten years or more.

Pat Fahey landed in the metropolis of London from the double parish of Bansha and Kilmoyler in the South Riding of County Tipperary, aged fourteen and alone. Against all the odds, he set about changing his fortunes. Blessed with a razor-sharp mind and a limitless capacity for hard slog, Pat, by the time I met him, had built a hugely successful property business, lived in Oscar Wilde's old house on the Thames, took delivery of a new Bentley every November and kept a stable of horses that would shake up a few Saudi pretenders.

By the time we were turfed out of that Down Street address, Pat and I were already pals and eager to meet up again. At that point he had no idea what I did for a living, which only served to accentuate the incongruity of his next comment.

"Do you know a place called the Wigmore Hall? Only I'm going to a concert there on Tuesday and I have a spare ticket."

You could have knocked me down with a feather.

"As a matter of fact, I do know that place and I'd love to go," said I.

As we entered the foyer, Pat was clearly intrigued as to how everyone seemed to know who I was, and I equally intrigued as to why this guy would choose to come to a Prussia Cove gig. Things got more baffling when, at the end of the show, Pat announced that he had to pop backstage to say hello to some people. Upon entering the Green Room, I was engulfed by all the sweaty performers and Pat, by the besuited organisers. It wasn't till we were in the restaurant later that I explained I was in the Brodsky Quartet, and he revealed that he'd been sponsoring IMS (International Music Seminar) events for the last couple of years.

Pat Fahey stories are a book in themselves – I am literally biting my lip as I write – but I guess I must stick to the task in hand. Pat remains a close family friend and the Brodsky Quartet owes him a great debt of gratitude for all the artistic projects he has got involved in over the years, not least our residencies at Cambridge and, subsequently, at the then-newly reopened Blackheath Concert Halls.

***

Apart from the joy of meeting one or two exceptionally gifted and lovely students, I have only two abiding memories of our time at Cambridge, and only one of them involves music.

We and the clarinettist Alan Hacker had taken on the unenviable challenge of learning the Birtwistle Quintet for a visit by the composer and had spent many hours slaving over this thankless work. The rambling central section in particular had caused much angst. It's one of those passages where everyone heads off on their own journey, all in different time signatures, but ultimately ends up at the same destination. Despite considerable probing, we never could meet up and were left bemused and perplexed. We diligently worked on it in vain right up to the last minute, whereupon we admitted defeat and agreed to wing it as best we could. When the orchestrator of our frustration arrived at the West Road Concert Hall, the scene of a public class on the piece, we were already in our positions as he shuffled onto the stage muttering greetings in a broad Yorkshire monotone. Before he had even got his overcoat off, he blurted out in a barely disguised snigger and without so much as a hint of embarrassment, "O' course, you know the first thing to realise about this piece is that the central section don't make any sense. The maths is all wrong so it's all a bit of a mess really."

My enthusiasm for the piece was already at a low ebb but with this information, any flicker of positivity drained away. A brief 'heads-up' in advance would have saved a lot of wasted time. Bach didn't make basic mathematical errors, did he? And he made his own fucking manuscript paper!

Certainly, it was mildly intriguing to get a glimpse of this quasi-fictional world, a world at the cutting edge of so much, yet Dickensian in reality. Cloaks and courtyards, gargoyles and gatekeepers, stone steps and shiny, dark-wood studies, ancient gas fires and inset inkwells, stuffy students and dusty Dons alike, sporting tweeds and brogues. A visit to the celebrated tea shop and a quick punt down the Cam took care of Monday afternoon... now what? Clearly, one stood in awe of the architecture and history of the place, and any chance to hear the choir of King's College was an undeniable treat, but the surprising influx of squaddies after dark left me feeling decidedly ill at ease.

The mention of squaddies and clarinets reminds me of a glorious 'coming of age' moment. We were standing in for the Gabrieli Quartet who had had to pull out of a concert, on the day, that included a performance of the Mozart Quintet with Jack Brymer. Jack was probably the most famous clarinettist in the country at that time and a pillar of the establishment. His sublime playing aside, visually he always put me in mind of a sergeant-major type and our rehearsal that day was undoubtedly an oft-repeated drill. If he was armed with a certain amount of trepidation at these youngsters' last-minute inclusion he certainly didn't show it – we, on the other hand, were clearly displaying rookie nerves.

We played our six-bar intro to the first movement and without blowing a single note, Jack piped up, "Oh, very nice. Beautifully balanced. We won't do the second repeat, obviously."

Jack had turned his page and was already inhaling in preparation for the heavenly second movement while we quickly fumbled with our mutes. We hadn't got to Bar 3 when he said, "Lovely tempo. I play the recap *pianissimo*."

The third movement was dismissed altogether with the wonderfully positive sentiment that, "We don't want to get in the way of spontaneity. Let's all have fun."

Nor did the maestro play a single note of the finale. We, having negotiated the notoriously troublesome opening rather niftily, elicited the sole comment, "Brilliant, chaps, you should have saved that for the show."

In a flash, he had skedaddled for a cuppa with his missus, leaving us to apply a bit of spit 'n' polish to the remainder of our evening's parade.

It was fun being back at West Road, the scene of our EBU triumph, and 'the first ever quartet-in-residence at Cambridge University' was undoubtedly a cool line to have cornered for our biography, but it was the wine cellars that would steal the show. We were affiliated to Trinity Hall and Clare

Colleges and were invited to gorge ourselves twice a day, three times if you include the indulgent breakfasts. This perk quickly wore thin, in direct opposition to our waistlines, and I found the abundance grotesque and the inevitable waste depressing.

Our first experience of dining at 'high table' was, admittedly, a blast. Sandy, as Alexander Goehr was affectionately known, had given us a few useful tips in terms of the perceived etiquette for such an occasion, labouring one point in particular – that which pertains to the passing of the port. This is one of the most crucial bits of knowledge required for a successful stay at this great house of learning. It's a pleasing coincidence that the port gets passed to the left. Now, had it been that the port gets passed to the right, that would of course be fine too; you would simply remember that the port gets passed in the opposite direction to the way in which the name suggests it might be passed, and all would be well. None of us being nautical types, it was still quite a lot of information to take in at short notice, and unnerving for a fastidious character like Ian, who found himself seated next to, of all people, the master. The experience was unreal, as if we'd entered a time warp. We were in an imposing baronial hall dripping with formal portraits of past alumni and professors. The be gowned boys and girls, who were seated at long trestle tables scoffing their gruel from lead plates, all stood to attention when we took our places at the top table. Grace was said and the butler service began. Course one – the soup – was easy enough to negotiate, but the second – the pear, walnut and chicory salad – heavens, which cutlery did we go for now? *Just work your way from the outside in, you eejit. Oh yeah, of course, that's it. But that doesn't half look like a fish knife and that's two courses away. No, that's for the butter. Weren't you listening to Sandy at all?* The cut-glass decanters of chardonnay and Bordeaux were invaluable in de-stressing this intimidating scene and worked wonders for poor Ian, whose tongue was finally beginning to loosen to the point where he and the master were chewing the fat like a pair of old sea captains. The embarrassing quiet that accompanied the start of the meal, where every minor clunk of glass or scrape of a knife seemed amplified to an almost deafening degree, had been replaced by a right din. Tom Brown and his mates had long since been excused and this rabble were fast losing their sense of decorum. It was into this melee that the infamous bottle of port was ceremoniously introduced and placed, as was the custom, in front of the master. At the appropriate moment the master passed the vessel to Ian, who was seated on his right. Ian, mindful of his earlier lesson and imagining that the master was breaking with protocol in a friendly gesture towards him, this being his first time, came down heavily on the side of tradition.

"Oh no, thank you, master. I will of course wait my turn."

"Oh, but I insist, Ian. Please, be my guest."

"No, no, couldn't possibly, sir."

This preposterous duet of diplomacy must have gone on for a full five minutes but no amount of coercing from the master would shake Ian's resolve and finally, with sudden, visible irritation, the master sent the heady liquid off on its long voyage round the table, leaving Ian's short-lived, burgeoning friendship prematurely on rocky ground. You see, Sandy (I told you he had a wicked sense of humour) had neglected to tell us one very important little detail in his port tutorial: the port always goes left *unless* you are seated to the right of the master. In this instance, you must accept the offer of the bottle, take some and then quickly return the valuable and much-needed resource to the master so that he can fill his goblet before it sets sail westward, where it's at the mercy of the drunken sailors, never to be seen again.

And so endeth the lesson.

'Reflections'

Pretty much everything about being in a group is counterintuitive. Any artist worth their salt strives daily to plumb the depths of their being in an effort to find out what, if anything, they have to say. What is the truth behind what drives them? They will try again and again to grasp that shapeshifting, abstract unknown. Then, if successful, there is a choice to be made: keep any revelations private or go public. Both avenues can be equally frustrating. A performer's life is ultimately a solitary one, so you can choose to keep these discoveries to yourself, leaving your colleagues to notice any changes by default; or alternatively, you can decide to share these moments of inspiration – by teaching, for example – but this can so often be an unpredictable, even empty experience. Given that much of what we're searching for is infuriatingly transient and nebulous anyway, one must be wary of strongly held convictions, keep an open mind and not expect too much by way of gratification from others who, remember, are on a similarly frustrating journey of their own.

Most of us will never really find that holy grail, so more often than not, it's the gruesome digging around that potentially gets aired like so much dirty laundry. There are days when you do feel convinced, when a luminous clarity surges through you and propels you forwards; sound, tempi, dynamics and, above all, style become clear and inevitable – life is good. Sometimes this feeling can last for hours, there are even rare periods when you can feel invincible for days, but this euphoria can slip back out through the door to your mind like quicksilver, only to return when it deems fit. These flashes of enlightenment are enormously important to any artist. Once you recognise them and learn how to grasp them, they can unlock some of the seemingly impenetrable puzzles we are faced with daily in our lives as interpreters of other people's thoughts. If you're lucky, the secret of a whole movement can be unearthed but, not being a greedy person, the answer to a single, enigmatic phrase will suffice.

We should work tirelessly on our techniques – these are the tools of our trade – but as with so many of life's problems, it is our minds that we must train and strive to control. This is where we can learn so much from sports people. Often the results of our poor technique can be difficult to discern and pinpoint, whereas for them it is painfully obvious. If Wayne Rooney unintentionally hits across the ball whilst leaning back slightly, that shot will go high and wide. If Tiger Woods doesn't execute that most infuriating of all movements, the dreaded golf swing, perfectly – if, when that ferocious 5-iron crunches that little white ball, it happens to be 2mm open – Mr Woods will be 20m right of the flag. No pay cheque for Mr Woods.

Where we seem to differ is that both Tiger and Wayne would know exactly what they did wrong and how to fix it. They would visit the practice area and work on improving that precise movement. We, on the other hand, are often flummoxed by our inaccuracies, not really knowing why our sound broke, why our intonation suffered, why we fluffed that run. Equally, all great athletes have the ability to slow down and focus their minds when under colossal pressure. They are calm and in complete control of their actions; for them, time stands still. This is an enormously important attribute for any musician, but not one that is ever talked about in the classroom. Not nearly enough emphasis is placed on the physics and physicality of what we do. We are, after all, athletes. We regularly perform a physical activity. You only have to witness the horrifying number of work-related injuries in our profession to figure that one out. I've learnt more about playing the viola in a single golf lesson than in four years at the Royal College of blinking Music.

It doesn't half wind me up when I hear people talk about the huge amounts of study time involved in becoming a doctor or a lawyer. How many people do you know who started reading medicine or law aged three and then devoted every day of their lives to their chosen vocation? That's what it takes to be a top-class player and there's no respite. As Yehudi once said, "If I miss a day's practice, I notice it. If I miss two, *they* notice it."

It's a constant battle to stay at the top of your game and this only gets more challenging as you get older. Most athletes bow out gracefully in their thirties or forties; many musicians go on into their eighties.

Fundamentally, performing musicians fall into three distinct categories: soloists, orchestral players and chamber musicians. I have little experience of the first two situations but it's fairly clear that to be a soloist, you would be advised to have a few basic attributes. You'll need to be reasonably happy with your own company, have a flawless technique, formidable memory, nerves of steel and, if not an ego the size of a house, then some serious self-belief.

Whilst an orchestral musician also needs a healthy technique, they are almost never called upon to memorise anything. They need to be able to live amongst people… lots of people, keep their mouths shut, take orders and compromise their playing so as to fit in. Their egos must be kept in check. Where a soloist can usually choose things like flights, hotels and even when to rehearse, the orchestral player's life is mapped out by other people. They have no choice but to toe the line.

A chamber musician occupies the middle ground. Though once again rarely called upon to memorise repertoire, a high level of technique is a must. Nerves are heavily tested here, since every time you put bow to string you are endangering not just your own reputation but also that of your colleagues.

Playing chamber music invariably starts out as a musical rush. It's a potent drug that satisfies so many desires – the repertoire, the technical challenges, having your voice heard whilst benefiting from that soul-enriching feeling of camaraderie. Once taken seriously, it quickly becomes all of that but under the confines of an ever-present reality – that it is also your job, your livelihood, and as such, it has to be viable. Be aware, that juvenile coming together over a pint, that intoxicating feeling of creating a gang, changes your collective status. With the clink of those half-empty glasses, you have entered into a bona fide, legally binding agreement called a 'Partnership at Will'. Be under no illusion, in that carefree moment you have compromised yourself. This cheery 'Cheers' can have far-reaching consequences that bring a sinister ring of truth to that old adage 'being in a quartet is like being in a marriage'.

Quartet players are unique in terms of the intense levels of scrutiny they face. In larger groups, personalities inevitably get watered down; in trios, you have the perfect two-against-one equation for sorting stuff out; but there is something in the mathematics of a foursome that lends it at once both formidable power and tremendous vulnerability. Three against one is intimidating, two versus two creates an impasse; it's so rare to achieve an 'all for one, one for all' situation that, if it happens, it immediately creates doubt.

It's an existence that calls for superhuman levels of endurance, and a relentless test of humility that would wear down a Zen master. The art itself reflects the life. You have to be dynamic, colourful and brilliant one minute, demure, sensitive, almost grey the next. Leader, follower, aggressive, passive, ruthless, understanding. At all times, both in playing and in everyday life, you have to challenge, relent, be assertive yet dubious, retain conviction whilst taking care to embrace other people's views. You absolutely must respect your colleagues, be understanding of their decisions and, if you don't achieve a heightened state of calm, considered awareness, you will fall ill. A small price to pay, I'm sure you'll agree.

'The Lyds and Stroke City'

My intense scepticism surrounding competitions has only been reinforced by sitting on juries. The experience of performing under pressure is undoubtedly valuable, but even if you fluke a win, the spoils are of no consequence if you haven't got the stamina. Early promise is all very well but can you grind it out over the long haul? One bonus, I'll grant you, is meeting like-minded individuals and forging friendships. Take the Lydian Quartet, for example. We met this all-female band at Banff and they became instant buddies, so much so that a couple of years later they invited us to give some concerts and classes at Brandeis University in Boston, where they were quartet-in-residence. Not long before our much-anticipated visit, a sad but all too common story unfolded. One of the members, their mercurial and charismatic first violin, Wilma Smith, got an offer she couldn't refuse. Though originally from Fiji, Wilma grew up in Auckland, and when she was approached to form the New Zealand String Quartet, the combination of quartet playing and roots was too powerful to resist. Hence, when we arrived in their midst, lovely Wilma was back in Auckland and the other three were going through that nightmare of trying to replace a colleague. As it happened, just at the time we arrived, they felt they had found that person. His name was Dan Stepner, and although their minds were pretty much made up, a nod of approval from the likes of us would be invaluable. During our stay they had a low-profile gig at a fancy men's club in downtown Boston; it would be Dan's first concert with them and a chance for all of them to see how things might work onstage. At their invitation, Jacky and I went along to offer support and lend a critical ear.

You can imagine the scene. Lots of silver-haired, fat guys drinking whiskey and smoking cigars, packed into a cramped space to endure some depressingly predictable string quartet music so they could cross 'culture' off their annual to-do list. When will people wake up to the fact that Mozart Quartets are not easy listening? They'd have so much more fun if they'd just let the musicians choose the programmes; Janacek, Sculthorpe, Stravinsky, Zemlinsky would so rock their boat, but instead they go for the same old, same old. Don't get me wrong here. I adore Mozart's Quartets; some of my favourite music lies in those hallowed pages. In point of fact, we had to all but give up playing these works way back because they caused us such heartache in rehearsal and performance. Only Bach rivals Mozart inasmuch as the interpretation has to be just so. It's simply too close to the bone.

These well-heeled Bostonians fidgeted and sniffed their way through the next hour till they had the opportunity to refill their tumblers and continue growling at each other. Hadn't they cleared their throats sufficiently during the performance, for goodness' sake?

Our mates, who had played brilliantly, soon emerged from backstage and hurriedly sought refuge in our company. We congratulated them and gave them as much encouragement as we could. They showed no signs of the undoubted stress they were under. Was it ok? Had Dan worked? Did he still want to do this? And on and on. Predictably, one of the gathered throng interrupted our chat and started rabbiting on about the concert. He literally turned his back on us and focused all his attention on Dan. He bent Dan's ear for a full five minutes before delivering his classic summation.

"Well, Mr Stepner, I thought your performance was top rate." Then, turning to the hitherto ignored three stooges, he uttered his parting remark. "And as for you young ladies, why, you done just fine."

One cannot begin to contemplate the thoughtlessness of this remark, particularly when it's delivered at such an inopportune moment, and for all to hear. These 'young ladies' had already devoted many years of their lives to this group. Their blood must have been boiling, being dismissed like a bunch of inconsequential chuggers while Mr Stepner, himself mortified by the situation, seemingly waltzed in off the street and took all the plaudits. I know we all have to deal with varying degrees of ignorance all the time but I do believe it is more commonplace in the arts, where it's felt more keenly. Much of what we do as artists is so personal, we really lay ourselves bare, and these uninvited, uninformed comments can be brutal.

"Must be wonderful to do something you really love."

"Piss off!"

"Amazing concert. What do you do for a living?"

"Amazing concerts, you twit." (Though, given what a plumber earns in comparison to us, they have a point.)

I'm happy to report, Dan got the job.

***

Coming from where I come from provides you with a lifelong affliction. There can't be many places where so much personal information can be unwittingly divulged just by answering the simple question, 'where are you from?'

'Derry' sticks in the throats of Unionists and 'Londonderry' sticks in the throats of Nationalists. A pleasing logic seems to have presided over the renaming of Caerdyf, Glas Cau and Dubh Linn, for example, as they became Cardiff, Glasgow and Dublin; one cannot help but wonder, therefore, what perplexed the momentarily tongue-twisted Sassenachs when it came to Doire.

One fine morning at Dartington Summer School, we were all standing around having coffee in the majestic courtyard when someone said to me, "Do you know David Jones?"

"No, I don't believe I do," I replied.

"Oh, but you should meet him. He's the choral conductor here and he's Irish. Look, there he is, right there. Come, I'll introduce you."

Immediately upon the introduction, I could tell from his accent that he was not only from Ireland but was undoubtedly from Derry. We didn't even need the tell-tale, giveaway line, we could see it in each other's eyes: we were different colours. Though we had both left all that behind many years before and made every effort to move forward with our lives, there is always a slight uneasiness in such encounters. The history is long and unsavoury and even within the most liberal and educated of minds, the wounds run deep. I've always thought that the astonishing facts of our ensuing five-minute conversation could make a fascinating documentary with a 'Sliding Doors' scenario. We stood there on the croquet lawn in a time capsule, aghast at the circumstances unfolding before us.

Only two children had been born in the tiny Northland Road Nursing

Home on 13.09.1959: myself and David. From there, we would take very different paths to ostensibly the same destination.

A once-pupil of Foyle High, he mentioned how scared he was of us St Columb's boys ever since an incident when he was standing with some fellow students waiting for his bus home. Along came a bus load of St Columb's boys, one of whom launched a seat cushion out the window towards them. He, seeing this quite large missile coming towards him at some speed, didn't have time to move and, transfixed to the spot, took the impact full on. I was in my first term at big school and, naively trying to impress the older boys, joined in with the general melee and mayhem that had overtaken the Shantallow Bus that afternoon. I had helped to launch the said projectile. I hasten to reassure readers that the offending missile was made of light foam and David sustained no injuries, but somehow I could not hide from the embarrassing truth and immediately owned up to my involvement in the regrettable incident just as I had done at the time, a confession that saw me suspended for six weeks.

It's such a shame David and I never met during our time in Derry; we would have had so much in common. Instead, circumstances beyond our control kept us apart, only for us to meet by chance, thirty-five years later in a foreign land. We had both become musicians and to this day live within a few streets of each other in North London. Sadly, we've not seen each other since.

'Whining 'n' dining'

Aside from delight at Middlesbrough winning a football match, unanimity within the Brodsky Quartet was a rare commodity invariably viewed with suspicion. It was never long before any fresh-faced idea was cynically scrutinised and pulled apart, its unsavoury underbelly laid bare before the jeering mob, all life-blood drained from its veins. Negativity is one of life's dark forces and one must be ever vigilant in the battle against its cheap, easy-going appeal that can effortlessly undermine a positive nature, sapping energy and shattering confidence.

One area where we seemed to have an unspoken agreement, however, was on the subject of touring. Those early offers of tours where you would hire a Chevy in Florida and do forty dates in as many days for measly fees, before ditching the crate in Maine prior to the red-eye home, held no appeal for us. I've always felt proud and not a little smug of the fact that, despite pressure from agents to take on such mindless escapades, we were astute enough to know that by South Carolina, not even one of those monstrous American cars would have had enough room for the four of us. We found that about six dates on the trot was our limit before relations deteriorated. *Why do it to yourselves? Just go home.*

One blatant dilemma is that, if you're that far away to begin with, why not make the most of the situation? That's all very well, but the picture looks strikingly different to a manager than to a travelling musician. Swinging by LA on the way to Oz seems logical if you're sitting in your London office, but absolutely hellish if you're standing in line at immigration or checking into yet another hotel. However, any self-employed person will tell you that it's never easy saying no to work, and it was with a giant dollop of reticence that we foolishly got talked into tagging South Korea and Hong Kong onto the end of an already too-long stint in Japan.

Finding out in Sapporo that the Japanese produce their own rather fine whiskey as you're coming to the end of an already boozy dinner in the company of an unusually generous promoter is perhaps not the ideal way to prepare for the next day in Sendai. To make matters worse, the lovely people in Sendai had decided that we absolutely had to have lunch in a specific restaurant renowned for its seafood but not open after the concert. The flight that morning had been at a most unfriendly hour and the scenic road from the airport featured one too many corkscrew bends. This was the main route south from the city and our hosts gleefully informed us that in bygone days, serious criminals would be tied up here along the roadside on their backs, their necks exposed. Resting lightly upon these necks would be a very fine and carefully serrated length of bamboo. The deal was that each and every passer-by, regardless of age, sex or purpose, had to pull or push this bamboo once, until sufficient travellers had passed for the gruesome punishment to have run its course and the wretch was put out of his or her misery. Now… lunchtime.

We were ushered into the bustling eatery down on the harbour and proudly shown to the top table, which was surrounded by huge seawater tanks, all stocked to the gills with everything from razor clams to blowfish. I was upset enough at being told to go and single out what I wanted to eat (a task I skillfully managed to pass on to our host by feigning an urgent need to visit the loo) but what happened next was something deeply shocking, a supreme test of one's diplomacy and anger management.

The waiter meticulously arranged a dizzying plethora of dishes on our table, expertly building in excitement till finally it was the turn of the magnificent centrepiece – a most impressive silver platter stacked with ice and decorated with breathtaking vegetable sculptures, each one more intricate than the next. It was at this precise moment that the chef entered the scene at a pace. All decked out in blue and white and brandishing an inordinately large landing net, he proceeded to isolate and capture our chosen fish, a proud and gleaming dorado. In one fleet, masterful movement, he produced a fearsome blade from a sheath on his belt and sliced the stunned creature in two along it's backbone. The side of the fish that still had its head and tail attached was immediately placed centre-stage, exposed cut-side down on the ice, while the stolen fillet was diced up into small cubes and dispatched onto our plates. Our hosts were beside themselves with delight and quickly scoffed their prized order. We, on the other hand, couldn't quite get over the fact that the stricken fish, hideously displayed on our centrepiece, was still flapping its tail and gasping for air. It was all I could do to sit there and fake absurd, polite conversation. I eventually tried one tiny square of what was causing all this excitement. Evidently, the tough quality of the flesh was due to the still-present adrenaline. This is desirable, apparently. I chewed my solitary morsel with long teeth while shovelling the rest under the rice in my bowl. The conclusion of that meal remains a blur. I know nature can be mind-bogglingly brutal, but surely we don't have to mimic it quite so meticulously. Would it have made such a difference to have given that poor creature a quick slap on the head before totally humiliating it and prolonging its agony? I grew up eating meat and fish that was so overcooked it was more akin to old leather than flesh; whilst this is hardly to be recommended, I just find this extreme to be downright unkind.

The concert in Seoul was in the main Symphony Hall. Everything in the build-up was routine until the moment we were summoned for the gig itself. We were escorted to the backstage area, shown into an absolutely tiny glass room barely big enough for the four of us, and the door firmly shut. At the designated moment, a man in a white boiler suit opened the door and gestured for us to make our way to the stage. We stifled giggles and tried to remain focused, although the overwhelming silence emanating from this enormous space was deflating. Upon entering from stage left you could have heard a pin drop; then, as if in a dream, three thousand impeccably behaved souls jumped to their feet and exploded into a cacophony of ecstatic applause, whoops and whistles. What a feeling. We had yet to play a note.

Before going to Korea, we had heard horror stories about some of their eating habits. In the aftermath of our recent Japanese experience, our invitation to an authentic restaurant after the concert meant my excitement was laced with a certain amount of foreboding. It was one of those places where your party gets its own room and, happily, everything arrives without you having to do anything, but as we took our places my worst nightmare seemed to be unfolding before my eyes. Our waitress came along and removed brass plates from three sections of the table, leaving circular gaps. One Korean delicacy I'd heard about, and the one that freaked me out the most, was the unimaginable practice of eating live monkeys' brains. The animals were presumably sedated, brought to the table, their heads protruding from these gaps, and their scalps duly removed. The live fish in Sendai was one thing but my diplomacy was not going to stretch to this. If anything resembling a primate appeared in that doorway, I was out of there. The very thought of this practice was turning my stomach and I could think of nothing else. Just when I thought I could bear it no longer, in came our waitress again, not with one of our forebears but a box of matches. She proceeded to light little fires in the three holes and pretty soon was cooking us a most glorious meal right there in our midst. Did I just sense a hunger pang?

Next up as we eased our way westward was a one-off in Hong Kong. This was back in the days of the old harbourside airport, which always added a buzz to any visit there. The very idea of a 747 gliding between business blocks and apartment buildings, so close you could see what people were having for breakfast, is mindblowing. Those people on the 52nd floor were taking a real chance hanging their washing out to dry and I giggled to myself at the thought of an airliner coming in to land bedecked with an array of underwear like a scene from *Airplane*.

With customary abandon we had plumbed for the night flight home. We knew it was going to be tight time-wise but this was a decision worth every grey hair. In the afternoon some of us went for a wander around one of those street markets for which Hong Kong is famous. We were having a fun time enjoying the riot of colours and general bustle of the place when we stumbled upon the bit dedicated to sea creatures. The sight of these majestic lifeforms being displayed in this way, fully alive but in an intensely alien environment, was upsetting. Now, if the divine oyster has a certain connotation with the female of our species, I guess for us lads, the delightful conch is somewhat unavoidable. Sorry, but what an ugly specimen the conch is, and – rather like their human counterparts – they seem to have a mind of their own. They were, understandably, not happy being confined to their buckets of seawater and were grotesquely making their way willy-nilly along the pavements, causing their 'owners' a real headache. If you've been crazy enough to buy one of these things, how on earth do you deal with it prior to cooking? Crabs and lobsters are bad enough, but the thought of having a giant appendage in your fridge is fairly unsettling. It's a cruel world.

In an effort to minimise stress and maximise the chances of making our flight, we booked a Limo to be on standby from 9.45pm outside the artist's entrance. We also agreed to have our suitcases packed and left in the backstage service lift; we would go to the airport in our concert clothes. The second half of our programme was 'Death and the Maiden' and although we poured as much emotion and gravitas into the opening movements as we could muster, I don't think the Tarantella finale has ever been dispatched with such alacrity. Luckily, Schubert did write Presto. But someone up there was feeling frivolous, trying not once but twice to trip us up as we danced with the devil. It was at the first of the two great horn-call moments that my chair collapsed. I have no idea how I managed it, but not only did I continue playing, I remained firmly rooted in the seated position with nothing to support me for the rest of the movement. Then, as we approached that magnificent final page, and for only the second time in my career, my C string snapped with a great thwack! The four of us eyed each other in horror but something in my manic demeanour made it very clear that I was not for stopping. Goodness knows what that coda sounded like, but as is often the case, some of our overflowing adrenaline must have found its way into the audience so that, as we unleashed those last demonic chords and I spontaneously jumped to my feet, so too did the whole auditorium. Luckily, a piece like that doesn't really lend itself to playing an encore, so by the time the generous applause had died away, we were already in the descending lift putting our instruments away.

Despite everything going like clockwork, and arriving at check-in just in time, fate would find a way to deliver another blow. Neither the chair nor the string had managed to waylay us, but the entire BA computer system crashing was another matter. There was pandemonium, even talk of the flight being cancelled and hotels booked. It was a horror show. Then the computers kicked in again and, despite the lateness of the hour, it was all systems go. We hurriedly checked in and sped off to passport control and security. Here there was an almighty queue and I think Mike and I must have momentarily lost it because we decided to try to bypass the security guards and make a dash for it. Next thing I remember was the concourse parting like the Red Sea. There was a lot of shouting and screaming and we both screeched to a halt. Turning round, we were confronted by three or four policemen on their knees, guns cocked and in the firing position. Hands in the air, we somehow managed to blag our way out of that nightmarish situation and, amazingly, were soon allowed to continue on our way to the gate. As we boarded the aircraft it became obvious that the computer failure had played havoc with the seating arrangements. There was chaos, with everyone standing around not knowing what to do. The poor attendants were frantic. Then something unprecedented happened. A very posh voice took to the tannoy system.

"Ladies and gentlemen, this is your captain speaking. I understand there's been a computer failure and that this has caused a problem with the seating plan but they are about to close the airport for the night, so unless you really want to spend another night in Hong Kong, will you for fuck's sake sit down anywhere for now and we can sort this out once we're airborne."

As I was in Business Class at that moment, I took our charming captain at his word, dived into the nearest seat and availed myself of a couple of glasses of free bubbly from a bemused-looking stewardess. At the same time, our captain, who was clearly my sort of guy, literally swung the great Jumbo round on a sixpence, raced out to the appropriate runway and, without so much as a 'doors to manual and cross-check', hit the throttle. Those foolish enough to be still standing soon found a spare seat and as we banked steeply across the Hong Kong skyline, I looked back to see the airport lights shut down. Our Captain Marvel commanded the second ovation of the evening and, against all the odds, we were finally heading home.

'Dartington'

It seemed as though every day of the Dartington Summer School's lengthy duration would contain a speech from its then-director, Gavin Henderson, in which he would issue a warning and a plea. *The School is facing financial ruin and will not be here next year – please give generously.* We, the artists, didn't have to dig too deep; our contribution was well reflected in the absurdity of the fee we were getting. For fourteen consecutive years we devoted weeks of our summer season to that worthy institution but eventually, after years of it actually costing us to go there (because we had families in tow), we had to concede defeat and hand over the baton that we had taken from the Lindsay Quartet, who in turn had received it from the Amadeus.

Without delving into our pockets, we often dreamt up things to do that might help the cause. One such scheme was to offer people the chance to play with us, a movement of their choice. In return for a donation, they could add to us in the form of a quintet, for example, or literally join us by kicking one of us into touch. Such was the response to this proposition that a marathon evening was planned for the next day in the Great Hall. It turned out to be a memorable and emotional occasion. Jacky's dad finally got his long-held wish by usurping Ian and joining us for the slow movement of Schubert's 'Death and the Maiden'. At one stage, we joined forces with the Guildhall String Ensemble so that the adorable Mr Theo Richardson could conduct the first movement of Elgar's glorious 'Serenade for Strings'. Theo was a great pal of Mr Thomas' and they played quartets together back in the North East, Theo taking the viola part. He was a judge by trade, the very image all cartoonists and comic book illustrators should turn to for inspiration in that regard. He was a ruddy, rotund old rascal and we all loved him.

It quickly became obvious that we would be playing the Elgar on autopilot since this conductor's fixed gaze and complete attention were focused solely on our Amazonian bass player, Mary Scully. Theo never once took his eyes off Mary and displayed an inane smile of total ecstasy throughout, drooling all the while through the involuntary parting at the side of his mouth where his crooked pipe should have been. Even before the last note had faded to silence, Theo couldn't help himself and, descending from the rostrum, made a beeline for our very own Northern Irish Jane Russell. Mary was such a sport and acted the part brilliantly.

Later that night, when a few of us had retired to the bar for what was to be an all-nighter, Mary continued to make Theo's night an unforgettable one; sitting on his knee, dancing with him and even, at one point, feigning a drag on his baccy. I have a great photo of this very moment that I sometimes hold Mary to ransom with. I could always keep our dear old friend Peter Sculthorpe sweet by not releasing the shot I've got of him from that night, resplendent in nothing but a black bin-liner. Peter had left the do in a suit and returned some time later sporting this rather more creative attire. No one mentioned his newly acquired fashion statement and Peter carried on as if nothing had happened. Another visual record of that night shows me and the violinist Peter Manning doing the tango, me with a red rose between my teeth. That one I tend to keep in the bottom drawer.

It was times like these that gave Dartington its incomparable charm. By lights out, we'd raised in excess of £1000.

Another game contestant on that show was Frank Taplin. Frank was one of those clever people who kept making music and making money two very separate endeavours. He consequently made a great deal of money whilst continuing to enjoy playing the piano to a high level. He joined us for a bash through the first movement of Schumann's quintet. Mr and Mrs Taplin were generous benefactors who were on the board of directors and I'm sure, helped bolster the Dartington cause. Their main residence was in Princeton, NJ, but they had a magnificent old-style apartment on the Upper East Side of Manhattan, which they kindly let Jacky and me use any time we were in town. On one occasion they had left us tickets for the Met. Upon taking our seats we found ourselves sitting not in any old seats, but in Frank and Peggy's very own seats. Their names were also all over the brochure. A modest couple, they had never mentioned this association in all the years we'd known them.

This was very different to another time Jacky and I were in New York and got last-minute standing-room tickets to hear Jessye Norman in Strauss' 'Ariadne auf Naxos'. While we were still applauding the first act, a couple approached us saying one of them was not feeling well and asking if we would like their silver tickets for the rest of the show. Sitting plumb centre, four rows back under the chandelier, witnessing the raw power of Jessye in full swing was quite an experience.

In those days we shared the same agent, David Sigall, and he told us one great story involving the majestic diva. Once, on her way to the Edinburgh Festival, she elected to take the train from King's Cross. Before attending to her luggage, the steward made it his business to escort Ms Norman onto the waiting locomotive, only to find that the girth of the steps didn't quite match that of the regal passenger.

"What to do?" giggled a genuinely amused Jessye.

"Why not try a sideways approach, ma'am?" suggested the steward demurely.

Lapsing briefly into a full Jamaican drawl, the great diva replied, "Sonny, with me there ain't no sideways!"

'Harry and Joao'

One day Jacky and I turned up at our gate in LHR for a flight to Ireland and who should be sitting there in full fishing garb, fly-rod in hand, but Harry Birtwistle. I had by now forgiven him for the Clarinet Quintet debacle and in fact, we seemed to get on very well. Intrigued to discover that Harry loved fly-fishing, we immediately engaged in one of those conversations riveting for those in the know, earth-shatteringly dull for those on the outside. Jacky therefore surreptitiously sneaked out her book while we two discussed the merits of a 'Coch y Bonddu' versus a 'Hare's Ear' and the incomparable joy of dapping a 'Daddy'.

As our flight was called and we parted company, Harry shouted after us, "What are you doing on the 22nd of May next year? One of my sons is getting married in France and I've said I'll organise the music."

I knew straight away this was not the sort of thing the quartet would do but we were free that day and Jacky and I thought it could be fun. We managed to con a couple of fiddle-playing friends from our respective pasts (Peter Fisher and Elspeth Cowie) into getting involved and when the time came, off we went and had ourselves a fine couple of days in the Lot.

The Birtwistles had a home there and their eldest son, Adam, had met and was now marrying a local girl by the name of Caroline Bouchard. In the short time we were there, Jacky and I became very friendly with the newlyweds and agreed to visit them as soon as possible in their new home near Rouen in Normandy. In point of fact, it was far from new, it was an ancient, half tumbled down barn-cum-house in that very attractive colombage style. In our efforts to escape Thatcher we'd been on the lookout for a faraway place for some time, eyeing up properties in Portugal, Spain, France and Ireland, and so it was inspiring for us to see this young couple living a simple life, rebuilding an old rundown place into a magical home, whilst carrying on a fruitful working life far from the green-eyed, greedy grocer.

This was a depressing time to be living in old Blighty. London was fast becoming less intoxicatingly international and vibrant, and more like Ballymena in mid-July. The grim granny of Grantham was riding high, waving her cheap little Union Jack flags on the cover of every gutter rag.

"We don't negotiate with terrorists." Yeah, sure thing, unless they happen to be called Bush or Pinochet. This was someone who had no time for one of the greatest examples of humanity, Nelson Mandela, but was happy to get into bed with the appalling regime of terror that incarcerated him for nearly thirty years. This was someone whose people skills were so non-existent that she simultaneously took the country into war over a wildlife sanctuary on the other side of the planet whilst allowing ten political prisoners to starve themselves to death in her own backyard just a few months shy of granting their five pathetic demands. The truth is, the greengrocer's offshoot didn't actually speak to anyone, as that Spitting Image sketch captured so beautifully. (She and her cabinet are seated for dinner. "I'll have the steak, medium rare," barks the PM. "And what about the vegetables, madam?" asks the waiter. "Oh, they'll have the same.")

Like so many others, Jacky and I were desperate to get away, eager to find somewhere more cultured and less cut-throat. Despite our increasingly hectic schedule, the quartet was dispersing too. Mike had married a Spaniard and was living in Granada. Ian's girlfriend was Swiss, which meant he was spending large amounts of time over there. We had always felt that being British with British names immediately put us into the second division of quartets internationally. Paul could never compete with Pavel in the cynical mind of the classical music world hierarchy and we had long since had plans to change our names accordingly. Funnily enough, for Mike and Jacky, the alteration could have been slight – Michel et Jacqueline Thomas was as french as you could get. Ian would become Ion Beltonoff (obviously!) and I would simply employ my Celtic heritage and become Pol O'Casaide. Given that the group was in fact one quarter Irish and one quarter Belgian (Mike and Jacky's mum), it was a bit of a misnomer to say we were British and we would have had every right to our new-fangled claims. The name-changing notion never actually happened but the geographical switch certainly did. Our Normandy visit would change our lives dramatically.

We were not taken with the austere architecture of that area along the north coast but one day made the fatal mistake of taking a drive south. It doesn't take long – less than an hour, in fact. You pass through Falaise and already things begin to change. By the time you trot past the stunning Haras du Pin, it's too late. That limestone fault that runs through County Westmeath and the Cotswolds arrives in France right here. Somehow, everything changes. The architecture becomes infinitely more beautiful, the light crystallizes, the landscape seems to unfold like a welcoming duvet. Suddenly the sun has come out and you are in the land of apples and cream, stud farms, dairy herds and Calvados.

By the next afternoon, with the help of a 100% mortgage, we had bought a 14th century ruin. It was the most beautiful ruin we'd ever seen, complete with a stone staircase up the outside, courtyard, orchard and a barn bigger than the house itself. We would simply sell our two flats in London and move here. What was in fact a tiny apartment, fashioned out of one corner of the great barn, with its prehistoric cooker and plastic portable shower would be our new home. We were blissfully unaware of the recent catastrophic financial situation in the UK with interest rates soaring to an unprecedented 17%. The reality was, we couldn't give away those London apartments and we would unwillingly carry three mortgages in the years to come, but we were in love on many levels. It was April 1st!

We passed many a happy time with the Birtwistles, both father and son, in Normandy and the Lot. We built up a strong working relationship with Adam, who came up with our logo and often exhibited in conjunction with specific concerts or residencies of ours. He painted dramatic portraits of us in oils, which set him off on a lifelong journey into that sphere, having previously been principally a painter of animals in watercolour. It was I who introduced him to Elvis Costello, a sitting which would eventually lead to Adam having his work on display in the National Portrait Gallery.

At the same time, I had many conversations with Harry about writing us a quartet. I had suggested to him that a set of short pieces, along the lines of Stravinsky's 'Three Pieces' would be a good idea in terms of programming. He seemed to like this suggestion and was already forming strong ideas when one day, during one of our visits, he called me into his study. Looking forlorn, he showed me a handwritten letter he had just received from a member of another well-known quartet. The letter said in no uncertain terms that if Harry went ahead with his plan to write the work for us, they would then choose to boycott that work henceforth. It went on to point out the undeniable fact that they were much better placed to both receive and programme the work and that in their hands, the work would stand a much better chance of success. They were the ones who frequented the heavyweight, squeaky-gate festivals, hell-bent on testing your dental nerves to their limits, whereas we were the light-cruiserweights, championing only music we loved with no emphasis on specialising. It was a brutal truth and Harry would have been a fool to ignore it, but it did come as a bit of a shock. We four were excited at the prospect of getting the first quartet from Britain's weightiest composer and our management were already in discussions with promoters from all over the world for the various premieres, but Harry is no fool and didn't ignore the well-timed advice within the pages of that correspondence. Our piece found a new home and all my efforts came to nothing.

The arrogance and determination behind this letter were a salutary lesson of how some people operate, but not one I ever felt inclined to employ. If I've learnt one thing over the years, it's to not get too upset over petty disasters. Stick around long enough and things almost always work out for the best in the end. Lugging Harry's piece around from pillar to post might have forced us in a direction we wouldn't have been comfortable with and if our esteemed colleagues wanted it so badly, frankly, they were welcome to it.

***

It was a Sunday morning in Hampstead when my old friend and neighbour, Didier de Cottignies, phoned, imploring me to come with him to a concert that afternoon at the Queen Elizabeth Hall. Didier was the head of something or other at Decca and the man responsible for Pavarotti singing a certain bit of Puccini at the 1990 World Cup, but also a friend of this pianist he was desperate for me to hear.

On entering the hall, it became clearer why he was waking me out of a nice Sunday morning snooze. A brief glance at the programme booklet showed me that this woman was a formidable and established musician, but she was unknown in the UK and the hall was embarrassingly empty. They had done what they could with lighting, flowers and stage screens to make it less obvious, but it was uncomfortable. At the appointed hour, a diminutive figure dressed in black appeared on stage, sidling up to the piano in an almost apologetic manner. She acknowledged the scant applause with an upward glance from the Princess Diana Collection and took her seat. What happened then was captivating and magical. The Bach Partita she teased into life before us made that piece special to me for the rest of my life. Likewise the Mozart, Schubert and Schumann that followed. This tiny figure, whose feet could barely reach the pedals, whose hands struggled to clear an octave, was playing the piano in a way I had never before witnessed.

When Didier introduced me to her after the show I was a blubbering idiot, but I did manage to beg her to consider playing with the Brodsky Quartet. She did not seem averse to the idea and said how much she loved playing chamber music, but suggested meeting properly and doing some informal playing together before making any concert plans. I assured her that her living in Switzerland was not a problem and we agreed to find a time for us all to meet sooner rather than later. This was the beginning of a beautiful relationship between us and the enchanting Maria Joao Pires.

I went raving to my colleagues. This would usually result in a backlash, with people rallying against the suspect fervour, but on this occasion they seemed to sense my genuineness and within days of meeting Joao, the four of us were on a flight to Zurich.

Joao and her adorable partner at the time, Rolf, picked us up at the airport – he in a sensible saloon, she at the wheel of a gorgeous red Alfa Spider. The moment I jumped into that little convertible I knew my instincts were right. These two people invited us not only into their home, but into their family. In the ensuing days, we ate, drank, chatted and played together endlessly. On the last afternoon before our flight home, Joao invited some strategic people over to hear an impromptu concert. My initial enthusiasm was now matched by everyone in the room and the industry wheels began to turn.

We enjoyed so many wonderful times with Joao and her family over the years but eventually, as was so often the case, management would get in the way. Time and time again our most fruitful collaborations were undermined, nipped in the bud by greedy agents. Why would Ms Pires waste her time playing some badly paid chamber music gig when she could be raking it in playing yet another concerto date? The artist's enjoyment or fulfillment soon takes second place to the size of the fee. This behaviour is horribly predictable but particularly galling when you actually share the same management. Slowly but surely, our fun was quashed. Joao would have to prioritise her solo profile and therefore not be seen playing chamber music. Invitations to play together stopped reaching our ears and sadly, we were forced our separate ways. Though we did reignite our relationship in later years, the vital chemistry and momentum had gone.

'Shostakovich'

In days gone by, record labels and managers wielded considerable power in their artist's career. With the collapse of the recording industry, only managers retain this influence. When I joined the quartet we had no record label, but we were on the books of the highly respected Ibbs and Tillett Agency for a short while before being enticed to join Ingpen and Williams under David Sigall. This relationship proved to be more fruitful. Ingpen operated in the new style of management, whereby the manager and artist are more of a team who go in search of work rather than, as historically, the manager dealing with promoters and then offering any work to various artists on their books. This new approach suited us much better. We wanted promoters to come looking for the Brodsky Quartet and not just a string quartet that ended up being us by default.

Towards the end of the '80s we were targeted again by another agent, Jasper Parrott. Jasper and his partner Terry Harrison had also left Ibbs and Tillett, back in 1969, and set up the now-famous Harrison and Parrott Agency. They took with them Andre Previn and Vladimir Ashkenazy, a reasonable starting point. During his time at Ibbs, Jasper had looked after the Amadeus Quartet; now he dreamed of finding a replacement group for his own agency and had decided we were it. Jasper's complimentary approach was a winning one and we signed on his dotted line. During our time at HP, we were expertly looked after by Lydia Connolly. Jasper's focus was on getting us a recording contract, one that would put us firmly on the international map, and with Lydia's help they persuaded Teldec to come to one of our London concerts. As it turned out, one concert was all it took; they offered us a contract before we'd even put our instruments away. Indeed, that concert carried the title 'End Games' and it became our first recording with Teldec.

Almost simultaneously, we received an invitation that would change our lives. We were asked to perform the Complete Shostakovich Quartets in the Queen Elizabeth Hall as part of a festival entitled 'Music from the Flames'. This festival would celebrate Shostakovich's Symphonies and String Quartets. The London Symphony Orcestra and the London Philharmonic Orchestra would share the symphonies; we would play all the quartets. It's difficult to imagine these days but back then, Shostakovich, surely one of the most formidable musicians since Beethoven, was almost universally considered a bit dodgy, second-rate, almost. Esteemed colleagues would say to us, "You're going to learn *all* those quartets? Aren't they basically just more of the same?"

Finding the scores and parts of these works would in itself prove quite a feat but we were not about to turn down this huge challenge and we set about our task. We had been playing Nos. 3,7,8 and 11 for many years already but this still left us with eleven substantial works to learn in a relatively short space of time.

Choosing repertoire is a perpetual nightmare for quartets. Unless you're very sure of yourself and determined to specialise from the outset, you have to begin by exploring all the different styles so that you get a feel for what you might be good at. Given that just between the four classical giants – Haydn, Mozart, Beethoven and Schubert – you have well over 100 pieces available to you, this exploration can take a wee while. For example, in the mid '80s we decided to check out the Haydn Quartets. We worked our way through them chronologically, spending an hour on each one as we went. It took us six months, but we ended up choosing only a handful that we felt we could do justice to. They were generally too first violin-driven for us and so we tended to avoid them, often persuading promoters to go for the equally extraordinary but hopelessly neglected Arriaga Quartets.

On the other hand, all the quartets of Beethoven and Schubert have remained firm friends throughout our careers. It's often the case that a particular group or player can have a unique insight into a particular composer, or even just a specific work by that composer, but any revelation is invaluable; it's very much a case of quality not quantity here. We were about to take on Shostakovich face to face and hoped for the best.

His fifteen quartets span over forty years, incorporate many different styles and arguably constitute the most striking and emotional journey in all of music. I can say this now with the benefit of hindsight but back then, we were facing a mountain of code that needed deciphering.

Our commitment to the cause was formidable and our preparation meticulous. We tried changing existing programmes so as to include as many of our new friends as we could, but it's never easy persuading promoters to undo what might have taken an age to agree on in the first place. Then there was the added difficulty of selling works we weren't overly familiar with ourselves, not knowing their impact or how they might sit in a programme. We also knew that we had to get a feel for the whole cycle and how best to present it. Back then it was hard work persuading a promoter to take just one Shostakovich quartet; imagine their response to the idea of a complete cycle of fifteen quartets in five concerts. Some intrepid warriors came out of the woodwork, however, like the inspirational William Jones at the Dovecot Arts Centre in Stockton-on-Tees. William was fearless and together we managed to bring a lot of edgy repertoire to that unlikely corner of the North East. William was a performing musician himself, an excellent singer-songwriter who fronted a band called The Friends. I cannot tell you how refreshing it was to be greeted at a venue by someone our own age, speaking our lingo and resplendent in full Punk garb. Our friendship continued through his years at the Dovecot and subsequently when he moved to the Arts Centre in Worksop, only fizzling out when he changed profession, cashing in his guitar for a laptop, his safety pins for cufflinks and his glorious Mohawk for an all-over No.2.

Our flirtations with the theatre had not gone away and we were determined to bring an air of theatricality to the performances. For some pieces we would come on at a pace and launch straight in, even while the audience were still clapping. Other works got a slow appearance and a more considered start. Some movements were played attacca, some pieces were played attacca. We would stare meaningfully at whoever had solo lines, pair off when it suited, be overly demonstrative or remain completely static. I know this isn't exactly groundbreaking and that a lot of this sort of thing can, and does, occur naturally within a performance, but it was the level of detail that we went into that was unusual, the rigidity of our approach and the seriousness of the decision-making. All these things were written down in our parts like stage directions and absolutely had to be adhered to. 'Lower head, take off mute immediately and aggressively, then wait for others before turning the page.' Sometimes with many bars' rest one was instructed to, 'remain ready to play so as not to disturb the music with unnecessary preparatory movements'.

Page turns and even bow retakes were real bones of contention and often one had to go to extreme lengths to make sure they didn't interfere with the ongoing drama. All this before we got on to vibrato/no vibrato, slow bow/fast bow, bridge/fingerboard, romantic/cold, funny/ironic, etc. etc. This intensity continued right up to the performances themselves, which were tremendously exciting and more than paid us back for all the hours we had put in.

We went directly from the South Bank to Berlin to begin recording the cycle. We were no longer youthful but we were naive. It was a naivety born out of a maverick approach to everything we did. It seemed to be in our DNA, an almost primal urge to challenge every perceived norm whilst diligently carrying on the great traditions. Our whole lives were devoted to this group and we prided ourselves on this fanatical single-mindedness.

Our pioneering spirit did not desert us when we set off for Berlin. It wasn't Hamburg in the early '60s, but from our perspective, it may as well have been. We were insisting to Teldec that we would record the whole cycle in five days, taking a day to play through and patch each of the five concerts in an effort to recreate the 'live' feel. (It's ironic to realise that, twenty-five years later, we would do just that; take five days to record those same pieces, live from the Muziekgebouw in Amsterdam. It's also encouraging to know that that early bravura had not abandoned us just yet).

Teldec, however, had their own way of doing things and flatly refused to listen to our whims; probably very sensible. Arguably less sensible was their decision to pair us up with an inexperienced young hotshot producer. This commendable notion of matching like with like didn't always work out for the best and the recording sessions became fraught, principally because there wasn't an experienced head to overrule some of the silliness that inevitably crept in. This silliness didn't only come from us; one side just seemed to inadvertently have a bad influence on the other. When a metronome gets played throughout an entire poignant, slow movement of music, you know you're in a bad place. We all decided that the pivotal and extraordinary 8th Quartet would benefit from being recorded in one day so as not to lose the thread of that amazing journey. This is all very well, but when one of you has to be taken to hospital at 1am because their body has literally seized up, here again, you're in a bad place.

Overall it was a memorable experience. Being in that great city during one of its most historic moments, the coming down of The Wall, was in itself worth all the angst. Walking around down by the Brandenburg Gate and experiencing that euphoria was electrifying. Sharing such a moment was a rare privilege. To be at the Israel Philharmonic's first performance in Berlin, at the Waldebuhne of all places, where they played Mahler No.1 and Dvorak No.7, complete with an encore of the Jewish National Anthem, was frankly overwhelming.

The Teldec studio was an old ballroom in the Lichterfelde district. It had a certain romance about it and a wonderful sound, but it was also quirky. For example, in dry weather the floor beneath our feet would start to creak. The high-tech Teldec solution to this problem was to send in the engineer with a watering can. Eberhart would soak the area where we were seated and the problem would disappear. Brilliant, except that we were now sitting in a very damp spot, which created havoc with our instruments and gave us all colds. By way of distraction, we had table tennis tournaments that became even more fraught than the recording sessions; memories of similarly stressful times back in the Thomas family garage, no doubt.

***

The daily challenges are such, that artists have to be driven individuals with one-track minds. We could really have benefitted from advice and nurturing while we got on with what we had to do musically. Once again, observe the sports world – the Rory McIlroys and Steffi Grafs of this world have people around them, helping them in every aspect of their survival. I fully understand the financial discrepancy involved here and do not for one minute expect a team of dieticians following a quartet around the world, but a little practical help from time to time would not go amiss. Another thing: they might be No.1 in the world, but these people continue having lessons. In our weird world, apart from maybe singers, this is almost unheard of. Once you've picked up your all-important diploma, you apparently know it all; you're suddenly in complete control, peerless till the end of your days. Sounds implausible, I know, but much of this reality could well be a result of financial implications. Many musicians are struggling to pay everyday bills, never mind pay for regular consultations with recognised pedagogues, which do not come cheap. And so we just blindly soldier on, often getting more and more disillusioned and lost.

I guess my gripe here is with the music education system. I mean, music college could be so much more than it currently is. One short lesson a week and some orchestral playing is not enough. Also, kids who have spent their lives grappling with the complexities of playing an instrument need to know what lies ahead business-wise, how to deal with the realities of the world they have chosen to inhabit. Using your precious art to make a living is not always the rose garden spectators make it out to be. Music is not an occupation to be taken lightly; it's as cut-throat as any other and your soppy dreams can be brutally dashed. It is a place filled with ambitious, single-minded people, many of whom would have been hailed as stars growing up, stars whose aura grew dimmer as they became more exposed to the ravages of reality, opening the door to cynicism and depression. Is it any wonder that the vast majority of people who follow their hearts into the murky world of chamber music hightail it after a short while? Apart from the paltry financial rewards, it's a massively complicated, daunting and lonely path that seemingly no one is prepared to enlighten. It's unbearable to witness how music continues to be taken for granted, to the extent that it has been taken off the state school curriculum these days. One can't help but wonder, would the Brodsky Quartet exist if those kids were growing up in Middlesbrough now?

The '90s

'Elvis and Juliet'

For some time now we had been aware of a regular visitor to our concerts. Though we never actually spied him, friends would come up after shows and say excitedly, "You know who we just saw?" or "You'll never guess who we were sitting next to."

Invariably, the answer to this question would be Elvis Costello.

Being very aware of his work, and having been to a few of his concerts ourselves, we were intrigued. We were both recording for Warner at the time and a bright spark employee there by the name of Ann-Louise Hyde spotted this game of cat and mouse and suggested a meeting. Now, we might have been forgiven for agreeing to sit around ogling a favourite rock star for an hour or so, but why would a rock star want to waste his time gazing at a string quartet? Apart from the odd moment of brilliance from the pen of George Martin or Nelson Riddle, historically these two worlds had little or nothing in common. Anyway, meet we did.

We revisited the scene of our Shostakovich success, the Queen Elizabeth Hall, for a lunchtime concert. Elvis attended the concert and we all met up afterwards in the Archduke, a wine bar across the street.

Elvis was in his 'wild man of Borneo' phase, which only served to accentuate the apparent difference between himself and the bunch of more predictably turned out geezers he had come to meet. But you should never judge a book by its cover, as they say, and this was certainly a case in point. From the time Ann-Louise introduced us and graciously bowed out of proceedings, there was never an awkward moment. We were instantly relaxed in each other's company and the conversation flowed effortlessly. So much so, that it was 7.15pm when Elvis apologised and, excusing himself, explained that he had to be somewhere at 7.30pm. This was perfectly understandable, given that no one could possibly have predicted our informal chat lasting five hours. We said our goodbyes and agreed to meet again as soon as possible. Then we found ourselves all crossing the road back in the direction of the South Bank and gradually realised that, by total chance, we all had tickets to Mahler No.6 that evening. If our coming together hadn't already felt like it had been written in the stars, this unlikely coincidence seemed spookily predestined.

Our concert had been on a Thursday lunchtime in November 1991. On the Friday, Elvis responded to a request from Wendy James, who had asked him if he would write her a song to put on her next album, saying that he wouldn't write her a song but he would write her the entire album. As the opening track ('This is a Test') of the ensuing CD testifies, he had taken this on in the form of a test. He would allow himself one weekend to compose a solid hour of music. If he failed, Wendy would get nothing, but if he was successful, she would get a whole album… given who we're talking about, pretty good odds, I would suggest.

The rather excellent album 'Now Ain't the Time for Your Tears' was indeed written in that short weekend and the subsequent demos rattled off the following Wednesday. We started work on the Monday in between.

Despite the fact that we had already worked with many vocalists and were thoroughly taken with the mix of voice and string quartet, we had never worked with a 'pop singer'. Equally, though Elvis had shown his ability to diversify musically, he had never worked with a string quartet. We were ostensibly meeting up simply to see what might happen, chat about one or two ideas and maybe play together a bit; it was flabbergasting how we immediately started writing new material, as naturally as could be. A euphoria set in, with musical ideas coming thick and fast. No songs were written on that first day but just like in our first meeting, the five of us were so excited, so inspired, so natural around each other, that it was clear we were collectively creating something. We kept an open mind but instrumentally, we sensed a raw power in the forces at hand; no need for drums, guitars or even keyboards; we could generate every conceivable emotion with strings, bows and vocal chords.

Those first sessions took place in mine and Jacky's apartment in Hampstead – in our bedroom, no less. Well, that's where the piano was. Even at this early stage we had decided on the idea that would inspire and propel the song cycle forwards. Yes, that's right, the 'song cycle' – it was already way too late, Elvis Costello and the Brodsky Quartet were writing an album.

Elvis had found this extraordinary article in the Guardian newspaper. It was an advertisement for a job. A professor in Verona had taken it upon himself to reply to the numerous letters addressed every day to the dead, imaginary woman who went by the name of Juliet Capulet. This seemingly charming deed was given a cruel twist, however, when one day the paparazzi found themselves with a dearth of dirt to dish and decided to expose our Robin Hood character as some kind of weirdo. Such aggressive, misplaced unpleasantness scared the professor off, the letters began to pile up and then, lo and behold, someone else decided it was a fine idea after all and the job was advertised. Our idea was to explore the dying art of letter writing. Not just love letters but all manner of letters, from suicide notes to junk mail. We exchanged musical ideas both verbally and on cassettes, a real mish-mash of stuff from Schubert and Bartok to George Jones and Tom Waits. Each day we would set ourselves homework, write a diatribe and a chorale, a love letter and a riff.

Working in each other's homes, as many quartets do, was something we had always tried to avoid. After a time, these daily rehearsals put undue stress on the host – making sure the space is conducive to work, providing refreshment, dealing with irate neighbours, etc. These are pressures any group can do without and we were always on the lookout for alternative places to rehearse. Fortuitously, we were contacted by some people who had taken over the running of a church in Maida Vale called the Amadeus Centre. They had plans to create an arts centre housing rehearsals and events, and thought that if we lent our name to the venue, that could be quite a valuable calling card for them. We jumped at the chance of having such a beautiful space in which to work; there was a fresh buzz about the place and the diversity of the space gave us the opportunity to encounter people from across the arts world.

Material came thick and fast and although we had never written anything before, inspired by our new pal, we collectively released some creative juices and managed to bring stuff to the table. It was an object lesson in democracy because the strength of the overall composition came from the fact that it was a real five-way collaboration. Many of the songs in *The Juliet Letters* are made up of a line from one person, a chorus from another, an intro from a third party and so on. Ideas were often brought in and then orchestrated on the hoof, the song taking shape under our fingers, there and then. It was incredibly exciting and massively liberating for us. Trained to be wholly subservient to composers, to see music as some magical black art that we were only fit to interpret, and even then, under the strictest rules, we were suddenly creating this magic ourselves, calling the shots and making our own rules, released from the shackles of an enforced inferiority complex and expressing these most natural feelings freely. This 'coming out' also gave us the confidence to fully embrace our long-held conviction that standing up to perform was infinitely preferable on so many levels to the seated arrangement. Having put it off for years, not wanting to antagonise the old guard with yet another breach of protocol, we finally took the plunge. Many groups have followed our lead; some have even told us that they would have loved to but didn't want to be seen as 'also-rans'. Bizarrely, the terrifying move went virtually unnoticed and we've only ever had positive comments about the decision. We have certainly never looked back.

The Christmas break came far too soon. I say 'break', some of us may have put our feet up and roasted a few chestnuts; Elvis, on the other hand, instantly frustrated by the fact that we had to write down any ideas he had through dictation, took the time off to learn how to read and write music. A feat most youngsters take many months to achieve, this grown man managed in a matter of weeks; indeed, by February, Elvis was coming to class with ideas completely scored and written out for quartet and voice.

During this period, we organised a series of concerts at the Amadeus Centre in aid of Children in Need. It was, if I may say so, a wonderfully eclectic set of six concerts featuring the likes of Barry Douglas, Evelyn Glennie and the soloists of the Orchestra of the Age of Enlightenment. The last of these shows, which received no special billing, was a performance of a 'work in progress' by ourselves and Elvis Costello. Granted, the Amadeus Centre is not a big hall, but all the dates sold out, which was hugely gratifying for us. The press inevitably got wind of the fact that something groundbreaking was about to happen in W9. The public, too, sensed this final concert was to be a unique event and the general fervour resulted in a bit of a bun fight come curtain-up. Nothing even close to this had ever happened before; ourselves and Elvis were making musical history.

I'll never forget Elvis' reaction as we came off for the interval.

"What the fuck was that?!" bellowed our bemused, bespectacled baritone.

"What was what?" I asked, thinking we hadn't done so badly.

"What were you guys doing out there?" he continued. "Scared the hell outta me!"

We soon realised what had spooked the rock star in our midst. Even though we'd spent much of the last few months up close and personal, we hadn't once gone into performance mode until that first half. Elvis had spent most of his life in a rock 'n' roll band. Obviously a string quartet cannot possibly match that noise level, but if you want to play louder in a rock band, no amount of flailing around will have any impact, you simply turn a knob and, hey presto, the decibels increase. In a string quartet, you have to physically produce that effect; there aren't any magic buttons. It was this huge increase in both the physical intensity and the subsequent noise level coming from us that had taken him by surprise. It was enormously gratifying to realise that little old we could be as engaging in our own way as any band and this realisation immediately dispelled any feelings of inadequacy we may have had in that respect. We quickly adopted a basic ambient miking system to suit everyone's needs, not too overpowering or visually distracting but sufficient for Elvis to be able to sing in a natural way.

Things in this new world moved at a pace one could only dream about in the classical world. We recorded the album at Church Studios in Crouch End using the analogue approach, which would often result in our saintly producer, Kevin Killen, getting on his hands and knees to wrestle with mountains of tape and scissors. Amelia Stein did the photoshoot for the cover using a camera from the last century, which, though it seemed a bit odd to me at the time, got us into just the right frame of mind for those moody period shots that would become synonymous with the album and ultimately delivered quite beautiful results. Philip King from Hummingbird Films shot a documentary about the making of the album, which took place at Ardmore Studios and culminated in a live performance at The Gate Theatre in Dublin.

Elvis' manager at the time was a guy called Jake Riviera. Jake was a bit of an East End-gangster type with a reputation to match. Though a formidable character in many ways, Jake had no feel for what we were doing and no understanding of *The Juliet Letters*' potential or what it represented. Consequently, when the phone started ringing off the hook, his stock reply to these promoters, hungry for something a little different to flog, was to put them off the scent, reassuring them that Elvis had just had one of his customary blips. "You know what he's like," he'd say. "It's just something he needed to get off his chest. He'll be back next year with a proper record. We'll be in touch then."

Our manager in those days, Jasper Parrott, also had a fearsome reputation as a bit of a gangster from a different part of town. He was busy fielding similar calls, reassuring classical promoters that we hadn't lost our minds. "They're just having a bit of fun. You know what they're like."

When Jake took us greenhorns aside and started talking about the 'promo tour' as being an unpaid tour of indiscriminate length, he knew exactly what he was doing and how we'd respond. We'd already devoted several months to this product, unpaid, and in our business no one made any money from CD sales; so all this talk of postponing concerts already in our diary and trotting around the world doing endless shows flogging this thing sent us into a panic. Tragically for us, when we discussed this with our management, they agreed with us. Acting on their advice, we set aside less than a month to circumvent the globe, less than a month to complete this absolutely crucial promotional tour.

We started the whistle-stop trip in Glasgow and backstage after the show, Jake gaily handed us a wad of cash.

"What's this?" we asked him, somewhat confusedly.

"That's your slice of tonight's action," he replied matter-of-factly.

"But I thought you said we wouldn't be getting paid for these shows?" we asked, incredulously.

"Well, you don't. I mean, you don't get an agreed fee, but you'll get a split of the box office, of course," he guffawed.

This way of working was pretty much unheard of in our world, but how had Jasper and co. failed to pick up on this in their negotiations? Every date on that tour yielded at least four times more than we could ever get for a quartet date, and we'd cut it short. We did four shows in America, where we could have done four hundred. But it was too late, the rollercoaster was in full swing, the window of opportunity had closed. The fever surrounding the record was high and even Elvis himself said he'd never encountered such a media response. I remember coming off stage in LA and not being able to get to our dressing rooms because of the celebrity wall that had gathered to say 'hi'. It was a bit like being on the set of *The Usual Suspects*, except at the centre of this mob was a little guy from a different film, *The Godfather* perhaps, puffin' on a cigar that was clearly a stand-in for something, flanked by a bevy of minders.

"Why didn't you tell us, Elvis?" he whined, arms outstretched. "Why didn't you tell us?"

It was at this point that Elvis had to be politely encouraged not to tear this eejit's head off. The head of Warner Bros. realised in the midst of this furore that he had missed a major opportunity and was already busy passing the buck.

With time at such a premium and demand so high, we found ourselves doing interviews in taxis, airport lounges, hotel lobbies, backstage, wherever we could possibly slot them in. One small fact that I believe is worth mentioning, because I think it's such a credit to Elvis in particular, is that, in all those hundreds of interviews and photoshoots, we never did a single one without Elvis and at least one or more of us present. We were collectively determined to honour this five-way collaboration.

One invitation we made time for was the Tonight Show. Being the first and maybe only quartet to have appeared on this iconic show with a TV audience of around 27 million was undoubtedly something worth making a little detour for. The sheer scale of a place like Burbank is hard to take in. This 'Media Centre of the World', as it's often referred to, is home to the likes of Disney, Warner and many more. Once you get past the private jets, the Limos and the fancy facades, the monotonous sea of utilitarian warehouses brings a stark reality to the dreamworld.

Even though that Tuesday he had probably only chosen a car from the third division of his world-famous collection, the machine parked outside the door where our bog-standard Limo had dropped us left us in no doubt that this was Jay Leno territory. Upon entering the warehouse, we were escorted down an endless corridor to our individual dressing rooms. I remember thinking how quaint it was that many of these rooms had been named after past Hollywood legends like Lauren Bacall, Doris Day and Sofia Loren, only to realise that these were not the names of the rooms but the names of the people actually in the rooms. A whole bunch of these women were filming a show about poodles on the stage next to ours. The mind boggles as to what might have been going down on the Disney stage that day.

It was on the flight from Europe to Japan that I realised we would be playing Boston Symphony Hall on St Paddy's Night. This was an opportunity too good to miss; something had to be done. On arrival at the hotel in Tokyo I cornered Robbie, 'Mr Fix-it' (Elvis' long-standing tour manager, Robbie McLeod) and asked him if he could please find me a piano for a couple of hours. By the time I got to my room, my wish had been granted. All I had to do was contact the concierge when I was ready and someone would escort me to the ivories. It turned out they had furnished me with not just any old joanna, but a magnificent Yamaha grand in the rooftop bar, with stunning views over the city. There I was, all on my own in this seriously swanky bar overlooking Tokyo with a pencil and a couple of old bits of manuscript. I felt like John bloomin' Lennon.

I had decided to do an arrangement of a Donegal ballad called 'She Moved Through the Fair'. It was a favourite of Jacky's and mine; we even had it as part of our wedding day music. Thankfully, the arrangement flowed easily and the following week we played it to close the mighty Boston gig. It was a poignant moment for me, one of those heartwarming moments when it feels good to have roots, and there's no better roots than those planted in the rich soil of Eire. My brother, Joe, had come down from Toronto for the concert and we didn't let the side down with our aftershow celebrations in the hotel bar. We awoke from our brief slumber too late for the hotel breakfast and, after consulting the front desk, decided to head across the street to a place on the corner just opposite the hotel entrance. I know we were both nursing heavy-duty hangovers but that remains the coldest I have ever been in my life. Even Joe, the Canadian, was paralysed. We literally couldn't make it across the street and resorted to room service. It's tough at the top.

The tour, which had taken in such iconic venues as the Palau de la Música in Barcelona and the Folies Bergère in Paris, ended as you might expect, in The Big Apple. The show was super slick by now. Each night we would play the song cycle faithfully to the recording and then get stuck into our lengthy encore set, which was becoming more and more colourful as people brought more and more new arrangements to the table. The NY show did not disappoint, and the Town Hall rocked so feverishly that we ended up releasing a 'live' EP to remember the night. Warner Bros. threw an end-of-tour party and it was at this lavish shindig that something truly remarkable happened.

I was minding my own business trying to run the champagne waiters off their feet when Paddy, Elvis' lifelong bodyguard, came up to me and said that there was a woman who was making a bit of a nuisance of herself, insisting she wanted to speak to one of us. Intrigued, I asked Paddy to bring me to her, but to not leave till I had had a chance to test the water, so to speak. The heart of *The Juliet Letters* is a song entitled 'I Thought I'd Write to Juliet', the central section of which quotes a letter, verbatim, sent to Elvis from a female soldier in the Iraq War. The writer of this letter stood before me now, a bright-eyed, bushy-tailed young woman. She extended her hand and exclaimed, "Hi, I'm Constance."

I thought we'd left all this fairytale nonsense behind on the west coast; weren't we now on the very real, hard-hitting east coast of this crazy country? Nevertheless, there she stood, smiling up at me. Fate had dictated that yesterday she would finish her military service, return to base somewhere in the Deep South, and today, jump on a train north, arriving just in time to catch the show. I managed to get everyone to sign a CD and poster for her and, in fact, we kept in touch for years after that, meeting several times on return US visits. It was a magical way to finish what had been an unforgettable trip.

Thankfully, this magical mystery tour finishing did not spell the end of our relationship with Elvis, which continues to bear fruit to this day. We have had so many wonderful times together since. He came to Dartington with us and taught songwriting for a week; we went to Roskilde with him. We made guest appearances on each other's albums and continued to perform *The Juliet Letters* all over the world, finally taking it to our beloved Australia in '06. We even appeared on Top of the Pops, since which time that show seems to have employed a full-time resident string quartet. It's hugely gratifying and endlessly rewarding that *The Juliet Letters* has stood the test of time and the cycle is constantly being performed in many guises all over the world. It has become a repertoire piece. How many contemporary composers can boast such a fact?

'Delfina – Jack and Vera'

Through two pianist friends, Peter Bridges and Elena Riu, we took part in a little festival in the south of Spain, in a village called Manilva. Though we were only supposed to do a couple of solo quartet concerts, we ended up staying for the whole week and getting involved in a production of *The Magic Flute*, scored for flute, piano and quartet. As befits the title, it was a magical week because it was one of those glorious community projects where everyone gets in on the act. The professionals inspire the villagers with their expertise and know-how, and the villagers in turn inspire the professionals with their openness and lack of cynicism, creating an infectious energy. The performance took place in the main square, which was completely taken over for the weekend and turned into a fantastical stage set. The HQ, another great asset of this festival, was the most imposing building in the whole village. Brimming with character, it dominated that main square and buzzed with activity morning, noon and night. The house belonged to a woman; not just any woman – an extraordinary woman, a true force of nature, a woman who would not only become a huge ally of the quartet's but, more importantly, a woman who would become a close, lifelong friend of mine and Jacky's: Delfina Entrecanales.

Delfina came from one of the great Spanish dynasties, an empire created by her father and consolidated by her brothers, which had grown into a colossal conglomerate spanning the world. To give you some idea of its magnitude, I recall that, on the sad day of her mother's death, the peseta was affected on the world markets.

We had been doing the rounds of the big, successful – yet equally useless – agencies in Spain, and getting more and more frustrated. Delfina mentioned someone, the wife of a senior employee of the Entrecanales, who happened to have a small agency and was very keen to talk with us. After the festival, we stayed on for a few days with Delfina at another one of her houses, in nearby Sotogrande, where a lunch was organised so we could meet. We seemed to attract wealthy middle-aged ladies with time on their hands and few contacts; we had been through a few already in various parts of Europe and were consequently apprehensive about the meeting. On this occasion, however, not only were our fears allayed, our prayers were answered.

Maria Angeles de Scals is another turbo-charged señora. She sprayed us with a relentless hail of machine-gun fire Spanish, little of which we understood, most of which we managed to dodge by a series of hmms and ahhs, various shakes of the head and two solid hours of inane, cheek-numbing smiles. Despite this onslaught, we could see that this was someone with not only a tremendous energy and a real passion for what she was doing, but someone with a warm heart and a kind soul. It was immediately obvious that Maria was a unique sort of person, an irresistible bundle of joy and enthusiasm. She finished the meeting by asking us how exactly we would want to go about tackling Spain. This is not a question you often get from an agent; mostly they're content with sticking your details on their website and waiting for the phone to ring… or not! We told her that Spain was a massively important country for us, a country we sought to infiltrate from the inside out. We wanted to get to the heart of that extraordinary country and embrace it fully. Over the next twenty years, Maria would help us fulfil those wishes.

Before leaving to come home later that day, Delfina, who was keen that we should not lose touch, wanted to know where we were performing next.

"In Switzerland," I replied.

"I love Switzerland. Whereabouts in Switzerland?" she asked.

"We're taking part in the Engadin Festival. We have four or five concerts in various towns there, starting next Sunday in a little place called Celerina," said I.

"Celerina. But I have a house in Celerina. You must stay with me," she insisted.

What were the chances? She did indeed have a house in this beautiful but unlikely village, and we did stay with her the following week. In fact, her house was nothing more than a gentle 7 iron from the venue. Something uncanny was going on with this Delfina person.

Back in London, where she lived, Delfina had been supporting the visual arts for some time already. She had a Foundation that offered scholarships to artists and, uniquely, provided these chosen artists with studios in which to work. Soon after we met, Delfina moved her studios from Stratford in London's East End to Bermondsey. Many people thought her mad buying a vast, deserted chocolate factory in what was then a very rundown, dangerous neighbourhood. Anyone familiar with Bermondsey Street these days will realise that this was not such a bad move. When she was finished with it, the new building had an apartment, an excellent café, several offices, two galleries and thirty-six studios.

This move of Delfina's coincided with a seismic shift we were making in our business. We'd had enough of agents endlessly taking and rarely giving. The final nail in that particular coffin was a letter we received from Jasper saying that from then on, he would be taking an individual's yearly salary (calculated on our best average) from us in advance. Not only was there no guarantee of securing this amount of work in the coming season, this was money taken from our accounts before we so much as put hair to gut.

Record companies were also becoming less and less attractive. You couldn't mix composers on the same disc whose names began with a different letter (this made it difficult to categorise). *We must have the artists on the cover, we mustn't have the artists on the cover. That repertoire is too modern, this repertoire doesn't sell. We'll give you one week to record all the Bartoks, two weeks to do all the Schubert.* You go into the studio, do the impossible, and then the first edit doesn't arrive till six months later, five minutes before the master should be delivered. In the end, the thing is released undercover, gets completely ignored by the press, and if you ever happen to spy it in a record store, you're a luckier man than me.

We signed for numerous labels throughout the '90s, often finding that although we signed with such and such a company, before the ink was dry we were with a completely different organisation. Companies were being sold or going under with such regularity that you had no idea where you stood. One more thing to remember – all this recording carry-on was done for the love of it, a feeble effort at leaving some kind of legacy. You don't get paid to record and any remuneration on the royalty front is a pipe dream.

And so, tired of all this nonsense, we decided to set up our own management company, recording company, publishing company, you-name-it company and, thanks to Delfina, this ambitious project would all be housed at the Delfina Studios. We spent twelve years at that address in Bermondsey with our very own personal manager, Marjon Koenekoop. All our rehearsals, meetings etc. took place there and during that time, we made records we wanted to make, how we wanted to make them, under the newly found Brodsky label. During those twelve years Marjon became like a fifth member of the group. She was as devoted to the cause as any of us and her tireless input went way beyond the call of duty.

***

Around this time, we began a love affair with the unlikely destination of Majorca. Our initial invitation came from an eccentric American by the name of Patrick Meadows. Patrick was one of many who, back in the '60s, had followed the hugely influential Robert Graves to Deia, that impossibly picturesque little village in the north of the island. Where Patrick differed from most of his compatriots, however, was in what he subsequently brought to the cultural life of that area. He lived a simple existence in a humble abode hidden away next to the path that leads from the village of Deia down to the Cala. Slowly but surely, Patrick built up an increasingly impressive series of concerts and events that took place in Deia church and the stunning nearby finca Son Marroig. That first visit consisted of four concerts over a five-day period and whilst the music-making was enjoyable and the general surroundings magnificent, our lodgings left something to be desired. We had been put in the Hotel del Mar in nearby Puerto Soller but, after enduring just one night in this frightful bootcamp, elected to spend every waking moment outdoors, thereby minimising the indignity of every moment spent within its walls. We were taking coffee in one of the seaside cafés on that first morning, drawing straws to decide who was going to phone Patrick and demand better accommodation, when a veritable vision of the archetypal hippy couple quietly approached our table. Little did we know that this mirage, this gentle zephyr of exotic aromas, would materialise into a treasured friendship. Jack Mutten and Vera Blum expressed how much they had enjoyed the concert the night before and how much they were looking forward to the rest of them. We explained how much we hated our hotel. They insisted we move in with them.

Hey presto, in the twinkling of an eye and without disturbing Patrick, we were following these two angels up a dirt track to their heavenly haven, tucked away within the Parc Nacional, not five minutes from where we had met them but a million miles from the Hotel del Mar. Not only did we spend the next few days in that paradisiacal setting but it would become an annual destination for myself, Jacky, and eventually our kids. This wasn't a one-way street. Jack and Vera would also make a habit of visiting our home in London as they made their way to and from their Majorcan home and their other home in India. We must have known this beautiful couple for the best part of ten years before they shared with us the secrets of their remarkable history. This story is a book in itself, but for the purposes of these pages, suffice to say, think Anne Frank meets Ernest Hemingway, and that's an understatement. They are tremendously artistic people. Vera's a wonderful violinist and Jack a fine painter and talented guitarist and keyboard player. They built their enchanting home with their own bare hands and employ an exemplary approach to life, one in which they quietly, happily and determinedly bend all the rules of survival in this merciless, dog-eat-dog world where notoriety is increasingly peddled as the only feature of any worth.

Majorca, like the rest of our glorious Spanish work, has all but disappeared since the financial crash of '08. Dear Patrick has sadly taken his leave, leaving us with the questionable pleasure of visiting that majestic island only to see our old friends, squeeze fresh orange juice from the tree by the patio, suck on figs plucked from the tree by the pool we dip in and out of between drinks and meals, over which we laze long into the night, putting the world to rights from our sacred, forgotten lair in the Sa Figuera Valley. On one such evening we found ourselves in the lamentable situation of having almost completely run out of aperitif material. In a state of barely controlled desperation, we cobbled together what we had: a dribble of Campari, a shot of gin and the dregs of a bottle of tonic. Feeling inspired, we added to this the juice of a freshly picked orange, some ice and a generous squeeze of lime. I may have to bring this chapter to a premature close right now as dribbling probably doesn't sit well with an Apple keyboard. The resulting cocktail, effectively a campari and orange mixed with a GnT, has become our signature drink. It is absolutely heavenly and carries the name, 'Jack and Vera'. Try one!

Meanwhile, that sleepy port of Soller that we first visited over twenty-five years ago is now an upmarket, pedestrianised, seaside resort worthy of the Riviera, with an impressive marina overlooked by an unlikely seven-star hotel, the shadow of which, thankfully, camouflages the dingy facade of that great hostelry, the Hotel del Mar.

'Dad'

Programming 'Black Angels' in the world of classical chamber music can be a nightmare. We have trouble getting four plausible music stands and rarely is the cello riser the dimensions stipulated in our simple rider, so to imagine getting all the stuff required to perform this piece is borderline fantasy. This frustrating situation reached an all-time low at the Berlin Festival, where they hadn't bothered to take the instructions seriously and we found ourselves in the bar of the Philharmonie ten minutes before showtime, not having a naughty snifter but tuning glasses for the God Music. This is not an ideal warm-up for the Smetana, which on this occasion opened the programme. It was a salutary lesson in life for any travelling musician: often, the bigger and more celebrated the venue, the lower you should make your expectations. More often than not, it's the little-known destination, the one that fills a space in the diary, a stepping stone from one city to another, that warms the heart.

This was a line in the sand as regards our life with George's piece. Determined not to let the work drop, we took it upon ourselves to buy much of what is required for its performance and take it with us wherever we went. This does not include the sound technician, however, so you're still at the mercy of their competence. It's a sad fact that the complications inherent in guaranteeing a satisfactory account of 'Black Angels' continue to restrict its accessibility and endanger its rightful place among the most important twentieth-century works for string quartet.

In 2009 there was a celebration of Crumb's orchestral music at the Barbican. Jacky and I went along to one of the concerts and were formally introduced to the composer. He told us of how one morning he had received a CD in the post. Upon opening it, he found that it was our

recently released Teldec recording of 'Black Angels' and one of the pieces
Crumb quotes in that work, Schubert's 'Death and the Maiden'. He was
dumbfounded as he hadn't been aware that we were making the recording,
and more worryingly, that we hadn't been in touch with him to discuss
the various complexities involved in the execution of the score. With
trepidation, he had simultaneously put on the kettle and the CD, fearing
a dubious document of his precious work. His coffee would have to wait,
however, because from the first screech that had so unsettled poor Max
he was captivated by our account, which to this day remains his favourite
recording. His words, not mine... I have witnesses.

**

It was my birthday, 13th September 1993. We were at the Seymour Centre
in Sydney, proudly brandishing all our newly acquired paraphernalia and
playing that programme, the Angels and the Maiden. Post-concert, I was
excitedly putting my viola away in readiness to party when Jacky came in
looking sombre. She had received a call before the show to say that my dad
had died that day. He had been poorly for some time, but these things are
always a shock when they finally come to pass. I thank Jacky for not telling
me beforehand as I may not have weathered that emotionally exhausting
programme had I known. The celebrations were cancelled and I returned
to my hotel room to gather my thoughts and see what was to happen next.
I quickly ascertained that there was no way I could physically get home
for his funeral, so I spent most of the night on the phone to my mum and
various siblings. She was wonderfully supportive and insisted I stay where
I was, get on with my work and come to see her upon my return, two
weeks later.

It's not something you imagine could ever happen and I was not
one bit happy about missing my own dad's funeral. Feeling the need to
mark the occasion in some way, I contacted Peter Sculthorpe and put
forward the idea of doing an impromptu performance of his 'Lament'
in memory of my dad. Next morning, the Sydney Morning Herald front
page announced that the Brodsky Quartet, with two friends from the
Australian Chamber Orchestra, were to perform Peter's 'Lament' in the
North Foyer of the Opera House at 6pm that day. Four hundred and fifty
beautiful people turned up to hear that fifteen-minute work and as the

tears rolled on that emotional event, 10,000 miles away my father was being taken feet first from the family home. Kebroyde, the house that had become such an important statement back in the '50s would soon be sold, closing the door on that era. It had been forty years since those smug drunkards had humiliated him with their snide, hurtful comments. Ridiculed from all sides for being 'too big for his boots', Joseph Cassidy stubbornly ploughed his own furrow, raised the bar and broke the mould. It may have taken a while, but by the time I left Derry, all ten of those staunch houses that proudly overlooked its northern exit had changed colour; a change he instigated.

'Lament – Bjork'

Working with Elvis felt totally natural for us and the fact that he was a pop star did not in any way signal some new departure. Much of the media had other ideas, however, so we had to be vigilant to avoid being pigeonholed. Having said that, we were in no mood to just roll over – rocking that old battleship was always high on our agenda. We were ploughing virgin soil, but music is the wondrous thing here, making it important for us to stay strong and follow our instincts.

Our next album release was that coupling of Schubert's 'Death and the Maiden' and Crumb's 'Black Angels'. The juxtaposition of these two iconic masterpieces would surely show that we had no intention of abandoning our life's work. Aside from having to play your own instrument in a variety of complicated ways, the Crumb score calls upon one to play, for example, maracas, the tam-tam and tuned glasses. As if this is not challenging enough, George makes us whistle (often while playing), whisper and, most embarrassing of all, scream and shout in several languages – such as 'one' to 'thirteen' in German. Getting '*eins*' to '*dreizehn*' past the uber-critical ears of the Teldec crew near enough finished us off.

Meanwhile, we composed the music for the BBC TV classic *The Antiques Hunt* and went to Toronto with Elvis to record our own version of 'Lost in the Stars' for a Hal Willner film about the music of Kurt Weill, entitled *September Songs*.

We released our own *Lament* CD, an important record for us because it encapsulated where we were artistically at that moment in time, incorporating as it did some classics, our own arrangements and one or two of our own compositions. This was released on Silva Records, and with Reynold da Silva's help, we approached the whole CD in a more 'pop' manner. We had special guests and a promo tour playing unconventional venues more associated with jazz than classical music – The Jazz Café in London, then seemingly all the North American venues with blue in the name, like The House of Blues in LA and The Blue Note in NY.

We became known as the 'Garage Band of Classical Music'. Someone in the press took a moment to read the opening paragraph of our biography, which truthfully stated that in the early days of the group, they used to rehearse in a garage. We never imagined that this tiny fact would become headline material. Given our increasing notoriety, with huge billboards everywhere, features in countless magazines, even our mugs on London buses, we needed to make sure that the gigs on this 'Lament' tour were sassy and cutting edge. The mere juxtaposition of the repertoire we were playing took care of most of this problem but there was real pressure to deliver. Every city we visited had a local rag wanting funky quotes and a radio station demanding something for everyone to enjoy. The concerts required some extra players and we agreed that we would pick up our 'special guests' as we went, which was lovely for us because it meant we made new friends and it always brought a spark to the concerts.

One problem remained: the vocal element. Though only a small part of the show, the songs we performed were all either written or arranged by us and were diverse stylistically. It was not an easy task to find the right person in so many different places. One day at rehearsals, Mike and I started mouthing off about how *we* could do the necessary vocals. This unsavoury prospect was nevertheless preferable to the proposed alternative – to play the songs as instrumentals. Neither of us felt comfortable singing in rehearsal but Mike threw down the gauntlet, saying, "If you sing 'She Moved Through the Fair'," (which came earlier in the set), "I'll sing 'Jacksons Monk and Rowe'."

The opening show was at the Orbit Club in Toronto and my heart was pounding as I played the intro to 'my number'. My plan was to play the game till the last second, make as though I was going to play the instrumental version, then suddenly burst into song. The problem was, would anything come out? Would I eventually start breathing, and would my dry throat produce anything other than a frog's chorus? There was a wonderful moment as I stepped forward and let fly; out of the corner of my eye, I caught Mike's astonished expression as he realised the ball was now in his court. He was next up. Not to be outdone, he rose to the occasion and we were off. Though we had sung a bit with Elvis on the Juliet tour, this was very different. Holding a tune, holding an audience throughout a whole song was a new kind of buzz. There was no stopping us now.

***

I'm not sure if it was the impact of the Lament tour or not, but something brought us to the attention of Dave Brubeck. He got in touch out of the blue and asked us if he could write a piece for us. We were thrilled and excited to see what he might come up with. The work that eventually landed on our stands was nothing like what we had imagined. Dave had studied with the likes of Milhaud and Schonberg and was obviously taking this opportunity to explore his classical roots. He had written a full-length, Bach-inspired tour de force. He attended several rehearsals and we played the piece quite often, eventually recording it alongside Stravinsky's Concertino and the quartet by Kurt Weill, a piece that always reminds me of the Delius in its dense curtness. These works, though interesting in a historic sense, provide little in the way of payback for the performer or listener alike, making them very difficult to programme. Consequently, they languish forever at the bottom of that lonely drawer. Well aware of this problem, Dave gave us permission to programme only the finale of his piece, the Chaconne. This opened up opportunities for getting at least some of the quartet aired and giving people a taste of what the whole work was like.

***

Elvis was in the habit of sending certain trusted colleagues demos of his next album in advance of its release, just to get a bit of feedback. With some songs – so many, in fact ('Country Darkness', 'Scarlet Tide', 'Either Side of the Same Town', the entire *North* album) I always remember where I was when I first heard them. In the case of the lads from U2, however, there's one song in particular that they can surely never forget where they first heard it. They were on tour in New Zealand when they received a demo of 'Brutal Youth', and on their way to the soundcheck decided to have a wee listen. When 'Rocking Horse Road' came on, one of them, no doubt bewitched by the beauty of what they were hearing, opened the blacked-out window of their Limousine in order to get some fresh air and promptly realised that they were actually on Rocking Horse Road. Bono immediately phoned Elvis, who verified the almost impossible truth. He had travelled that very same road on his way to yet another soundcheck of his own and passed the time by writing another classic. I hate him sometimes.

Speaking of U2… their mind-bending Zooropa tour had reached Wembley, and Elvis asked Jacky and me if we'd like to go. Hearing U2 on a crummy tape deck can already be thrilling, but to hear these guys letting rip in a stadium is a whole other ball game. The concert was monumental and afterwards we headed backstage to congratulate them and say thanks for the tickets. As we stood there waiting for them to appear, Elvis spied Bjork sitting alone over in the corner and went to say hello. He returned a few minutes later grinning from ear to ear and reported the following conversation.

"Hi there, I just wanted to say how much I enjoyed your *Debut* album. It's really beautiful."

"Aw, well, thank you," she replied. "And I loved your last album too. I listened to it on repeat. Absolutely gorgeous."

"Hey, I'm so glad you liked it."

"Yeah, I'm a big fan of the Brodsky Quartet."

I remember thinking to myself that if there was another human on this planet I'd like to work with, this girl would surely top the list.

A year passed before the invitation came in, Bjork asking if we would be interested in doing an arrangement of a new song. We were tremendously excited at the prospect of working with this unique musician and asked her to please send over a demo ASAP. The bewildering demo was nothing more than a series of three repeated sounds, so low and distorted that they were indecipherable, above which hung a melody. That was the verse. In the chorus, the distorted sounds were replaced by a beat that once again underpinned a soaring melody. That was it. I set to work, completing the arrangement over the Christmas holiday. She loved the result and we recorded it first thing that next January. The song I had worked on was called 'Cowboy Leemings', later known as 'Hyperballad' and would be the first of twenty-three arrangements we did together.

'Jacky's cello'

Our Italian tour kicked off with a Sunday afternoon concert in Rimini. It was a nasty old day as we touched down in Bologna with just enough time to make it to the coastal town for a quick rehearsal before the performance. When Jacky's cello appeared on the carousel with all the other bags instead of being brought by hand to the oversized luggage section, we were already concerned. Jacky quickly opened up the case to make sure the instrument was alright, only to find, to our horror, that it most certainly was not. Remember, this cello was in a great white Stephenson's flight case covered in bright red Fragile stickers, and yet the charming baggage handlers had found a way to mistreat this clearly valuable item so badly that the cello lay before us in three or four pieces, bridge collapsed, fingerboard off, strings flopping around like an inebriated life-size marionette. As if this wasn't bad enough, BA had expertly managed to lose both mine and Jacky's bags into the bargain. So here we were, in a tiny airport on a Sunday morning, ninety minutes from our destination, with time running out, no cello, no stage clothes and, did I mention, no music.

This was back in the days when we used to try to sneak the cello onto the flight, a feat we often accomplished, incredibly, insisting it went in Hold B (the one for livestock) if we were rumbled. Normally, we would at least insist on carrying the cello to the aircraft and witnessing its placement, but on this occasion, with Jacky being pregnant, we just didn't have the energy for the fight – and besides, they promised us they would take extra care. It was also in that far-gone age when we would put our music in our luggage. If nothing else, this dismal Sunday in Northern Italy would teach us a couple of important lessons for the travelling musician. It was difficult to know where to start. We were borderline hysterical. We decided that

Mike and Ian would go on ahead to the venue, alert them to our plight and start trying to piece together some music we could play, also maybe find some clothes for us to wear and, last but not least, go on the hunt for a cello. Meanwhile Jacky and I would go through the necessary motions of filling out forms for our errant bags and complaint forms for the damaged cello. These formalities led us upstairs to the tiny broom cupboard that doubled as the BA office. Inside sat the entire contingent of BA staff in the Bologna area and, though I doubt my credibility as I relate this tale to you now, it turned out *both* these people played the cello! Whilst this mind-boggling fact took some getting one's head around, one has to remember there are levels of cello playing and different standards of instrument to cater for those levels. Furthermore, these two people were at work and their respective homes quite some distance away. But they were delightful, and the whole cello slant gave them a vested interest in helping us as best they could. Having discerned which of the instruments was the more feasible – i.e. which one had a full complement of strings – we set about having it delivered to the airport, pronto. Meanwhile, I got a car sorted and awaited the package.

The cello arrived in a soft case and Jacky gave it a quick check. Given the woman's kindness, we didn't have the heart to tell her just how awful this thing was. It was like the worst kind of school instrument, the kind they use on cheap ads, where someone who has clearly never set eyes on a musical instrument in their lives makes a botched attempt at mimicking something they've never witnessed, their alien nail varnish applied with the same shovel and brush as that of the instrument. It was the kind of garish eyesore you trip over when you're getting out the badminton equipment from the dusty recesses of a stinky school gym cupboard. We kept our mouths shut and loaded the gift-horse onto the back seat, thanking the lady profusely and setting up a time for its return the next day. Having accomplished the impossible, we jumped in the car and sped east to Rimini.

We arrived at the hall to find Mike and Ian struggling under a giant pile of fax paper, which they were busy cutting and pasting. Not all of the pieces we were to play that day were readily available but by chance, we had extra copies at home and had managed to contact our next-door neighbour, who took on the unenviable task of finding those parts and faxing them to Rimini. The organiser was a helpful young woman about the same size as Jacky and she turned up with a simple black two-piece which would have been perfect but for the small fact that Jacky was several months pregnant with Holly. Somehow she managed. I cobbled something together with the help of the violin section. We took to the stage on time having had no time to warm up, with sticky fingers, nerves in tatters and two of us facing horribly haphazard parts that we could only hope were in the right order. Jacky, squeezed into a straitjacket, had the unenviable task of teasing a pleasing sound – indeed, any sound – out of the second-rate piece of furniture she had in her hands and the small matter of Beethoven's Op.18/6 to negotiate. The less said about that performance the better, I would suggest. Poor Jacky had to resort to playing much of her part up the octave as the C string simply didn't work. The rest of the instrument, even in her hands, sounded somewhere between a comb and paper and a didgeridoo. Not our finest hour.

The next day we dropped the cello back with the lovely woman in Bologna, picked up our suitcases, which had arrived on that day's flight, and continued westward to our next port of call, Genoa. We had spent the remainder of Sunday liaising with the promoter in Genoa to see if he could possibly set us up with a decent cello for that night's concert, a considerably more grand affair than the Rimini gig. Unlike the understanding and charming young lady in Rimini, the belligerent, self-important git in Genoa was entirely without sympathy. The simple phone call he had to make to the principal cello of the local orchestra was such an effort, such a disruption to his Groundhog Day existence that he became deeply unsettled and unreasonable. He went on and on about how stupid and unprofessional we had been to put the cello in the hold. Nowadays, I would have to agree with him, but back then it was common practice to do this. The vast majority of cellists invested in these flight cases and insisted on the instrument being placed in Hold B. This versus the expense of extra seats on a hundred flights a year, pre-budget airlines, was a no-brainer. Furthermore, I can just imagine the reaction of our little friend in Genoa had we asked for a small increase in the pitiful fee to help with our extra expense.

Anyway, in the end, the principal cellist was only too happy to lend Jacky his beautiful cello for the evening and that concert went very well.

By this stage, we had organised for our manager to fetch and bring Jacky's spare cello to Genoa the next morning. We were out of the woods;

we'd somehow survived this mini-disaster and our tour was back on track. Hugely relieved, we all went for a gloriously boozy meal in a restaurant not far from the hotel in the *centro historico*. We'd heard a lot about Genoa in advance of our visit – how it is a famously edgy sort of a place – and it wasn't about to let us down. Later, as we wandered somewhat the worse for wear back through the tiny, ancient streets to our hotel, we actually witnessed a gunfight between the local police and a couple of armed guys who had just robbed a bank. It was surreal. There we were, looking every bit the part, clutching our fiddle cases, pinned to the wall as these robbers bombed past at full tilt, being chased by police on foot and in vehicles, bullets flying. All this seen through a haze of limoncello was doubly intoxicating. I felt strangely at home.

The rest of the trip went smoothly and we could see the finish line when we turned up for our final gig in Milan. Though we had played two or three different programmes on the tour, this concert was unique in that it was the only one which included Bartok's 6th Quartet. Everything was going swimmingly until Ian turned his first page. In a quartet, you can immediately sense even the slightest feeling of unease within the ranks; his was more of a red alert. After his initial panic and obvious distress, Ian coped with the situation brilliantly. He had turned his page to find the faxed viola part of Beethoven's Op.18/6 sellotaped in place over his Bartok music. This is a really horrible thing to have to deal with – to be reading music and then suddenly have it taken away from you without warning – particularly in a highly pressured concert environment. Amazingly, Ian kept his cool and managed to negotiate the final two pages of the first movement. The Bartok Quartets are works we know inside out and works we have often performed from memory in rehearsal in an effort to encourage a natural freedom, but even so, it was impressive and we were relieved not to have had to stop the performance. I could see that Ian had a job on his hands to unearth the rest of his Bartok music, so in an effort to buy him some time, I smacked my fingerboard with my bow, *col legno* style, and pretended I had snapped a string. Though I always carry a spare set of strings in my back pocket, I excused myself and hurried off stage, where I stood watching through a crack in the door till I could see that Ian had surreptitiously accomplished his task, whereupon I re-entered the fray. We took a moment to compose ourselves and finished the first half with no further dramas other than the ones

Bartok had intended. There may have been an extra bottle of barolo ordered that evening.

***

As the quartet entered its third decade we had arrived at another place on our journey. Though no longer the new kids on the block, our magic mix of youth and experience was beginning to reap rewards. Our potentially lightweight, adventurous spirit now carried the kudos of past heavyweight concerts and critically acclaimed recordings. It was a time when we could have rested on our laurels somewhat and, with the success of the CDs, become the go-to specialists for Shostakovich. Instead, we more or less turned our backs on Shostakovich for a time and started playing all the Bartoks. Once again, William Jones up at the Dovecot in Stockton gave us our first airing of these great masterpieces before we took them on the road. The BBC had licked any wounds leftover from the EBU days in Cambridge and were embracing us fully. We played all the Schoenberg Quartets alongside the late quartets of Beethoven for them at Bangor University, and all Mozart's chamber music with wind and piano at Pebble Mill in Birmingham with Christian Blackshaw, Michael Collins and others.

The IBA were not to be outdone, however, and Granada TV made a full-length documentary about us, shot in Manchester. Croft Sherry asked us to do an ad which took nearly as long as the film to shoot. Pinewood Studios was the venue for this ad, in which we were supposedly hard at work trying to capture just the right mood in the Nocturne from Borodin's 2nd Quartet. Time and again that elusive quality we were searching for would escape us and we would throw looks of disdain at each other until the magic moment arrived – group satisfaction (likely story) – and we would collectively elicit a smug, toe-curling smirk. At this poignant moment, the all-important punchline would appear on your screens: 'One instinctively knows when something is right.'

It was a plausible concept and the finished product looked amazing. Indeed, people up and down the country were very taken with the ad; the only problem was, they could never remember what it was for. This may well have had something to do with the fact that the camera could not pull itself away from our mesmeric cellist. Any red-blooded human watching would surely have had something other than a tipple of amontillado on their minds. Quite why we lads were woken up at some unearthly hour and whisked out to Pinewood to spend an hour in makeup in order to just sit there like eejits next to the angelic focus of attention remains a moot point.

Each morning, on our way to makeup, we would pass this guy polishing an array of sherry glasses to within an inch of their lives and diligently practising filling them, again and again. At the appointed time, he would choose one of the receptacles, place it with the utmost delicacy on the prescribed spot, then administer with the aid of a syringe a measure of the honey-coloured liquid, taking great care not to spill a drop or, God forbid, leave a smudge on the glass. His attention to detail was a valuable lesson. Though Jacky gave it a run for its money, the glass, remember, was the star of the show. This was the money shot, the one that made you instinctively know that you simply had to have a shot – nay, a schooner – of the old Jerez.

Continuing our burgeoning career in film, the legendary Swiss director Adrian Marthaler asked us to do a film centred around Schonberg's masterpiece 'Verklarte Nacht'. Though originally written for string sextet, Schonberg himself did an arrangement for string orchestra, and for the purposes of this film, we did a version that incorporated both orchestrations, teaming up with Tim Hugh (then principal cello of the LSO), Rushen Gunes (then principal viola of the BBC), and the Basel Symphony Orchestra, conducted by James Judd. It was filmed in the dramatic Basel Railway Station, which, though it dates from the mid-1800s, had undergone a massive regeneration at the beginning of the 20th century when the Schonberg had been written. One of the curiosities of this great rail artery is that its platforms span three countries – Switzerland, France and Germany. Thus, when we went to work (we filmed through the night), we had to show our passports to get from one platform to another; we were staying in Switzerland but filming in France. It was an inspired choice of location – the geography of the place was so evocative, and this, combined with the old steam train belching out its own version of dry ice, made every shot tremendously atmospheric and moody. Then there was the platform itself, untouched from the day it was built save for the opulent chandeliers and imposing portraits, painted by the composer himself, the sole props brought into this already perfect scene.

An extra bonus for me was the fact that the principal viola of the orchestra was a guy called Max Lesueur who had played on those wonderful Mozart Quintet recordings with Arthur Grumiaux and co. Though we were only there for a short time, he and I got on famously and I was deeply touched by the fact that before I left, he actually offered me a job sitting next to him, which he assured me would then become his job, as he was closing in on retirement. Touching offer, but maybe in another life.

'Holly – Macca'

Our relationship with Elvis happily continued. In 1995 we travelled to Gothenburg to witness the premiere of a theatre production of *The Juliet Letters*, and took part in the Meltdown Festival at the South Bank, which Elvis was curating. The artistic direction of this festival, still in its infancy, had gone from George Benjamin to Louis Andriessen to Elvis Costello, a most welcome and brave departure, but a departure nonetheless. Things were showing signs of change; great musicians were being acknowledged as such, regardless of their chosen genre. One memorable event from this week's festivities was playing in what would turn out to be Jeff Buckley's last appearance before his tragic and imminent death. His extraordinary rendition of Purcell's 'Dido' was a real high point, if you know what I mean.

Earlier in the year, we had taken Juliet back to Spain for a six-date tour, courtesy of Maria Angeles. It was during this trip that Elvis took me aside and told me that he had been approached by an old friend asking about the possibility of working with us on a very specific project. Elvis assured him that the combination could work beautifully and suggested that this gentleman give me a call upon our return to England. And so it was that, at the appointed moment, my phone rang and I found myself talking to Paul McCartney.

Now that's an odd experience, suddenly speaking to someone you've idolised all your life, someone whose songs you know by heart, inside out; someone who feels like your best mate and yet you've never met. We had a long chat, me mumbling gibberish, him being gracious and charming. He explained that he wanted us to join him for a concert at St James' Palace on 23rd March to celebrate his recent award of an Hon. Fellowship from the Royal College of Music. Various half-formed platitudes dribbled from my lips before Paul wound up the conversation, cutting me loose in never-never land. We were about to work with Macca.

Our first meeting was in the recital room at the RCM, on the very stage where I had performed many times as a student. There was an inordinate amount of people around, mostly Paul's entourage. Managers and minders, cooks, guitar gurus, photographers, runners – the list went on – and yet there was Paul in the middle of all this, cool and friendly as you like. He was an expert at making us feel relaxed but standing right next to him, I found myself unable to take my eyes off him and incapable of concentrating on what I was doing. Consequently, I rather embarrassingly played a wrong note in the very first song we rehearsed; 'Yesterday', no less.

Without even thinking, Paul looked round and started the second verse, "Yesterday, the viola was such an easy thing to play."

Soon I was asking him if he'd ever received the letter I'd written him when I was about twelve years old – not very likely.

"Sadly, I don't recall that correspondence, Paul. What was it about?" he asked.

"It was a heartfelt letter in which I pointed out that you had weirdly missed an obvious scan in one of your songs," said I, smiling.

"Really? Do you remember which song, or what the error was?" asked Paul.

"Absolutely," I answered. "I couldn't understand how you could possibly have missed, 'Still they lead me back… to the long winding track'."

After nearly choking on his coffee, he agreed. "My God, you're right. Such an obvious one. Idiot!"

How we laughed.

As we reconvened on stage, Paul started playing the opening of 'Blackbird'. Upon reaching the vocal, he stopped.

"Hey," I said, involuntarily. "You can't do that."

"Can't do what?" he replied.

"You can't just play the opening to 'Blackbird' and then stop… it's not fair," I complained.

He explained how he and George had come up with that beautiful sequence after being inspired by an old book of ancient keyboard music, and then played us the song. It was amazing to hear him playing all these things that one had grown up with. The command of playing something you've actually written yourself is a liberating experience. His wonderfully carefree approach to that um-cha-cha-cha opening of 'Yesterday' is exactly how I like to think of the opening of Shostakovich's 3rd Quartet.

Which reminds me… When the Borodin Quartet turned up to play that piece to the composer for the first time, their cellist Berlinsky played those opening downbeats pizzicato, giving Shostakovich such a shock that he fell off his chair, losing his glasses and sending the many pages of his handwritten score hither and thither across the floor. Picking himself up, he approached the cellist.

"My dear Valentin, does it say pizzicato here, in your part?"

"Ah no, maestro. It says arco, but in rehearsal we thought it sounded better pizzicato. What do *you* think, maestro?"

"Yes, yes… much better, Valentin, much better," replied Shostakovich. Then, with a gentle smile, he added, "Just play arco."

We had so much fun working with Paul; it was a pure delight. As for the concert, we stood there in St James' Palace with the biggest full-length portrait of Henry VIII you've ever seen overlooking proceedings, surrounded by all kinds of royalty, both in the audience and on the stage itself. The highlight of the show was playing 'The One After 909' with Paul and Elvis singing together live for the first and maybe last time. These two giants had so much love and respect for each other, it was palpable. Remember, Paul once remarked that Elvis was the closest thing to John he'd ever come across. That'll do!

After the concert, Paul invited us to dinner at a restaurant near the Burlington Arcade. As if having dinner with the McCartney family wasn't spicy enough, there was an extra ingredient to that evening's menu that added a certain piquancy for me. A short time before, Man U had made an infamous visit to Crystal Palace. For the most part it was just another Premier League game but then some eejit in the crowd got a bit too vocal with our magnificent Gallic talisman Eric Cantona. I have no idea what that guy said but whatever it was, it was enough to destabilise our Eric's fragile temperament. He took a run at the thug, who was standing jeering and gesticulating wildly from the perceived safety of his second-row seat, and delivered a characteristically dramatic Kung-Fu kick. Though no doubt taken aback somewhat, the guy wasn't hurt, but the game was interrupted and King Eric banished with a red card. During the subsequent FA inquiry and court case, Eric was suspended pending the court's decision. This just happened to be the day of that court case, which turned out favourably for Eric and therefore Man U. The only other people in that restaurant were at the next table: Sir Alex Ferguson (or, as our little Celia used to call him, St Fergus Aniston) and, presumably, the lawyers who had done the business. I remember Paul clearly wondering why I kept looking past him, till the Liverpool contingent at our table realised who was in their midst. We had just beaten Arsenal 3-0 and at one stage I caught Alex's eye and held up the 3-0 result with my fingers whereupon the two of us had a quiet fist pump and a giggle to ourselves. He did approach the table to say hello before leaving, knowing he had at least one ally seated there, and I must say, the Kop handled themselves admirably.

I often ask myself, what's the point? Why practise all day long when there's William Primrose? Faced with greatness, who needs mediocrity? But then I think of people like Eric. He was not Ronaldo. He came from the shadows, playing average football for Leeds and not even in the French team, but he blossomed into a true United legend, providing us fans with oh-so many wonderful memories. He maybe wasn't blessed with blistering pace or out-and-out brilliance, but he could command a football pitch and dictate a game better than anyone I've ever seen. Man U's history would be missing a hugely important dash of flair without Eric Cantona. It takes all sorts, and this thought keeps me going.

***

It was at this moment that mine and Jacky's life took a seismic shift. Holly, the most immaculate little bundle of perfection you could possibly conceptualise, appeared from that rhubarb patch in the sky. Jacky and I had agreed that, if we were to have kids, we couldn't possibly leave them at home while we went off working. They – and the inevitable nanny – would have to come with us, and if this meant sacrificing one of our salaries, then so be it. Though we stuck to the task, our resolve would certainly be tested over the next ten to twelve years. Our relentless regime of travel coupled with the stress of the job, the late nights etc. is taxing enough to cope with just by yourself; throw in a helpless wee human and, worst of all, the accompanying paraphernalia, and you have a nightmarish scenario.

Within weeks of Holly's birth we were back up to speed, working in South Africa with the singer Sibongile Kumalu. We stayed in a brand-new hotel in Sandton – now a well-known suburb of Johannesburg – then under construction. In the short time we were there we watched it being built… twenty-four hours a day. It was shocking to see. Those people slaving away on this massive project were there 24/7; they never went home. In the evening and at night the whole place was floodlit and the builders worked non-stop until they could work no more, then they simply went to sleep on the grass verges till they felt able to carry on. In our naivety, we tried to insist that local people were given tickets to our concerts but in the end, we played to a thoroughly white audience. Sibongile lived in Soweto, however, so we did get a chance to go there and socialise a bit, which was an education. That short drive up over the hill from affluent Sandton to run-down Soweto doesn't do much for your faith in the human spirit.

'Anne Sofie and Dr No'

Our artistic life at this point in the mid-90s was about as colourful as we could ever have wished for. We would go from tours with Bjork and Elvis to a Shostakovich Cycle in Spain, from more concerts with Anne Sofie von Otter to a Schubert Cycle in Germany.

One tour with Bjork took in many of the major UK pop venues like Manchester GMex, Sheffield Arena, Wembley Arena etc. They were daunting affairs. We would open the show with about twenty-five minutes of solo quartet music, then she would appear for another twenty-five-minute set with just us, and finally, my arrangement of 'Army of Me' would gradually morph from solo quartet to quartet and band, to just the band, and they were off.

Each time it was nervy. Thousands of people had turned up to see and hear the global star of the moment and instead got treated to a load of string quartet music. We fully expected the rotten tomato treatment or worse, and yet each and every time, we had them dancing and clapping along to Stravinsky and Shostakovich. When Bjork took to the stage, I must say, my pristine, middle-class ears were shocked by some of the things I heard directed from the audience at my elfin friend. I concur, she did look undeniably sexy in what could only be described as a torn tissue of a dress, but really, ladies and gentlemen, some decorum, please.

Thanks to the hard work of Liz Turnbull and Nic Pendlebury, Trinity College had developed a thriving chamber music department. String quartets in particular were encouraged and we were lucky enough to be engaged to go in and lend a hand. The strength in depth, to use a footballing term, was so impressive that we suggested doing all the Shostakovich quartets, a different group for each work. Not content with that already impressive feat, we got them to play them all in one day in the gallery at The Delfina Studios, with us all joining together in an arrangement of No.8 as the finale. It was a marathon, but it delivered a tremendous feeling of achievement and gave us all a day to remember.

One of our outings with Elvis that season was a trip to the Montreux Jazz Festival. After the show, the festival director came into our dressing room full of warm greetings and congratulations for the performance. He carried with him a selection of gifts for us all; a car crash of a Missoni necktie for me, Mike and Ian, a scarf by the same designer for Jacky, and for Elvis... a Tag Heuer wristwatch. I stood open-mouthed at this transaction, for this was not just any old timepiece; this was the exact watch I had been coveting for many years. It was doubly upsetting as I never wear ties and, up to that point, I had never seen Elvis wear a watch. Had I told him of my plight at the time, he would almost certainly have happily given it to me. I elected to remain silent.

One day Frank Taplin called me to ask a favour. It was a request that caused within me quite a dilemma. Would we join him in a performance of the Elgar Quintet to celebrate Sir Edward Heath's 80th birthday? On the one hand, why would I want to give my services to celebrate this man who had ushered in internment in Northern Ireland? Equally, history has taught us that the mere love of music is not necessarily a saving grace.

It was the combination of two things that swung it for me. One was that my dad, who had been tremendously interested in politics and was fiercely opinionated, always had a bit of a soft spot for the Jolly Giant on account of the fact that, as he put it, "One Thursday afternoon he marched up to Stormont and, locking the front door, declared, 'fifty years of misrule is long enough'."

And two, being a great believer in 'the pen is mightier than the sword', I decided an ambassadorial approach might serve to remind him for a brief moment about the reality of what was still going on in his backyard.

Our two fiddle players were unavailable for the proposed date, so Jacky and I elicited the help of two old pals, Jacqueline Shave and Patrick Kiernan, the violinists of the Brindisi Quartet. On arrival at the venue, Heath's sumptuous Queen Anne residence across the green from Salisbury

Cathedral, the security felt overly intense, given that Ted hadn't been in the hot seat for quite some time, the dogs and the machine guns ironing out the lilt in my voice somewhat. We were allotted two bedrooms to get changed in and the soirée took place in the main sitting room, where seating had been arranged for the forty or so invited guests. We tried our best to enjoy the occasion despite the fact that as we came out to start Mozart's Eb Quartet, which Ted had asked for to begin the programme, we noticed that sitting pride of place on the front row was the great violinist Iona Brown. Whoever chose that seating plan was a heartless soul. She can't have relished the proximity any more than we did.

After the music and the fairly meagre buffet, the guests took to their carriages rather abruptly, no doubt anxious not to overstay their welcome and, God forbid, tire out the birthday boy. We, on the other hand, totally ignored such protocol and soon found ourselves relaxing with the man himself, who was in no hurry to call it a night. The velvety claret put to bed, Ted moved us all onto his preferred tipple, a fine single malt. This is hardly noteworthy but for the fact that he was pouring his very own whisky; the label read, 'Sir Edward Heath's Malt Whisky'. Now that's cool.

By the time we were imbibing our second helping of this stuff, I sensed my moment to broach the 'Stormont on a Thursday afternoon' story. In the event, he was pleased I brought it up and vehemently reaffirmed his conviction of twenty years earlier – that fifty years had been long enough. I was dying to push my luck but decided to leave it there, happy enough with this tiny chink of light. How my dad would have loved this evening. Somehow I fancied he might be smugly looking down on the scene as we toasted his memory.

Anne Sofie von Otter is an artist who shares our ideals that music is for everyone, and that good music should be hunted down and celebrated regardless of its genre. I'd like to think that our work together reflected this aim. We played standard classics like Respighi's extraordinary 'Il Tramonto' but also visited folk, jazz and popular song. We commissioned works from Elvis Costello and Peter Sculthorpe, made a couple of CDs together, and passed some enormously happy times performing throughout Europe. Here again, the shameful pettiness of the classical music industry appeared from some dusty recess. Anne Sofie's record company, whose name I prefer not to waste energy writing, refused to let our record company put a photo of her on the cover of either CD. We rallied by replacing her adorable face with a rather fetching photo of an otter.

Throughout our time together we only ever had one issue, and that was when it came to deciding on a London venue. She, like so many foreign visitors, wanted to play at the Wigmore Hall, whereas we wanted to play at the South Bank or Barbican. We tried to sway her by pointing out that we'd have to do two nights at the Wigmore, whereas we could probably get away with only one in either of the other venues, but she had her heart set on this place and we did not want to disappoint her. So, two nights at the Wigmore it was.

Now, why did we not want to play in this place? Was it the unbearably pompous vibe surrounding the place? No. The ludicrously small stage, then, which already feels horribly cramped with only four people on it? Not that either. Ah, then I guess it was the endless rumble of tube trains adding a little tingle to the bass of that supposedly wonderful acoustic? Wrong again, I'm afraid.

No, it was none of these admittedly irritating truths. The reason we wanted to avoid this place was because, for ten years now, it had avoided us. After an almost obsessive love affair that saw us regularly perform there five or six times in a single season, we were unceremoniously and inexplicably dumped. Over the years I have become aware that we are not the only people to have found ourselves on the end of such brutal actions; this is a place whose sole aim is to keep classical music elitist. They actively pursue and wish to embrace the very thing that we have spent our entire careers trying to abolish. Added to this is an inherent distrust of anything homegrown; they prefer to invest in and hide behind the cheap patina of the exotic.

Many times over the years I have amused myself by imagining some irritating little runt who has woken up to find himself at the helm of this conservative dinosaur of a place. A character devoid of invention who works with whimsy; many fall foul of his fancy. There he will be, reclining empirically, sipping a Nero d'Avola and stroking his fluffy, white pussy. In my daydream, this Ceasarito figure fixates on his less-than-perfect reflection in the glass of a slightly-too-imposing portrait of his predecessor, infuriatingly hung opposite his curule. Struggling with his shortage of artistic flair and an inadequate frame that could never do his trabea justice, he decrees that that very day, he will wield his sneaky, silent power and some unsuspecting, undeserving lowlifes will pay the price for his neuroses.

"Let me see, now… eenie, meenie, miny, moe… *ecco*… Il Quartetto Brodsky, *perfecto*! Arrogant bunch of Northerners, if you ask me, and I never did like that mouthy Paddy. *Arrivederci bambini*, hahahahaha!!!"

This all takes place in my own little fantasy world, of course; Ceasarito and his white pussy are as fictitious as Dr No and his feline sidekick. Back in the real world, it had been ten years since we'd received an invitation to that ancient arena; it's now been thirty years without an invite, and counting.

Enough navel-gazing. Away from all this petty nonsense, real life was forging ahead at a pace. We got a residency at an emerging venue, the Cabot Hall in Canary Wharf. You would leave your home in North London and within thirty minutes find yourself seemingly in downtown Chicago. But as we found out time and time again, starting a new venue is a frustrating occupation. Even if you have the most beautiful space, get the acoustics right and find an inspired programmer, you still have the public to persuade. There's nowt so queer as folk, and gaining their trust is a perilous business. Problem was, in those days at least, the area was too far removed from normality and that potentially captive audience either poured into the strategically placed wine bars, never to be seen again, or shot off home at 5.30pm, leaving the place derelict come showtime.

The BBC asked if we would take part in some weird and wonderful rehash of a Lou Reed song in aid of Children in Need. Intrigued but wary, we asked what it would entail and who might be involved. Due to the nature of the idea, they were able to assure us that it would take us no time at all to do our bit and, by way of a carrot, went on to list a who's who of stars already signed up for the gig. We, along with Lesley Garrett, Thomas Allen, Andrew Davis and the BBC Symphony, would constitute the classos.

We didn't believe a word of it, fully imagining we were being screwed in some way, but it was the Beeb so we reluctantly agreed. It wasn't until we turned up at the studios in West London to record our two-bar, um-cha-cha riff and bumped into David Bowie on his way out that we began to realise this might be something proper after all. That recording of 'Perfect Day', with its accompanying video, went platinum, going straight to No.1, where it spent the next three weeks.

We were back on the road with Elvis again and accompanied Bjork to Oslo, where we performed at the presentation ceremony of the Nordic Council Music Award, which she had won. It always tickles me when I recall the rehearsal for that show. She came running over to me in a right tizzy and, jumping up and down on the spot, proceeded to reveal the reason for this display of unbridled joy.

"I knew it, I knew it. I've always known it," she squealed. "The DNA results are out. Don't you see, it's undeniable proof. When the Vikings invaded Ireland from the north, they raped and pillaged in their normal way but the local hierarchy, the chieftains and so on, they put on boats, cast adrift and warned never to return. That's who landed in Iceland. *They* are our ancestors. I'm not Scandinavian, I'm Irish!"

Seeing someone that happy to be Irish was crackin' and we danced around the room like a pair of banshees.

'Joe and Ash out and about'

Having had such a lovely time with Paul McCartney at the St James' Palace concert, he invited us to get involved in his next project, his 'Standing Stone' Oratorio. We had the relatively straightforward task of playing his string quartet in the concerts, although the rhapsodic slow movement turned out to be a challenging duet for viola and cello, which Paul had written specially for myself and Jacky. This touching gesture did bring an added pressure to the concerts, given that the two gigs were in the Albert Hall with the London Symphony Orchestra and Carnegie Hall with the New York Philharmonic, and we had to perform our set in front of the entire band. Hanging out with Paul in London was one thing, but being with him in New York was quite another. It always surprises me that one of the reasons John Lennon gave for choosing to reside in the Big Apple was that he could operate with a degree of anonymity. Given the hysteria I witnessed surrounding this other Beatle's presence, I can't imagine how any of them could ever have had a moment's peace, even there.

Warming up before the show, I heard hysterical screaming coming from outside. Rushing to the window, I could see that it was the arrival of Paul's Limousine that had caused the madness currently unfolding on a cordoned-off and packed West 56th Street. As he emerged from the vehicle he was engulfed by a sea of love, over-excited well-wishers clambering over each other in a frantic attempt to catch a brief glimpse of this icon who had helped pen the fantasy storybook of their childhoods. They weren't all middle-aged humans, either; many of these manic creatures were teenagers, powerless to resist the heady potion this foursome had concocted before they were even a twinkle in their hippy parents' bloodshot eyes. Elvis had warned us from the start that, though we had experienced some stuff, this was Beatlemania. Even twenty-five years after the event, this was something else.

My brother Joe, who had helped ignite my passion for the Beatles all those years ago, and his family had come down from Toronto for the occasion, and I managed to get him – and only him – past the intense security by getting him to carry Jacky's cello and introducing him as our roadie. Joe acted the part perfectly. So, I had got him into the same space as his idol, but how to now affect an introduction? This was clearly a big day for Paul on many levels and I could see he was under pressure. In my little life, however, this was an even bigger day, I could get my favourite big brother to meet Macca. I chose my moment carefully and asked Paul if he could possibly, at some point during proceedings, just say a brief hello to Joe.

"Where is he?" asked Paul.

"There," said I, pointing to the big, cuddly bear standing alone in the auditorium.

"Tell him to stay there and I'll be along when I can."

I thanked Paul profusely and ran to warn Joe of what might be about to happen. By now the orchestra had taken their seats and were tuning up. The rehearsal kicked in and Paul was in constant demand. By the break, I had all but given up the ghost. How could anyone under these circumstances remember to come and say hello to a total stranger? Paul, who had been clearing up some phrasing issues with the concertmaster, suddenly fixed us with his gaze from afar and, jumping down off the stage, came haring up the aisle towards us. He started shadow-boxing and fooling around, teasing Joe.

"Hey Joe, Joe Cassidy. Come on, then, let's do this thing, right here, right now."

Joe rose to the challenge and, for a moment, two of my favourite men in the world sparred together. Paul soon dropped his guard and gave Joe a huge embrace, and the two men chatted fondly for what seemed like an age. That infernal A from the oboe alerted Paul that it was time to get back to work, but before he departed he said to Joe, "You must come to the party tonight after the show."

"Aw, I'd absolutely love to, but I've got my wife and kids with me," said Joe, not wanting to impose.

"Bring them along. They're very welcome and I'd like to meet them. T'rah, then." And he was off.

Nora and the girls did come to the aftershow party, which was a blast. The girls flirted with Billy Baldwin and Joe and Nora shot the breeze with Paul Simon. It was the other Paul, however, who had made all this possible. Through being ultra kind and considerate, he had given a whole load of people, me included, a day to remember.

Through it all, Joe had been so cool. It's not easy meeting such famous people, especially if they happen to be your idol. I remember Elvis telling me that he had introduced his son Matt to *his* hero, Suggs, and been quite taken aback by the fact that Matt could neither move nor speak to this guy who, after all, was only Suggs! Then, some days later, Elvis – in the backstage bar of Wembley Arena after a Macca concert – found himself similarly dumbstruck when Kenny Dalglish walked in and said hello. EC tongue-tied is an amonoly if ever I erred one!

My nemesis came in the shape of Princess Diana. We had played during some function or other at Mansion House and afterwards were presented to her and her then-husband, Prince Charles. I had met Charles before and was able to blurt out some nonsense – albeit in an alien, plummy accent that appeared from I-know-not-where – but when she offered me her hand, I just stood there smiling inanely. Then, in the twinkling of an emerald, she was gone. What on earth do you say in such circumstances? I have no idea.

Her tragic and untimely death was one of those events that you always remember where you were when it happened. I had just arrived home in London having driven through the night. We had been on one of our Irish west coast holidays, only this time, Jacky and the girls had flown over and I had driven with a carload of useful kiddie stuff. Having dropped them at Dublin Airport for the return, I hit some terrible traffic and found myself arriving at Dun Laoghaire just as the boat set sail. It was a beautiful summer's afternoon and the next crossing wasn't for hours. I couldn't just sit there feeling sorry for myself. I suddenly thought of Elvis. In those days, he lived up in the Wicklow Hills, a stone's throw from this very spot. Incredibly, he answered the phone, saying he was indeed at home and the kettle was on. I wound my way up those country lanes and was soon chilling with a cup of Barry's Red Label, enjoying the extraordinary view of Dublin's Fair City stretching away to the North. Before I had drained my brew, a helicopter appeared from nowhere and landed at a nearby residence.

"Ah, that'll be the lads heading off for their soundcheck," said Elvis.

With that, the aircraft took to the skies again and this time swooped right down and hovered just above us. I joined Elvis in waving to the mystery airmen before recognising, even from that distance, that it was the members of U2 who were extending us a cordial greeting.

"I'm actually going tonight. Why don't you join me?" said Elvis.

"Oh my goodness, I would so love to, but I'd better get home. There's a boat in an hour and I should be on it." Now those were the words of a committed family man.

I mustn't have been listening to the radio during that drive because I only learnt of the covert Paris mission over breakfast at home. London was an extraordinary place to be in the aftermath of her death. The atmosphere was other-worldly. An overwhelming stillness fell about the place; the shock of the event resulted in an eerie hush. After a couple of days of this, Jacky and I felt a strong pull to go downtown, see what was going on and soak up this atmosphere for ourselves. We parked on Bayswater and walked over the park towards Kensington Palace. Now, our Holly had taken to a dummy like a duck to water and by the time we reached the royal household and the mountains of flowers it was twilight, and our usually perfectly behaved little angel was becoming a tad cranky – but we had mistakenly left her magic dummy in the car. For some inexplicable reason, Holly had always referred to her dummy as her 'dodi'. Can you imagine the looks we got, carrying this slightly hysterical child through that massed throng of people, crying and screaming, "Dodi, Dodi... I want my Dodi!"

***

For obvious reasons, it's always nice when Middlesbrough FC joins us in the Premier League, even though, truth be known, it can be a bit of a bogey team for Man U. In their heyday back in the '90s, with Bryan Robson at the helm, they managed to attract players like Juninho, Ravenelli – and do you remember Emerson? Emerson was a charismatic Brazilian who, with his shock of tight curls and wide, toothy grin, resembled a giant poodle patrolling the midfield. Unlikely though it may seem, rumour has it that his agent somehow struck the £4 million signing-on deal without Captain Marvel's approval. Sadly, as the club began to struggle and slip-slide away towards the dreaded Championship, so these 'southerners' would nervously make for the door.

We just happened to be on the same flight as young Emerson as he headed for sunnier climes in La Liga. He looked for all the world like an Avenger action figure in his metallic silver suit, permanently wedded to his mobile device despite the persistent attentions of the tiny doll-like creature hanging on his left arm. Whilst we got off at Madrid, 'Curly' continued on to wherever it was he had signed for next – Tenerife, as it happened. At the airport café the next morning, we happened to catch his first press conference on the telly. Having covered all the usual bullshit about how he'd enjoyed his spell in the Premier League and what position he was likely to play in this new system etc. the interviewer asked him,

"So, Señor Emerson, you have a couple of free days off before your first training session on Wednesday. Have you got any plans?"

"Oh, I don't know," said Emerson. "My girlfriend and I thought we might take a drive up to Madrid. I hear it's a wonderful city."

One can only assume that his wily agent was up to his tricks again, cleverly informing his overly trusting charge of the favourable financial implications of his move to the highly coveted La Liga without fully explaining the geographical details.

***

Do you know how Bono maintains his almost God-like persona year after year? Well, allow me to enlighten you. I have come to the conclusion that he's got some kind of retina recognition device linked to a deeply implanted earphone, so that when the eye registers a heightened state of awareness, this triggers a hive of activity back at U2 HQ, and from that moment on, everything the object of his attention says or does is closely scrutinized and acted upon with breathtaking speed, allowing the great man to effortlessly become the erudite, all-encompassing raconteur his idol status demands. Should the conversation drift to such and such a war, the names of influential generals and strategic battles will be softly fed into the hidden earpiece. A brief dalliance into the potentially hairy subject of cats and dogs, and a wealth of feline facts and canine chatter will be magically intoned.

This, at least, is my take on what must have happened on that memorable night when my princess-like niece, Ashlinn, met the King of Rock.

Ashlinn is the middle one of Joe and Nora's three daughters and is, as her name suggests, an out-and-out dreamboat.

Joe, physically the most impressive of us Cassidys, and Nora Gallen, who comes from a long line of Donegal giants (one of her brothers once carried the coveted title of 'The Strongest Man in Ireland', lifting impossibly large farm animals off the ground and dragging around enormous agricultural vehicles with his bare hands), produced three of the most striking girls imaginable.

Flanked by two gorgeous blondes, Shawna and Meghan, Ashlinn is a statuesque brunette, a heady cocktail of femininity who packs a punch that can leave even the most confident and capable of men flailing around on the ropes, tongue-tied.

Ashlinn left her native Toronto to study at McGill University. She fell in love with Montreal, subsequently making her home there and recently setting up a magnificent beauty salon by the name of Barbarella. While still a student, she would take on the usual waitressing type jobs to make ends meet. One day an agency contacted her asking if she would like to work that evening at a major party in one of the premier addresses of the city. She took the invitation and found herself at the home of Daniel Lamarre, the man behind the extraordinary Cirque du Soleil. During the course of the evening, she and the host got talking and quickly became firm friends, resulting in Ash finding her way onto the guest list for such events in the future, and not as a helper.

It was at just such a knees-up that the famous encounter took place. U2 were on one of their legendary world tours, about to play Montreal, and Bono was staying with his good friend, Mr Lamarre. The party was in full swing when the guest of honour descended the sweeping staircase and made a beeline for Barbarella. I reckon that by now, the dilated pupils of Mr P D Hewson must have been sending the boys back home into overdrive. His opening shot was a bit of a giveaway.

"You must be Irish."

Now, how did he know that? Was it a shot in the dark? Was it something in her eyes, perhaps? He came up with some fanciful yarn about the fact that only Irish people stand, as she was, with their backs to the fire, but I don't believe a word of it. I reckon those glasses had relayed her image, the check had been carried out and, hearing the name Ashlinn, he figured it was a safe bet to assume she was one of ours.

Ok, if you think this a trifle fanciful, how else do you explain the fact that, once they'd got over the initial banter and Ash had decided to mention that her uncle and aunt were musicians in the Brodsky Quartet, Bono immediately got very animated, saying how much he loved the quartet's work, and in particular, those amazing Paul Cassidy arrangements of Bjork songs? The fact that Bono knew my name and professed to value my work was both perplexing and undeniably cool. Believe me, those leprechauns, wherever they were, were putting in quite a shift.

Bono and Ashlinn got on like a house on fire and spent most of the rest of the evening chatting ten to the dozen. The 'wee folk' could have had a well-earned break because never once did Bono need to employ useless facts about the antics of John 'Black Jack' Pershing or concern himself with the dwindling numbers of the Dutch Stabyhoun. Their conversation flowed effortlessly; he, no doubt, relieved to have found someone who was at once eloquent, easygoing and no threat. Ash got VIP tickets to the show and the U2 juggernaut moved on to the next port.

Back home, Teesside University bestowed an honorary MA upon us. It was a proud moment, and undeniably gratifying and encouraging to have one's work acknowledged in that way.

We played at Linda McCartney's memorial service in St Martin-in-the-Fields Church on Trafalgar Square. Every effort was made to make this a celebration of Linda's life, but it's a fight to not feel great sadness at the passing of such a beautiful human being. It was an immensely moving tribute; the church was filled with cornflowers (Linda's favourite), rock stars and the extraordinary music, courtesy of us, that Paul had written for his wife over the course of their time together. It's difficult enough for us normal people to sustain a loving relationship in this ever-changing world we live in; I cannot begin to imagine what it must be like for a couple burdened with the kind of fame they had. They were bricks, shining examples of good, old-fashioned values. Linda could not have been nicer to us. She made no secret of the fact that she loved the work we were doing with Paul, and I'm absolutely sure that if that horrible illness hadn't taken her, Paul would have had no choice but to find more things for us to do together. The world is a lesser place without her sunny disposition and well-placed conscience.

'Celia – Andrew'

In 1998, Mike finally took the decision that had been brewing in his mind for many years. He left the quartet and, together with his Spanish wife and growing family, went to live in Spain. This left the three of us in a difficult place. The clue is in the name – a quartet tends to have four people, and we were a player short.

These moments are monumentally stressful for any group, whatever the circumstances, but the timing of this split could hardly have been worse. In the previous season, thanks to our wizard Maria Angeles, we had done over sixty concerts in Spain alone. Now, between the 8th January in York and the 26th March in Wellington, we had played seventy-two pieces in forty-three concerts; these included the complete quartets of Schubert, Bartok, Schonberg, Webern, Zemlinsky and Berg, not to mention a Complete Shostakovich Cycle across the major cities of Australia, live to ABC. The quartet was flying high but with one engine down.

Finding the time and energy to hunt down a new comrade was a challenge. Being in a quartet can be an insular existence; we were so wrapped up in our own little world, we didn't have a clue where to begin looking. Past quartet players, orchestral leaders who maybe fancied a change, soloists with the right temperament who could perhaps juggle two diaries? It was a jungle out there and we were ill-equipped.

One day, before any of us had so much as contacted a single candidate, Ian was talking to a musician friend called Chris Windass. Upon hearing our predicament, Chris said quite categorically; "If you're looking for a violinist, look no further than Andrew Haveron."

We trusted Chris' word and were excited by his vehemence, but deflated by the news that this Haveron chap was still in his early twenties. Could we seriously hook up with someone fifteen years our junior? The harsh reality of the situation meant that we had to start somewhere, so why not here? It turned out that Andrew was already in a quartet (a good sign) but that that group was about to fold (an even better sign). One of their final concerts was to be in the Holywell Room in Oxford the following Sunday morning. We agreed to go.

It felt like the beginning of an interminable journey as we set off from Crouch End that morning. We almost didn't go and several times nearly turned back. We felt horribly self-conscious as we took our seats high up at the back of that historic hall, falsely imagining that everyone in the audience would know why we were there. Apparently Andrew did, Chris having alerted him to our presence. Their programme that morning consisted of Webern and Beethoven. It was already clear in the 'Langsamer Satz' that this guy looked the part and could seriously play the violin, but it was the masterful way in which he negotiated the explosive semi-quaver runs at the beginning of Op.132 that was so impressive, the consummate ease with which he executed that seemingly endless down-bow, the command, the coordination, the dexterity, the beauty of sound, the inflection. It sounds implausible, I know, but in that moment I knew this was our boy. I prayed Jacky and Ian felt the same way.

Although I diligently sat through the rest of the performance, I didn't really take in much else, to be honest. My mind was racing, already trying to picture how our future diary might work out. The masterwork unfolded somewhat predictably. Andrew broke a string halfway through the first movement but he dealt with this often-disturbing hiccup with minimum fuss. Nothing seemed to bother him.

In the pub afterwards, not a word was said between the three of us, save a nodded agreement that we should talk to him and, if he agreed, meet as soon as possible. As luck would have it, I turned away from the counter with my pint and who should be standing there but the man himself? I was suddenly nervous and chose to ignore him in an effort to buy myself some time. When he took his drink and went outside for a smoke, I plucked up the courage to make a move. I congratulated him on the concert and said how much I loved his playing. With barely a pause for breath, I told him who I was and what I was up to. He replied that he knew exactly who I was, what I was up to, and that he would be thrilled to try for the job. We agreed to meet the following week at our office in Bermondsey.

"What would you like to play?" I asked.

"Whatever you like," said he. This guy was super cool and totally unflappable.

"Take your pick," I rallied.

"Let's decide when we meet."

Advantage Andrew.

Those first playthroughs took me back to my first weekend with the quartet up in Edge Lane. Here was someone who was either the best sight-reader I'd ever encountered, or who knew one hell of a lot of quartets. Everything we played felt so totally natural and effortless. I had never known anyone who made playing the violin look so easy. The question of age never entered into it and a strong feeling of camaraderie was there from the outset. This feeling only strengthened as the day progressed. Going downstairs for lunch, we could see that Andrew was, like us, a food lover. The look of hurt and astonishment on his face when I foolishly suggested sharing a dessert was a carbon copy of the look that would have been on our faces at his age.

On returning to our rehearsal room, there seemed little point in playing any more; instead we chatted about life in general, past and future. My one reservation was that he was bound to have aspirations to be a soloist. With this in mind, I asked him a loaded question. "Who would you say is your ideal violinist?"

Expecting a stock answer such as, Oistrakh, Menuhin or Kremer, I nearly fell off my seat when he said Slatkin.

This sealed the deal. Any slight worries or fears went out the window. Felix Slatkin had been the first violin of the Hollywood Quartet and someone whose playing we all held in very high esteem. His was not a household name and Andrew could not have chosen a more appropriate idol if he had wanted to endear himself to the three other people in that room. Right there and then, we discussed how great it would be to do a homage to this inspirational group, and by teatime we were complete again. It was as easy as that. Somehow, miraculously, the perfect person had entered our lives at the perfect moment.

Throughout our career we have maintained a special bond with one of the great chamber music venues in the UK: St George's, Bristol. Relationships like this are hugely important to any artist, and to have such solid support from an important institution is invaluable. This kind of solidarity works best if it's a two-way street and I think that where St George's is concerned, that is certainly the case. Many of the artistic ventures we have undertaken over the years, we have brought to that glorious Bristol stage. In 1998 it was Bjork's turn.

If the stadium tour was surreal from our perspective, I think we managed to get our own back here. It's fascinating to see someone for whom performing in front of 10,000 people is no big deal get increasingly uncomfortable at the prospect of singing for 500. Paul McCartney wouldn't perform without a guitar or piano, simply because he never had. They were like his props, his disguise, almost. In Bjork's case, it had probably been a wee while since she had done a gig like this, if indeed she had ever – a gig where there's no electricity to hide behind, where you can see the whites of people's eyes. It can make you feel naked and vulnerable. Coming out to find the members of Radiohead on the front row didn't exactly help matters much but it was, despite the absence of wires, an electric concert that undoubtedly paved the way for the Union Chapel shows we would do the following year.

In the midst of all this stress and chaos, our very own miracle-caterer was conjuring up another breathtaking show of mind-boggling brilliance – Jacky gave birth to Celia.

We played 'Black Angels' to a packed Barbican that night and within five hours of negotiating those haunting final sounds, a very different kind of angel appeared to us. Such timing, such consideration, coupled with a tenacious determination gave us an early insight into the formidable character who had just joined our world.

It began to feel as though we were single-handedly keeping BA airborne since now, every time we flew, Jacky and I required six seats. Add to this the extra hotel rooms, taxis, meals and so on. There's no denying that the lifestyle we chose was taxing, but equally, as a family, it has furnished us with many extraordinary memories.

Our concertizing with Elvis happily continued. We also had a nice little thing going where we would appear on each other's albums. For example, he sang on 'Lament', and we played on 'All This Useless Beauty'. In March of '99 we were the final act on the TV extravaganza, Comic Relief, playing a little ditty called 'You'll Never Walk Alone'. All very well for Elvis but, much as I adore that song, my Man U allegiances had to be put to one side for a minute or two.

Bjork had been trying to persuade us to get involved in her next album *Homogenic* but, hugely tempting though that was, we decided against it because it would have involved a lot of amplification and the introduction of other instruments, beats and so on. We felt very proud and protective of what we had created with her acoustically and didn't want to compromise this achievement. So the Icelandic Octet was born for the purposes of *Homogenic* whilst we five aired the fruits of our work together up to that point with a pair of concerts at a relatively unknown venue in North London, The Union Chapel. These concerts were a huge success, garnering the sort of reviews you can only dream about. We played our full repertoire of twenty-three songs; the place looked amazing, bathed in candlelight; and thirty DVD cameras captured every sound and move we made. So successful were the concerts and so charming the recordings that we wanted to release a CD of the whole event straight away. Unfortunately Bjork had other ideas and only ten of the songs eventually found their way onto disc, hidden away in her 'Family Tree' box-set under the title 'Strings'. Go seek.

The '00s

'Moodswings'

In the years leading up to the Millennium, promoters everywhere had been asking us for our ideas for the milestone event; a clear indication, in case it got overlooked, that we are indeed in the entertainment business. This always puts a lot of pressure on me because that's a big part of my role in the group, programming ideas. The idea for the Millenium ended up being a celebration of the Op.18 Quartets of Beethoven. These six masterpieces were his first in the medium and, rather conveniently from our perspective, were written and published in 1800. So, two hundred years later we would commission six composers – three women and three men, with a married couple at the centre of things – to each write a short work inspired by one of the Beethoven pieces. In numerical order, Javier Alvarez, Tunde Jegede, Karen Tanaka, Sally Beamish, Dmitri Smirnov and Elena Firsova went to work and created six beautiful reflections on the Op.18 we had issued them. It went under the catchy title of 'The Op.18 Project', which we subsequently recorded for Challenge Records. It made a lovely three-concert package that promoters clearly found attractive because we played that series a great many times over the Millennium and beyond, the premiere taking place in The Cabot Hall.

I thought it would be nice to have some relevant encores ready for these concerts and asked a diverse bunch of friends if they would write a variation on Beethoven's 'Ode to Joy' theme. The contributions came from Django Bates, Fabrizio Festa, Peter Sculthorpe, Pam Liebeck, John Tavener, Ray Davies and Dave Brubeck, and we called the collection the 'Euro Variations'.

One night, late, I got a call from Dave, which went something like this:

"Hey Paul, guess what? You won't believe this. I'm so excited... so excited... only, don't tell anyone," whispered a clearly upbeat Mr Brubeck.

"Of course, Dave, my lips are sealed. But what is it?" I enquired, suitably conspiratorially.

"It works in five, Paul. The Beethoven… it works in five!"

It was so touching to hear the childlike quality in his voice at this discovery – the man who, for many, put 5/4 on the map.

We were contacted by the Sociedad Generale des Autores y Editores and embarked on a lengthy project to record the sadly ignored quartets of some of Spain's most important composers, namely Conrado del Campo, Fernando Remacha and Ruperto Chapi. After the genius of Arriaga string quartet writing had literally disappeared from Spanish music, and we owe a lot to these three composers for reintroducing it. Whilst the music is maybe not up to the highest standards, the quality of the writing impressed us tremendously, and I consider it one of our more worthwhile forays into the shady underworld of lost quartets.

We've been fortunate enough to enjoy a prolific recording career. By now we were with Challenge Records and working our way through some more neglected works (Korngold, Kriesler, Zemlinsky, Respighi) as well as some more famous ones (Beethoven, Tchaikovsky, the Shostakovich Piano Quintet with Christian Blackshaw, Britten). I always find recording a massively stressful ordeal, but committing those three big Britten masterpieces to disc, in the Maltings – the arts complex which owes its very existence to the composer – with Colin Matthews (who had been with the composer as he wrote his last quartet) producing and me playing Ben's very own viola with all that history attached, was downright terrifying. Admittedly there were perks to the process. Working with Colin was a delight and we even got to stay in the Red House. For the whole team to be able to relax after a long day, have a chat and a glass of something warming by the fire in the composer's home, was a privilege and truly inspirational.

Through our work with Elvis, we inevitably got to know the various members of the Attractions (or Imposters, as they became later), especially their mercurial keyboard player Steve Nieve, who we performed with many times. Steve composed an opera – libretto by his wife Muriel Teodori – entitled 'Welcome to the Voice'. It was purposefully scored for our combined forces plus voices and having worked on it for some time, in June of 2000 we set sail for New York, where the premiere would take place at the Town Hall, with the vocal talents of Elvis and Ron Sexsmith amongst others. We were staying at the Tribeca Grand, a hotel we'd never heard of, in an area of Manhattan we were not familiar with. It turned out that we'd arrived on the opening weekend of the hotel and that Tribeca was the new, cool NY hotspot. In case we were in any doubt, we bumped into Bjork, of all people, in the lobby and as I was checking in, I had to physically hold on to the front desk as I realised I was standing next to Joni Mitchell, looking glamorous and gorgeous. The temptation to run over and hug this inspirational human was huge; instead, I observed her quietly as she went about her business.

The hotel threw an opening party that night, which was pretty unavoidable given that it took over the whole ground floor and was mostly filled with weird and wonderful people doing more and more wacky things as they nailed ever-increasing amounts of the beautifully presented cocktails containing heaven knows what. After the premiere of Steve's opera the next night, we had a little opening celebration of our own, eating and drinking at the Algonquin till the wee hours. It was such a quintessentially New York sort of a weekend. There is nowhere else on Earth that can give you a buzz like that. On our return, little old London felt so quaint and civilised.

I had been working on an idea that was simple in my mind but in reality, grew and grew into a monster – a nice monster – that was brought to life by the Contemporary Music Network.

Sensing that teenagers can often get overlooked by education projects (visiting musicians seem to concentrate their efforts on the younger age groups), the notion was to go into secondary schools, take the English, Art and Music students, mix them up and get them, over the course of a week, to write songs for string quartet and voice. Only string quartet and voice, mind – no guitar, piano or drums – no cheating. They would also be asked to produce stage design for the end-of-week concert of the material produced; design and produce a CD, merchandise, and anything else they felt inspired to do. What I hadn't understood was just what a leap of faith this was for any school, to lose their English, Art and Music classes for a whole week. Also, for the idea to reach its full potential, we would need a team of people – a composer, a singer, a writer, a designer. We needed some serious financial help if we were to make this happen. After endless research, phone calls, emails, meetings and form-filling, myself and Marjon, our then manager arrived at the door of an organisation called NESTA. Rarely had I come across such an impressive group of people with such high standards. They quite rightly put us through the mill, but with the superhuman efforts of Marjon in particular, they eventually got behind us and my crazy scheme. Notwithstanding that Marjon had always displayed an exemplary work ethic, the ethos of this project seemed to really click with her, resulting in a drive and determination that were infectious and inspiring to behold. She spearheaded the idea, enabling us all to realise the dream.

We gathered together not one but two amazing teams and visited six schools from Manchester to Portsmouth. The students composed over one hundred songs, made six CDs and created unique and beautiful stage sets, not to mention T-shirts, waistcoats and all manner of memorabilia. It was an emotional and unforgettable experience for us.

The legacy of the escapade was to be a commercial CD. We undertook the unenviable task of choosing one song from each school, which would then sit alongside songs by some more established songwriters. Sophie Grimmer and Adey Grummet, our amazing songstresses on the project, took a kid's song each, and the magnificent Jacqui Dankworth and Ian Shaw, who would eventually join us as vocalists on the concert tour, took two each of the remaining four.

Naturally we started the hunt for the more established songwriters with our co-conspirators, Elvis and Bjork. I had asked Elvis for an obscure song, maybe even one he hadn't yet recorded. He duly obliged, sending over a song he had written in a taxi on the way to the studio to record it for the film *The Big Lebowski*. You have to be concentrating to spot the song in the film, but I loved 'My Mood Swings' from the first moment I heard it. Its raw, raunchy power and effortless, throw-away lyric just hit the spot for me. Furthermore, it has to be said, it threw up a happy coincidence in that teenagers do have a bit of a reputation for the odd mood swing. Aware of the challenge of making a string quartet sound like a rock band, Elvis sent an alternative 'get out of jail' song. 'Shot With His Own Gun' is a big, flowery drama of a song that would have lent itself perfectly to a quartet arrangement, but my mind was made up; 'My Mood Swings' was our song.

Having recently witnessed and loved *Dancer in the Dark* at the cinema, Bjork's subdued epic 'I've Seen it All' more or less chose itself. Bjork had introduced us to the work of Meredith Monk and her hypnotic 'Gotham Lullaby' certainly struck a chord. Originally Bjork was going to do the vocal, but in the end, Meredith insisted she wanted to do it herself.

Richard Rodney Bennett was a good friend of Andrew's and together, they prepared Richard's touching love song, 'I Never Went Away'. Sting was amazingly kind and canny, immediately realising that 'Until' would be the perfect track. Errollyn Wallen, an old friend of the quartet's, had written several pieces for us already; her extraordinary 'Daedalus' was a no-brainer, surely one of my Desert Island Discs.

Ron Sexsmith, like Elvis, sent two songs and, as with Elvis, I ended up choosing what he had undoubtedly considered the B-side. Ron sent 'On a Whim', yet another brilliant oeuvre from that man's pen, but alongside it was the quirky, childlike, heartbreaking 'Dumptruck'. I was powerless to resist; 'Dumptruck' stole my heart.

The whole CD was recorded in London except for 'Until'. For this pleasure, Sting invited us to Il Palaggio, his home in Italy, where he and his gang were busy working on a new CD of their own. We spent three glorious days there, quite a lot of time for one five-minute track, I know, but we hadn't worked together before and it was lovely to have a bit of space to gel and get to know the arrangement.

On arrival we got straight down to business. Halfway through the second playthrough of the song, Sting, who had naturally enough been strumming along on his guitar, stopped, looked at me and said, "We don't really need the guitar, do we?"

"Maybe not," said I, relieved that *I* didn't have to be the one to say it.

It was so easy working with him. He's such a fantastic musician that very little needed to be said; we just adjusted where necessary without the need for troublesome words.

After that second playthrough, I tentatively asked him if the arrangement was ok, not knowing what we would do if he didn't like it.

"The arrangement's great, Paul," he said. " I love it. There's one tiny thing. In that little bridge between the second chorus and third verse, I stay a bit longer on the G minor chord before resolving it."

"Oh, sorry," I said, "I must have missed that."

We quickly found the errant spot and corrected it. On playing it again, a happier Sting smiled and exclaimed, "Aw, that's better. You know me, delayed gratification and all that."

We all fell about laughing. It was so great that he could take the piss out of himself like that.

Later that night, when we got back to the kitchen, the thought of a big dinner didn't really appeal. What to do?

"I could rustle you up a chilli pasta in five minutes, how would that be?" asked Joe Sponzo, Sting's chef at that time.

"Perfect," we chorused.

Now, chilli pasta isn't exactly haute cuisine. I've thrown this dish together myself many a time. But this was not your average chilli pasta. Sure, the pasta was homemade on the premises; the oil also came from the very farm where we were staying, as did the garlic and chillies – maybe even the parmesan, who knows? But still, I found myself in the kitchen nagging Joe to divulge the secret of turning this humdrum dish into something memorable. It was nothing more complicated than a splash of the pasta water. That's all it took to release the flavours and create this transformation. It was Joe who informed me that in an authentic Italian restaurant, they would never dream of changing the pasta water. So often, the magic is in the detail. This, washed down with a delicious bottle of homebrew, Sting-style.

Each morning, while we stumbled in monosyllabic and bleary eyed, our host would appear all wrapped up like a prize fighter, having already done ninety minutes of Ashtanga yoga. Taking his place at the head of the table, a perfectly crafted cappuccino would be placed under his nose. I was beginning to better understand that New Yorker cartoon that depicts a couple of guys chatting at the bar: "How are you anyway?" one asks. "Oh, I'm happy enough – I just wish my life were more like Sting's."

When we started working with Elvis back in 1992 and were constantly exchanging recorded ideas, there was a song on the very first tape he gave us that had totally blown me away. Randy Newman's 'Real Emotional Girl' really was emotional, but also, its content again seemed heaven-sent for a CD celebrating the work of teenagers. Elvis came to the studio to record 'My Mood Swings', now the title track on what would become our *Moodswings* album, and as he was leaving I asked him if we could play him my arrangement of Randy's song. The poignancy of the moment hung heavy in the air of that cramped studio.

"That's beautiful, man. Is that going on the album?" asked Elvis.

"Yes. We thought of it as a kind of encore, actually," said I.

"But who's going to sing it?" he enquired.

"Well, we're in touch with Randy but trying to find a suitable time is proving difficult."

"Please let me do it. Let's do it right now!"

And so, right there and then, we laid it down. Having heard the arrangement once and with no printed lyrics, Elvis took the mic and together we recorded the track in one take. It was one of those rare, impromptu, magical moments that is somehow meant to be. The album was complete, with our old pal fittingly opening and closing the affair.

If the album was complicated to assemble, the resulting concert would prove even more so. Even though the original idea was to get youngsters to write songs for us, we were less than enthusiastic about going out and playing one song after another for the entirety of the show. This programme needed something, something a bit more substantial to offset the string of songs. In those days, our gorgeous daughters were finding more and more interesting things to watch on telly and had recently graduated from *Teletubbies* to *Wallace and Gromit*. Now here was something the whole family could enjoy, and even if I got tired of the visual plot, there was always that amazing soundtrack to enjoy. Permanently aware of their education even while watching the box, we would avidly encourage things like 'Fantasia', a perfect way of exposing them to some great classical music without forcing it down their throats. Whilst working with Sting we had come across a fantastic set of films done by the Spitting Image crew, one of which was Prokofiev's ingenious 'Peter and the Wolf', narrated by Mr Sumner himself. It was probably the umpteenth time of watching this enchanting video that it suddenly struck me: *of course, this is exactly what we need for our show – a story.*

I'd heard Prokofiev was difficult to get hold of, so instead decided to pursue whoever was responsible for that wonderful *Wallace and Gromit* score I enjoyed so much. For the story itself, I remembered an intriguing guy we'd met through Bjork. He had worked with her on some of her lyrics and was a writer in his own right; I even had a book of his in the downstairs loo that entertained me on more than one visit.

Sjon turned out to be heaven-sent. He already spent his summers doing children's workshops in Iceland, helping them to express themselves artistically, including by writing stories. From the moment he heard our plan he was fully committed, and we subsequently met our composer, Julian Nott, at his club in Soho. I must confess, I was a trifle taken aback by the almost comical plumminess of Julian's voice when I spoke to him on the phone and could hardly have been more surprised when a Punk in full garb, crossed those Olde English oak floorboards and offered me his hand. Mind you, what must he have made of me, ill at ease in my only suit and mumbling away ten to the dozen in broad Derry? There's no doubt that the three of us were an unlikely bunch and my two new conspirators uttered a collective nervous giggle when, after a couple of hours, Sjon asked, by way of wrapping up the meeting, "Paul, before we adjourn, may I ask – what exactly is our brief?"

"Well, what we want is a twenty-minute piece for narrator and string quartet along the lines of 'Peter and the Wolf'," said I, matter-of-factly.

"Ah, so write a timeless classic, then?" quipped Julian.

"Exactly lads. A timeless classic."

These two guys certainly stayed true to the unrealistic brief and together created what I believe to be just that, a timeless classic entitled 'Anna and the Moods'. Anna, a delicious coming-of-age story, was precisely what 'The Brodsky Song Show' needed, and she would travel the world with us, captivating young audiences wherever we went.

'2001:
A Place Oddity'

Ok, here's a pub quiz question for you: What do Newgrange, Swarovski HQ and Teletubbyland have in common?

No idea? Well, I urge you to have a look at these three seemingly disparate places because, apart from the small matter of about five thousand years, you'd swear that these grassy igloos must all be the work of the same architect.

Newgrange is a vast Neolithic tunnel-tomb in the East of Ireland dating from 3200 BC. A feat of engineering to rival the Pyramids, the huge quantities of white quartz that decorate its exterior came from the Wicklow Hills, all of one hundred and fifty miles to the south. Even more astonishing is the small passageway built into the roof that allows the sunlight, only on the dawn of the winter solstice, to bathe the central chamber in light thereby heralding in the new year and encouraging past friends into renewed life.

Teletubbyland is that fictional place you visit 'again again' on your TV set if you're a sleep-deprived parent or a confused teenager who's had one puff too many of the magic dragon.

Swarovski HQ is a happy coming together of these two tales, a make-believe world built on semi-precious stones.

This is where we found ourselves on 11th September 2001. Just a short drive from Innsbruck in the Tyrolean Mountains lies the unlikely looking headquarters of this sparkly business, and every now and then they put on concerts in the little recital hall down in the bowels of their extraordinary green and white fantasy land. They picked us up from the airport and deposited us in an enchanting ski hotel on top of a nearby mountain.

The place was remarkable in many respects but prided itself on the fact that there was no contact with the outside world. No TVs or radios, no telephones or internet. Once you had accepted this state of affairs, you just got on with your day, albeit in a different way; it certainly made for a blissful afternoon snooze. We had only been isolated for a couple of hours when the driver came to take us back down the mountain for our rehearsal, but what a deafening period of silence that turned out to be.

Our limited grasp of German allowed us to decipher the gist of what was being reported over the car radio whilst postponing reality for a while yet. The driver did his best to ram the truth home with a series of noises and gestures, which resulted in him taking an alarming percentage of hairpin bends with only one hand on the wheel. We were playing 'Verklarte Nacht' that evening with a couple of Austrian musicians and so our rehearsal was absolutely imperative but, in all honesty, both rehearsal and concert went by in a bit of a haze. Even from this remote corner of Europe, the events taking place in America were numbing. After the show, we tried to put off returning to the silent hotel for as long as possible, but our driver had had a long day too and understandably wanted to ditch us and get home himself. Frustrated and despondent, we pushed open the huge wooden doors to the lodge having not yet seen a single image or heard a word in English about '9/11'. Unable to retire for the night, we managed to gather together some like-minded individuals in the bar and eventually forced the staff to dig out an ancient, wooden, black-and-white TV set and attempt to set it up. Hence, the first sight we all had of those surreal pictures was through a fuzzy screen that, given where we were, made it look for all the world as if we were gazing out the window through the falling snow at a distant mirage. One still struggles to view those scenes as anything other than science fiction, but for us, the unfolding reality of that attack on the Twin Towers in New York will somehow always carry an extra degree of poignancy.

'Chelsea 0 – Green Day 4'

There's something cloying and gut-wrenching about a whole load of privileged dicks and debs letting it all hang out. With all its choreographed decadence, attending the Chelsea Arts Ball is like being an extra on one of those Peter Greenaway movies. That said – even though he famously made it clear that he didn't want to go – we didn't exactly turn down the invitation to play there with Elvis back in the early '90s, and Jacky and I happily returned some years later to lend him some support when he appeared with the Count Basie Band. Not that that set wasn't great, you understand, but what really stuck in my memory from that night was the appearance of Tom Jones. I'm one of those people who grew up with Tom; I was an ardent fan of his TV show, hooked, like everyone else, on that potent chemistry he exuded. As the jacket came off, then the bow tie, the excitement grew. By the time the shirt got unbuttoned to the navel there was palpable hysteria. But to witness this fever at first hand was a whole other experience. Tom came on late in the proceedings, by which time the toffs were exhibiting freely, sweating out all that anger left behind by years of loveless boarding. A security cordon was erected around the Albert Hall stage and a posse of giants in dinner suits took up position just behind it. Tom exploded onto the stage and immediately the minders were put to work. By the time he got to 'What's New Pussycat?', not even this hand-picked crew of muscle could cope. Every conceivable undergarment was launched at the miner's son and the song climaxed with a throng of naked female bodies breaking through the barrier, overwhelming the heavies, and thrusting themselves upon the singer. Mr Jones remained totally calm and, supporting one particularly feisty blonde with his left hand, used his right to execute impeccable microphone technique in order to deliver the final chorus. The frenzy was brought under control quite quickly with the burly boys regaining their composure and literally flinging these nubile nudes back into the auditorium where, by that stage, they blended in naturally with the increasingly naked mob.

I've only ever heard that song live twice in my life – that night, and when KD Lang sang it at the equivalent moment in her show at Wembley Arena. She was a fantastic performer – what a voice – and not surprisingly, the song had the same effect on her audience. Though no one actually breached security and got onto the stage, I would say that the underwear was, if anything, more imaginative. I remember looking around at the bethonged throng and not spotting a single other male. On a quick visit to the gents' after the show, I was charmed to find myself standing at the urinal flanked only by women, happily relieving themselves.

The invitation from Complicité to get involved in their new play about Shostakovich is the sort of request that can strike dread in one's heart. Crazy, isn't it, that something so monumentally exciting should instill anything other than a feeling of euphoria, but a quartet is a warped beast, a great dollop of ego and fear hanging on by a thread, and so introducing anything unusual that could potentially threaten the perceived status quo can be treacherous. We hadn't done any theatre work since those workshops with Di Trevis way back in the '80s, and heaven knows, in everyday life, just an overly flamboyant up-bow could spark an inquest. As a general rule, quartets don't take kindly to being told what to do. They spend so much time in each other's pockets, constantly adjusting to each other and endlessly compromising, that when that delicate balance is tampered with, all bets are off. People can react badly, causing embarrassment and unwelcome time-wasting.

Then there was the small matter of having to perform Shostakovich No.15 from memory. We had played many quartets from memory in rehearsal, but never in public. This was another pressure, an added pressure no string quartet needs. I'm happy to report, however, that all this paranoia came from another life. The quartet we had now become had none of these hang-ups. On the contrary, we wholeheartedly embraced the many challenges, and had an amazing experience under the inspirational guidance of Complicité's director, Simon McBurney.

Dipping your toe in another art form at such a high level is exhilarating. Learning new tricks, doing their exercises, embracing their daily timetable is such an education. One thing I found intriguing was how easily we understood each other; our working language was so similar. We talked about intonation, phrasing, dynamics and architecture, and quickly recognised in each other that intoxicating devotion to the art, the emphasis on technique and the manic attention to detail.

Our performance of No.15, which made up the second half of the show, took place in near darkness with minimal choreography. The scene prior to our entrance could not have been more ideal, considering what we were about to have to do. The set was Shostakovich's front room, where two men sat in the half-light. There was complete silence but for the ticking of a clock. As the light gradually gave way to darkness and the clock diminuendoed al niente, the gauze lifted and we were off. This understated nothing of a scene was so moving and powerful not just because it came after a high-decibel, action-packed first forty-five minutes, but because it told of the fact that, from time to time, Shostakovich would phone certain close friends (on this occasion Rostropovich), invite them over and then, having welcomed them in with an affectionate hug, just sit there silently; both men so comfortable in their own company and so relieved to be able to enjoy a brief respite from the angst of everyday life – no words were needed. After an hour or so, Dmitri would get to his feet and escort his friend to the door saying, "My dear Slava, thank you so much. We must do this again soon. I love you," before getting on with his day.

The already emotionally charged music took on an extra dimension when the staging, with us on it, inched forwards imperceptibly out into the audience so that it practically touched those sitting on the front row. The manoeuvre took about fifteen minutes to complete and, though it might seem trivial, had a dramatic impact. We took this magnificent production to several European destinations during its short existence. How I wish someone would bring it back.

One day I met up with Bjork to chat about this and that. We were in that cute tea shop overlooking the canal in London's Little Venice. It was busy and becoming a tad uncomfortable as more and more of our fellow customers realised who was in their midst. If it wasn't obvious enough, the Lego platform shoes and Liquorice Allsorts handbag probably reinforced their suspicions. Bjork asked me if I knew the music of John Tavener, saying that she had recently got to know it and absolutely loved it. I explained that not only was I acquainted with his music, but that we had played a few of his pieces and that he had actually written stuff for us, a fact that appeared to interest her greatly.

"If you like his music so much, why don't we ask him to write something for us?" I asked.

"You're shitting me, right? I mean, that's crazy. How would we go about that?" countered my increasingly excited companion.

"Well, I'll just call him and ask him," said I, blagging my arse off.

"What, you can do that? Just like that?"

"Sure."

It was a gamble, of course, but I had a feeling John was no fool, and frankly, only an eejit would turn down an opportunity like this. I didn't phone him directly but called our manager and urged her to get in touch and pose the question as a matter of urgency. Even I wasn't ready for the overwhelmingly positive response we received not five minutes later. We were still sipping our tea when my phone rang with the good news. Bjork instantly jumped up from her seat and ran around the café, punching the air and making adorable little squealing noises. For those few doubting Thomases still uncertain as to the identity of their fellow customer, this was clear confirmation.

It did not take John long to come up with our piece. A couple of weeks later, he called to say that he had something for us to look at and invited us to join him for dinner at his home in Sussex. Derek Birkett, Bjork's manager, drove us down on that Friday evening. On arrival, we went straight into John's studio, where he showed us the score and talked us through his offering, entitled 'Prayer of the Heart'. As so often with his music, it was simple but brilliant. Bjork would intone a series of chants, namely, 'Lord Jesus Christ, Lamb of God, have mercy upon me', over a series of chords played by us.

As the chords rise in pitch and volume, the chants move through a series of languages, both elements climaxing in the English rendition and then falling away again in a mirror image. Underpinning the whole work is a recording of John's own heartbeat on a loop, adding an extra degree of poignancy, given the many health issues this heart had given him. As luck would have it, John's heart had a particularly catchy beat to it, which not only created a certain fascination but helped propel us through the work.

With this bit of the evening successfully negotiated, John popped some champagne and we made our way through to dinner. I'm not sure how much Retsina was imbibed that night but I can tell you one thing – I was bottles, not glasses, behind John. He was formidable, and yet remained coherent throughout. There was one slightly uncomfortable moment when the commission fee was mentioned but it was mercifully short-lived because when Derek heard the figure, he gaily chirped, "I would have paid that just to be here this evening," and promptly wrote out a cheque for the whole amount.

It was not an insubstantial amount, and Derek was not being derogatory in any way – he meant what he said – but it didn't half highlight the gulf between the two worlds. Undoubtedly, the high point of the shindig was much later when John took to the piano and Bjork led us all in a fairly lengthy singsong, during which we managed to wreck a sizeable number of big show tunes from the last hundred years, before Derek whisked us out of there and back to the relative calm of the Big Smoke. Things can get pretty scary out there in the wild, late at night. Though we recorded the 'Prayer' for John's sixtieth birthday CD, we never actually performed it live together. Perhaps this joy awaits us in the future.

We performed Haydn's magnificent 'Seven Last Words on the Cross', to celebrate the 225th anniversary of its premiere, in the very place it had been commissioned back in 1786, The Oratorio de la Santa Cuevo, in Cadiz. We coupled it with a specially commissioned work of the same name, written for us by Jose Luis Turina, grandson of Joaquin and a terrific composer in his own right.

We were given Honorary Doctorates by the University of Kent, where we had built up a long-standing relationship, thanks to that human dynamo Sue Wanless. This was an honour indeed. Among many wonderful memories, the Gulbenkian Theatre there would provide the backdrop for our first complete Beethoven Cycle.

We made a guest appearance on Elvis' album 'North', that most extraordinary CD that celebrates his renaissance in the form of Diana

Krall. With Elvis and Steve in a studio in NY, we made our way to Abbey Road, where we co-wrote and recorded the string chart for 'Still'. We would soon attend the fairytale wedding of Elvis and Diana, which was a magical day. As you might imagine, the live music was fantastic, not necessarily our bit but everything else, and Jacky and I rather embarrassingly hogged the dance floor for hours on end. One surreal moment was dancing to 'Back in the USSR', one of my all-time favourite Beatles songs, and finding ourselves actually dancing with Paul himself and Elton John. I remember getting pissed off with Elton because he clearly knew all the words... all the words to *my* song.

"Who does he think he is?" I muttered to myself, refusing to accept this affront, even from the guy who had famously covered that track for a couple of little shows in... where was it now?... ah yes, the USSR.

In the fifteen or so years that I had known Elvis, I had never called upon his considerable influence for anything, until now. Our Holly (aged 9) had become a huge Green Day fan, so when they came to London I made it my business to get tickets. Their thirteen-concert run at the Hammersmith Apollo sold out before I had even begun to look, and despite best efforts over many months, I could not secure a ticket. With about twenty-four hours to go till the final show, I relented and called Elvis, saying that I was in trouble. Daddy had screwed up. Why was I so surprised when he phoned back a short time later, exclaiming, "Cinderella can go to the ball!" Not only had he got us two tickets for the last show, but he'd told Billie Joe to look out for the dodgy-looking classo with the little girl.

The following evening as we finished dinner, I turned to Holly and said, "Hadn't you better get a move on? We don't want to be late now, do we?"

"What do you mean, Dad, late for what?" she innocently enquired.

"Well, Green Day, of course. It'd be a shame to miss any of it," I said nonchalantly.

Never have I seen such a reaction from anyone about anything. Her face became two enormous eyes, which began to stream with tears. Having ascertained that this really was no joke, the little darling became delirious with joy and ran about the place, trying to do ten things at once without achieving any. I whisked her up in my arms and pretty soon we were cruising through London town with the top down, listening to the lads at full volume. Holly, never one to waste time, was in the front seat making an elaborate card, which we would later give to her heroes. It was wonderful to share her innocent enthusiasm, witness her bursting with pride every time she explained to us that this was a 'concept album' and that not one but two of the songs were 'over nine minutes long!'; just like her parents would have done thirty years earlier whilst raving about the latest Yes, Black Sabbath or Pink Floyd offering. We got to the venue bang on time and, having picked up our tickets, I got Holly the T-shirt from the merch. stall in the foyer.

"I'll be right back," she said.

"Now where are you going?" I shouted after her.

Oblivious of the snaking queue, she stole into the loo, re-emerging moments later resplendent in her new top, which, though I got the XS size, came to just below her knees. As we entered the auditorium, I realised the next major hurdle to getting the kid what she wanted. The place was jammed and she was tiny. This would never do. I put her on my shoulders and started shamelessly pushing past people. Normally this sort of behaviour would be met with considerable resentment and resistance, but on this occasion, when each person in turn wheeled round to see by far the oldest punter in the place, looking desperate, and carrying by far the youngest person in the place, looking angelic, they each and every one let out an involuntary 'Awwww' and let us past. In no time we were standing not four rows back and before we could say Tres Cool, there they were, running onto the stage and taking up their positions right in front of our eyes.

My final worry was that Holly's love for these guys centred on one single album; at that stage, her knowledge of Green Day only incorporated the nine magnificent tracks on this one CD. This was the last gig of a massive world tour. These guys had been around for years. What would happen if they'd had enough of flogging 'American Idiot' and started digging into the back catalogue or, worse still, started airing loads of new stuff they'd been writing on the road? My worries were allayed when, after the opening tune, Billie Joe grabbed the mike and announced, "Good evening, London. We're gonna do something now you're not strictly supposed to do, but we don't care. We're just gonna play the whole fucking album from start to finish!"

This was music to my ears, and Holly's. There was one more extraordinary moment that capped an already unforgettable evening.

During 'Boulevard of Broken Dreams', BJ jumped up onto the speaker stack right in front of us and, having clearly spotted the old fogey with the kid that Elvis had warned him about, sang the whole song directly to Holly. A few brownie points for old daddy there… thanks EC :)

'Mum'

I guess that of all the countries we've visited over the years, Spain and Holland have proved to be our greatest allies, and within those countries, certain cities have been particularly welcoming. In Spain, Barcelona, Valencia, Madrid and Zaragoza were the hotspots, whilst in Holland, Amsterdam, Rotterdam and Utrecht seemed to never tire of our screeching and scratching. In January 2003, we were in the middle of a week-long residency at the Vredenburg in Utrecht when my breakfast was interrupted by that dreaded, once-in-a-lifetime phone call. The one that tells you your mum has died. Ten years younger than my dad, she outlasted him by the same margin. Weirdly, if you visit the tombs of my departed family, who are interred in the cemetery at Ballybrack Church, Inishowen, it's a glaring and slightly disturbing fact that they all appear to have thrown in the towel aged eighty-six. I suppose I'd take that if it were offered right now.

Even though, like her husband, she had been unwell for some time, I did not expect her to leave us at that point. Having missed my dad's send-off, I was sure as hell not going to miss my mum's.

An ingenious plan was hatched that enabled us (me, Jacky, Holly and Celia) to attend the funeral *and* complete the residency with minimum fuss. To begin with, we did the concert that night and the one the next night, after which the four of us jumped into a waiting car containing two drivers, who would whisk us off through the night in an effort to catch the morning flight from Stansted to Derry. Flying from Holland wasn't an option without cancelling one of our concerts; morning flights would have had us arrive too late for the funeral. Though exhausting, everything worked like clockwork, except that it became increasingly obvious that these two young drivers had never left the outskirts of Utrecht before, and Jacky and I had to remain constantly vigilant for fear we might end up in Luxembourg, perish the thought. The stakes were raised when we arrived on English soil because the drivers' preoccupation and amusement at having to 'prenez la gauche' only exacerbated the absolute conviction they both carried that – having been told by some Dutch barman to head for Canterbury – every single time they saw a sign for Canterbury, they were determined to leave the motorway. It took all our combined guile and powers of persuasion to convince them that Canterbury was merely a point of reference on the way to Stansted Airport, which in fact lay much further to the north.

Miraculously, we made the flight and entered Mum's crowded wake house with twenty minutes to spare before they nailed down the lid, forcibly taking this arrangement of dust and bone from my life's stage.

Before we'd even reached the front door, we had been made aware, in no uncertain terms, of the edict for this event. There was to be no crying. Did you hear that? No crying! It had been decreed that this was to be a 'celebration' of Mum's life, and therefore not the time for tears. This is the deplorable sort of nonsense that tends to float to the surface in large families, like some giant, gaseous turd. Hierarchies inevitably form and the self-appointed rulers begin to dictate.

If you don't mind, this was *my* mother – not ours, *mine*. *She* gave birth to *me*, and *I* had a relationship with *her* that had nothing to do with anyone else, it was private and personal. *My* mother.

I closed the door on this soap opera, allowing my own family to pass a few moments with mum, mother-in-law, granny, before the next scene. The minutes that followed were surreal. The four of us, cooped up alone with a mannequin who only vaguely resembled the tragic figure who, for the last ten years, had called this tiny, uninspiring space her bedroom. I say tragic because here lay a woman whom fate had dealt a cruel hand. A beautiful, capable, but above all, spiritual woman, who inhabited a rarified space in which mere material things held no value. True love would have been a bonus but with or without it, she would have been oh-so much happier to have passed her time quietly, among her own kind in rural Inishowen. Instead of which, she found herself unwillingly exposed to an alien world she didn't understand and had no sympathy with, being perpetually pregnant, and playing a bit part to her husband's starring role in a farce about social embetterment. With no help and no 'mod-cons', she quietly took it on the chin.

'You've made your bed, now lie in it' was, ironically, one of her oft-used phrases. Well, she certainly practised what she preached and suffered her lot with immense dignity. A substantial house to keep up, a self-employed husband working all hours, sixteen self-opinionated, hungry kids/adults to deal with, three sittings for all meals, laundry on an industrial scale, endless fights to referee, never a day off, never a holiday, rarely a gift or any show of love or appreciation. It conjures up in my mind a terrifying mixture of *Groundhog Day* and *One Flew Over the Cuckoo's Nest*. Only a saint could endure such a penance. It's no wonder that in later years, at the slightest sign of trouble, she took to putting her hands over her ears, lamenting, "My head's deeved!"

Even this gesture, only recently so frustrating to me, would have been welcome now, but the disturbing waxwork dummy before us lay motionless and silent. Mum was not in that room; she had moved on, hopefully finally released to a more tranquil, happier place. Whatever this was, laid out in her old room, had retained none of her aura – a fact not lost on her young namesake.

Whereas the scene had rendered Jacky and me rather awkward and Holly slightly shocked and bemused, the effect on our four-year-old Celia was remarkable. She took one look at the effigy and blurted out, "But that's not Granny – her hair's all wrong… and where are her glasses?"

With this, she proceeded to hunt out a comb and began to carefully 'fix' granny's hair. Her glasses were procured from a bedside drawer and delicately placed upon those fragile blue eyes, whose once sorrowful gaze haunts me to this day. All Mass Cards and letters of condolence were gathered up from the dressing table and rearranged about her person. A favourite scarf seemed to complete the picture to Celia's satisfaction.

"Now, that's much better. That's more like Granny," she announced, before spinning round and leaving her old friend to the Dickens characters who had just entered with their hammer and nails.

This would not be little Celia's last performance of the day. Later, when we all returned to the house after the service, burial and meal, she disappeared. Understandably distracted by ongoing events, her parents only gradually became aware of her absence. When a brief recce of the rooms and copious enquiries as to her whereabouts yielded nothing, we began to panic. Surely she wouldn't have ventured out into what was a cold, dark, wet, January night? But where, then, could she be? We eventually found her, hidden away in the eaves of Mum's modest abode. She had discovered a camouflaged pine trapdoor in the spare bedroom that led to a space only big enough for a couple of suitcases to be stored. This cramped space had just the right mix of privacy and intimacy that she'd been looking for, and taking all the religious ornaments and holy pictures she could lay her hands on, she set about building a shrine to her granny. Cushions and candles completed the heartfelt, highly evocative scene. Oblivious to all our increasingly desperate shouts and calls, she was totally lost in her own world, chatting ten to the dozen with her granny. We thanked our lucky stars that she hadn't burnt the house down and persuaded her to allow us to leave the trap door open so we could surreptitiously keep a watchful eye on proceedings. This is where she spent the rest of the day.

Witnessing a woman being carried to church for the last time, by her sons, is an undeniably moving sight. Actually, being one of those bearers plumbs the emotional depths of any semi-conscious individual. Having to watch as the person who gave you life is returned to the earth within sight of where her own life was gifted her; these are profound milestones on this perplexing path of life. Where losing one parent changes the dynamic, leaving you feeling somewhat at sea, losing both casts you adrift altogether; the rule book effectively gets torn up.

Leaving home at sixteen, I had cut the cord early on. But I had also made a very conscious decision to visit my parents as often as I could and include them in my life as much as I could. Consequently, their passing left me feeling that much more alone, the current in both directions that bit stronger on my voyage toward the precipice.

Numb, protocol helped us struggle through that dark day and we managed to get back to Utrecht the next day in time for the climax of our week-long residency. Peter Tra and all the people there could not have been nicer, and I thank them again for their gracious understanding.

I wonder how those two young lads are enjoying Canterbury.

'Betty and Brian'

2004 presented us with a happy coincidence. Our US tour dovetailed with Elvis' and so we hooked up and did some shows together. After a concert in the Library of Congress we headed for the final destination on our leg of the trip, Montgomery, Alabama. Not long into the flight we were told that we were being diverted to Birmingham, about ninety miles north, where ground transportation would be arranged. This was not music to our ears; we'd been on the road for a while at this point, our concert the next day was in the afternoon, and in addition to our instruments and luggage, Jacky and I had two young whippersnappers in tow (no, not Andrew and Ian... Holly and Celia). The thought of sitting around waiting for some boneshaker, then enduring the endless diversions to various drop-off points before getting dumped at Montgomery Central Bus Station, was just too depressing. The aircraft phone came equipped with an old-fashioned Yellow Pages and one glance at the Airport Taxi section drew me irresistibly to Betty's Taxi Service in Montgomery. Feeling bothered and with little or no confidence in my actions, I dialled the number. My call was answered in an instant by an angel whose soft, southern tones immediately calmed my frazzled nerves and soothed my jumbled mind.

"Now, you don't worry 'bout a thing, Mr Paul. Soon as you got yo' bags 'n all, you just make yo' way outside 'n Betty'll be awaitin'," she purred.

Betty assured me that she had room in her vehicle for all of us *and* our luggage and that, incredibly, there would be no extra charge; everything was included in the very reasonable price.

"How will I recognise you, Betty?" I asked.

"Aw, honey, you ain't gonna have no problem recognising Betty. Now, y'all have a safe flight 'n' I'll see you real soon."

My oh my, how right she was. We exited the terminal building into the usual, foul-smelling stampede of buses and taxis, and I did think for a moment, *how the heck are we going to find this woman in the middle of all this?*, when out of the corner of my eye I spotted an oasis of calm, a picture postcard that made me question if we hadn't been diverted to Havana by mistake. Perched on the trunk of the biggest, pinkest '50s Cadillac DeVille sedan I have ever seen was a movie star, not a taxi driver. Reclining there as naturally as if she were on a chaise longue and drawing gently on a Winston Extra Long, Betty was impossibly glamorous. From her ten-gallon hat to her figure-hugging, brown leather pants, neatly tucked into her calfskin Tecovas, she was the picture of elegance. Upon seeing us she jumped to attention, and in a flash had deposited all suitcases, pushchairs, instruments, the lot, into the cavernous trunk of this monstrous automobile. We equally seemed to make little impact on the vastness of its interior. Jacky, Ian and Andrew disappeared into the back, while I, Holly and Celia took our places on the magnificent, white-leather front bench-seat with Betty. Did I mention, this pin-up was nearly seventy years old! The girls were spellbound; they never took their eyes off her for a second, mesmerised by her hair, her makeup, her elongated, highly-decorated nails. By the time we dismounted this fairytale carriage, we and Betty were best friends, so much so that I decided to ask her what she had planned for the next day. She was so laidback that I don't think she ever thought that far in advance.

"Why, I aint doin' nuttin' special, honey," she said. "What's on yo' mind?"

"Well, I just wondered if you might be interested in picking us up, taking us to the venue and looking after Holly and Celia for a couple of hours while we do our concert?"

"Why sure, dahlin', that would be a pleasure," she replied.

And that's exactly what happened. Betty rolled up, deposited us at the Montgomery Museum of Fine Arts and continued on her way with our kids, still in their hypnotised state next to her, as natural and happy as if they'd known each other all their lives.

The Montgomery Chamber Music Society is an established and impressive set-up. Their concerts take place in a magnificent space within the Museum and the five hundred or so punters are treated to high tea after the show. I'm talking proper tea in teapots, with everything from cucumber sandwiches to Victoria sponges, all homemade and served on bone china. That's quite a feat, and the good people of that society who take the time to make something like that a success deserve our appreciation and encouragement. There was an awkward moment when Betty arrived back with our kids, a stark reminder of where we were in the world, when she found it impossible to enter that tea room – a place she was clearly not welcome – because of the colour of her skin. No amount of cajoling would change her mind and so we ended up having our tea outside with her.

Elvis' tour with the Imposters had originally given them a day to get from New Orleans up to Nashville, but they had been offered a last-minute opportunity in New York that meant that, with only a small detour, Elvis' tour bus could swing by Montgomery and whisk us lot on up to Tennessee on the day we finished off in Alabama. Now we had a couple of kids used to cruising around in a pink Cadillac, the expectation placed upon this bus was unfairly ambitious. On the way down to the lobby I was doing my best to rationalise their imaginings, trying to prepare them for a nice, upmarket coach. Their increasing excitement was matched by my increasing trepidation. I needn't have worried; good old Elvis did not disappoint. The thing that glided round the corner into view could never be described as an upmarket coach; this was a futuristic dreamliner in the shape of a silver bullet.

Climbing aboard, the interior kept up the comic book imagery. At the back was a round double bedroom complete with its own sound system, TV etc. Midway, there were some bunk beds and a bathroom, then further forward, a mini kitchen/dining area opened up into a sumptuous lounge with leather seating, an enormous surround-sound TV and an extensive DVD library. While we nonchalantly took our seats and tried to remain cool, Holly and Celia fully exercised their right to be blown away. Constant, needless trips to the bathroom were punctuated by snacks in the kitchen and snoozes on the bunks, *Finding Nemo* whilst reclining on the satin-covered double bed, *A Bug's Life,* intertwined on the leather sofa. The hours flew by. It was a fun experience for us adults too, by the way, had it not been for the relentless, incendiary signage all along that hellish highway – Jesus Saves, Repent Sinner, God Gave His Life – all of which left me incandescent and terrified; it was as if we'd taken a wrong turn up the Antrim coast. That one-off bus ride left its occupants with mixed emotions as we disembarked in Nashville, but at least we had the Grand Ole Opry to look forward to.

'Sterling Mossy'

After the critically acclaimed performances of Steve Nieve's opera *Welcome to the Voice*, we went into Air Studios in London and recorded it for Deutsche Grammophon with the final line-up of singers, which included Sting, Barbara Bonney, EC and Robert Wyatt. We got along famously with Robert, who, it turned out, was an old friend of Delfina's and used to be a regular at her legendary parties down in Wiltshire back in the '60s. We came close to doing a comeback concert with him (he hadn't performed in public for many years) at the Queen Elizabeth Hall some years later but sadly it wasn't to be in the end.

We did the opening concert of the Kenwood Open Air Summer Festival with Elvis. That was such a happy occasion, playing a neighbourhood concert right there where we would so often go for walks, *en famille*. We were blessed with a fine evening and the place was packed with chilled-out people doing the picnic thing. The acoustics were surprisingly good and, whilst I sympathise greatly with Roy Keane's assertion that, all too often, certain people place more importance on the food and drink instead of the spectacle they've come to witness, it was nevertheless heartwarming in this scenario to see everyone dancing around on the grass in between mouthfuls of lobster salad and swigs of champagne.

Oh, allow me to digress for a moment. The inspirational Roy Keane is the type of character I know well. I grew up with people like that – hell, he's the spit of one of my brothers, for goodness' sake. Though they are scary individuals, their uncompromising attitude often turns out to be infuriatingly true. Apropos of nothing, here's a wee yarn I absolutely love, which elucidates that most glorious characteristic of the Irish race, their wit. If nothing else, these people are seriously switched on in terms of the craic.

Roy's dad, back in Cork, had always carried the nickname 'Mossy' till his son signed that life-changing and undoubtedly lucrative contract with Man U. Suddenly, Roy would invariably have a little more than dirty underwear in his overnight bag on visits home. Before the ink had dried in Lancashire, Roy's dad's nickname had changed to 'Sterling'!

Sotheby's had got their hands on the original score of an arrangement of the Grosse Fuge for two pianos by Beethoven himself, and had organised a private concert in which we were to perform the piece in its original form, for string quartet. That's not a piece to mess with, and it was made all the more challenging in that confined space when we took to the stage and spied Martin Lovett, cellist of the Amadeus Quartet, seated on the front row. While the performance took years off our lives, the score went for a cool £1.1m.

From here we went to a series of concerts in Madrid. The intensity of rehearsals and concerts makes life in a group tremendously challenging; quartets operate on maximum stress. But often it's the other day-to-day stuff that can really test one's character – travelling, eating, socialising etc. We were queuing up to check into the hotel, and though the place was not all that busy, the procedure was taking forever because the lone receptionist insisted on doing that infuriating thing of answering the phone every time it rang. You're standing in front of her and she's busy taking bookings for next month or explaining to someone in Room 101 how to use the trouser press. At a certain point when this had become, frankly, farcical, Andrew quietly got out his phone and called the hotel.

"Hola, Hotel NH Calderon, buenos dias," she whined.

"Oh, hello madam. I wonder if you'd be so kind as to check me in, please?" said Andrew.

"I'm sorry, sir, but we can't check you in on the phone. I'm afraid you have to be here in person," she countered.

"Well, that's just fine and dandy, miss. You see, I'm actually standing right in front of you, but if it's ok with you, I'm going to stay on the phone until you've checked me and my colleagues into our rooms. Thank you."

It was a genius move that worked brilliantly.

Andrew's prank must have been infectious because later, at rehearsal, we were all in a funny mood. We've always been keen on presenting inventive encores and Andrew had tracked down the music for the Nokia phone ringtone, the 'Gran Vals' by Francisco Tarrega, thinking it could be fun in the right situation. We decided this was to be the night. Given the mood in the dressing room, the fun wasn't going to end there. The encore section would end with the Tarrega and, at the famous Nokia waltz bit, the stage manager would come on stage holding up my phone (a Nokia), announcing that I had a call. Embarrassed, we would stop playing, and I would take the call from the stage.

"Hola… Si, soy yo, Señor Cassidy… Una mesa por quatro?… Ah si, correcto, señor… la mesa es lista ahora… aha… y las cervezas también… d'accuerdo, senor. Muchísimas gracias. Hasta ahora!"

With this pretend conversation over and the hall in hysterics, we waved goodbye and left the stage for the real restaurant and the real beers. The scenario wasn't completely fictitious.

In January '06 we had undertaken a residency at the Sydney Festival that included solo dates, a concert with Elvis and a kids' show, featuring *Anna and the Moods*. Back home, we had found our dream narrator in the form of the multi-talented John Telfer. John lived in Bristol, had a BBC accent and played the vicar in *The Archers*, no less. We had known each other for quite some time when one day an innocuous conversation revealed a most surprising fact. We were quizzing him as to how he had got into the arts world. He explained without hesitation that it had all been as a result of one single teacher who had transformed not just his life, but the life of many youngsters at that school.

"How extraordinary," said Jacky. "How did he manage that?"

"Well, for example, he would play classical music over the tannoy system every day in assembly," said John.

"But that can only have been Mr Starling," piped up Jacky.

"Good heavens. How on earth do you know Mr Starling?" screeched an incredulous Mr Telfer.

"Because he was the head of our school," concluded an equally flabbergasted Jacky.

In that moment, John's origins moved several degrees north and with this collective realisation, our already-close relationship ramped up a gear.

Our Antipodean narrator was, shall we say, not the sort of character one would normally associate with the industrial north-east of England. This incarnation of Anna was a larger-than-life feast for the eyes, a wonderfully flamboyant TV personality who wafted into our lives in suburban Parramatta on a zephyr of perfume and powder. He really camped it up and insisted on having arguably the most opulent chaise longue I think I've ever seen, in cerise, purple and gold.

Holly and Celia had, as usual, joined us for this trip and were in the audience with some local friends of ours who also had a little girl about Celia's age. I thought it would be a laugh to organise a simple game during the show, in which I would ask a fairly obvious question about something that was going on on stage. Celia's mate, who had been tipped off, would raise her hand and I would choose her to give the correct answer. When it came to the crucial moment, however, the poor wee thing had fallen asleep and I was instead faced with my own little darling, jumping up and down, arms in the air, grinning from ear to ear. What could I do? I pointed to her, naturally, she gave me the right answer, amazingly, and then skipped to the side of the stage to pick up her very special prize – one of our CDs. As I handed it to her she gave me a huge hug and bellowed out in an unnaturally loud Hollywood-style voice, "Thanks daddy!"

Never work with children or animals, as they say.

Since our stint with Complicité we were thoroughly converted thespians, eager for the next opportunity to tread the boards. These positive vibes soon resulted in a call from a guy called Lou Stein asking if we would like to get involved in Brian Friel's recent play, *Performances*. Not only was Friel one of the great playwrights of the world, he was a Derryman, lived down the road from us and had even taught some of my brothers. The play is about the intense love affair between a seventy-year-old married man by the name of Leos Janacek and a thirty-something, married mother of two, Kamila Stosslova. It involves a string quartet, which is called upon to act as well as provide the music. That music is Janacek's 2nd Quartet 'Intimate Letters', so named because of the more than seven hundred passionate love letters the old man wrote to his muse over three years. Lou cajoled Henry Goodman into playing Janacek and Rosamund Pike into playing the young PHD student studying the late works of Mr Janacek, and in no time we were in rehearsals at the wonderfully characterful Wilton's Music Hall in London's East End, where we would do a two-week run.

Trying to act was hugely challenging and required tremendous concentration if we weren't to let the side down. It was thrilling, putting ourselves on the line like that, and we could not have had two more kind, patient, understanding experts to guide us along.

Brian turned up for the press night. The performance went swimmingly but afterwards, the reception was getting a bit intense with all the reporters getting sozzled and wanting to get chatting. Not long into the proceedings, Brian sidled over to me and whispered, "There's a pub outside the back entrance, on the left. That's where I'll be."

With that, he gently and expertly disappeared. I informed Jacky of the plan and we quickly followed the bard.

When we got there, he was suitably impressed with our *vitesse* and immediately offered to buy us a drink.

"Oh no, you don't," I insisted. "You're *our* guest here. It's such a pleasure to meet you, and your magnificent play is a joy to behold. I'm getting this round. What'll you have?"

"Aw, that's very kind of you. I loved what you all did with it. If you're absolutely sure?" said he.

"Absolutely," I confirmed.

Brian was an enchanting wee red-faced leprechaun of a man. Of late he walked with the aid of a stick as a result of a serious illness and by rights, shouldn't even have travelled over to London, and certainly shouldn't have been in the pub sucking fiercely on a huge cigar.

"Since you insist, mine's a triple vodka and tonic."

Well, it was my fault for insisting, and I only got what I deserved. You'd have thought I'd have learnt my lesson since this was the cripplingly expensive chosen tipple of both Eleanor Warren and Terry Weil as they held up the bar way back in the RNCM days.

* * *

Also in 2006, we performed all the Shostakovich in Bristol to celebrate the great man's centenary, and started a residency at a beautiful new hall in London, the Cadogan Hall. I say 'new', the building is a church dating from 1907 that fell into disrepair till it was bought by the Cadogan

Estate and turned into a concert hall, home to ourselves and the Royal Philharmonic Orchestra. You would be forgiven for thinking that a hall overlooking Sloane Square would be an instant hit, but it's never easy getting a new venue off the ground and to begin with, all comers struggled to get an audience there. Having said that, by the time we moved on, five years later, our regular public had grown fourfold.

The most noteworthy event in this period, as far as we were concerned, was the departure of our beloved Andrew. Andrew had been such a fantastic colleague and never once questioned the endless unpaid hours required to play in a quartet. But he was young and massively talented, so inevitably the sharks were out and about, making him offers no one could resist, until finally the pressure became too much. It is touching to know that dear old Hugh Maguire phoned Andrew and tried to persuade him not to make the same mistake he had made forty years earlier, leaving the Allegri Quartet for the London Symphony Orchestra, but Andrew was on his way by then and we had a huge void to fill.

In the eight years we had spent together, we had done so much: Shostakovich Cycles, Beethoven Cycles (including the Op.18 Project), all the Anne Sofie and Bjork stuff, countless EC concerts, The Education Project, Anna. We had made no fewer than twenty CDs, including all Tchaikovsky, Britten, Chapi, Remacha and Respighi. Mostly, though, we had had a wonderfully enriching time with never a sour word spoken, and Andrew left the Brodsky Quartet an infinitely better group than when he'd joined it.

'Daniel Goes to Hollywood'

All well and good, but for the second time in our careers, we found ourselves light in the violin department. The energy required at a time like this is colossal. You feel extremely vulnerable. Clearly, you do not have to love the other people in your group, but you do have to appreciate them, trust them, and spend an inordinate amount of time with them. Building a serious group is a massive commitment; it requires tremendous focus, which can often lead to a very insular existence. Hence, when someone decides to move on, it can be horribly unnerving. What's good enough for you is no longer good enough for them. All that energy you invested has come to nothing. Just the logistics of how to break the news, when to break the news so as to minimise the impact. Then compiling a list of potential replacements, contacting them, doing auditions. The endless rehearsals of music you could play in your sleep, and often did. Wasted conversations about repertoire, travel, dress. *I don't like flying, I don't like encores, I don't like standing up to play, I don't like Mozart; I like rehearsing in the morning, I like to have my own life outside of the group, I like having no input into the running of the group…*

I like, I don't like – just when you've got a way of working together sussed, the enforced change brings along another bellyload of compromise. It's monumentally tiring.

Given the ease with which we had found Andrew, we might have been forgiven for thinking that we could perform the same trick again. We were about to have that thought well and truly quashed.

Over the course of the next year or so, we would meet with sixteen violinists from all over the world and give concerts with seven of them. At one stage we had pretty much given up but decided to fulfil our commitments to the remaining few who were yet to audition. We agreed to draw a line in the sand on a particular Thursday afternoon. Whatever we had at that stage, that would be it, and we would either move forward with someone or throw in the towel.

As we finished our lunch together on that chosen day, there wasn't much repartee. Our spirits were rock-bottom and we didn't hold out much hope for what the afternoon might bring. Looking on the bright side, there was one exceptional candidate whom we loved working with, but there were some serious complications that might be unsurmountable in terms of her current employment and place of residence. It was at this quiet low point that our final violinist rang the doorbell and Daniel entered our lives.

It's fascinating how knowing if you can coexist with someone on a personal level can take quite some time, but in terms of playing, the answer to this question is clear within a few bars. By the time we were halfway down the first page of the Brahms A minor, we four knew that musically, we'd struck gold. After months of hell and uncertainty, we had a future again. We had potential, a persona we felt comfortable with. The life-force began to course through our collective veins, and boy, did we need it. Sussing each other out, finding a way of working, developing a profile, building a repertoire, the whole re-moulding process is gargantuan. Frustratingly, for every fiddle player who was dissatisfied with the financial rewards on offer, there was another who was shocked by how full-time the position would be. Apart from his exceptional playing, Daniel was also perfect in this respect; an experienced chamber musician, he was well used to the laughable spoils this life afforded one, but also loved to be busy. Considering our enormous repertoire, we needed someone with a voracious appetite for music and a fearless approach to performing.

It seemed like a good omen that our first concert together would be an all-Elgar affair amongst friends. It was 21st May 2007 at Champs Hill, with the very special and dear David and Mary Bowerman. The concert was a roaring success, which they still talk about to this day. Pride was restored within our ranks and we were off.

Very often, the ideas one has either take forever to get off the ground or don't happen at all. A good example of this was the plan we agreed on *Andrew's* first day with us, to do a homage to the Hollywood Quartet.

As it turned out, we did do this homage, but it took place ten years later in '08, with Daniel. The final draft ended up being a set of three concerts highlighting the Hollywood's diversity and brilliance, with particular reference to their recorded legacy. As the project gradually unfolded, I spoke to the Slatkin children – Leonard, the conductor, and Freddie, the cellist – their parents were Felix Slatkin (first violin) and Eleanor Aller, cellist of the renowned group. They were helpful and told me familiar sounding stories about growing up with string quartet parents, which I found fascinating.

One of our concerts would focus on the work the quartet did with the legendary Frank Sinatra, resulting in the 1956 record 'Close to You'. Frank and the quartet were close friends; indeed, Frank wouldn't record with the Hollywood orchestra if the quartet wasn't leading the sections. 'Close to You' was an unusual album in that it was a lengthy collection of ballads, one after the other, but it was close to Frank's heart and, though some of the tracks are forgettable, there are some – not least of all, the title track – that are about as heavenly as it gets. The orchestration is along the lines of Ravel's 'Introduction and Allegro' and the masterful arrangements by none other than the great Nelson Riddle. (I was lucky enough to have played on his last recording sessions in London back in the '80s.)

Incredibly, the Hollywood Quartet only visited the UK once in their illustrious career, playing at the Edinburgh and Dartington Festivals in 1957. I managed to track down the only surviving member of the group, the second violinist Paul Shure, who had recently retired and was living in Seattle. We had a couple of lovely phone calls together and towards the end of one of them, I thanked him for all the wonderful work he had done with the quartet, especially those timeless recordings that have enriched the lives of so many subsequent listeners. At this point he remained quiet, as though he was testing me. There was an awkward pause…

"I mean, the Schubert Quintet, 'Verklarte Nacht'."

Silence…

"Oh, and the Brahms A minor, not to mention Prokofiev No.2 and Turina," I offered.

More silence…

Finally he piped up, "So, you didn't like the Beethoven then?!"

On the one hand it was comical, but on the other, horribly real. This encapsulated the relentlessly thankless existence of a performing musician. Always unsure, unsatisfied, looking over one's shoulder. Only ever as good as the last few notes you play, and even those are a matter of opinion. This is where people involved in sport are fortunate. Of course, luck can often play a part, but in the end, those with the most points win and that's that. In the brutal world of the arts, some failed practitioner decides if you shall win or not. What a ludicrous state of affairs – a world that surely thrives on innovation, imagination and brilliance is presided over by 'experts' with little or none of these attributes.

Taking my seat in the Barbican for a rare performance of Golijov's extraordinary St Mark Passion, I overheard a pair of well-known critics, seated uncomfortably nearby, greeting each other with the following:

"Hi. How are you?"

"Well, I was fine up until now. Don't know how I'm going to get through the next three hours."

"Oh, I know. I've decided, when it gets to the bit that goes – 'I wanna be in America', I'm outta here."

This overheard banter took place *before* the concert had begun, by the way. I found it doubly hurtful because Osvaldo Golijov is not only a truly remarkable composer but a good friend. His groundbreaking Clarinet Quintet 'The Dreams and Prayers of Isaac the Blind', the intoxicating song cycle 'Ayre' – which we played many times with Dawn Upshaw and the gang – and his touching quartet 'Tenebrae' are just three examples of his invention and brilliance, and yet here were these losers sharpening their pencils in anticipation of a kill.

The ensuing performance of his Passion was one of the most exciting musical experiences of my life, and a packed Barbican – as it had been for the whole Golijov Weekend – rose involuntarily to its feet, giving an ovation the likes of which I have not witnessed before or since. Our two friends missed all this, of course; they'd already long gone. Such an unbridled show of emotion would only have angered them all the more anyway, a sure sign that all could not be right if people were responding in such an uncouth manner. This musical highlight was ferociously panned and I have not been aware of Osvaldo or his music enriching the lives of Londoners since – outside of *our* concert programmes, that is.

Back to the Hollywood Quartet. In the end we devised a set of three programmes. The first two were easy and basically chose themselves, though we made sure to include a Beethoven! The crucial third programme, however, was infinitely more testing and caused some considerable angst. We thought of simply recreating the 'Close to You' record, but sourcing the arrangements and getting all the extra players would become prohibitively expensive. Furthermore, though the repertoire works fine as a recording, it wouldn't make for a thrilling concert. Instead, we carefully chose repertoire that reflected the work of the Hollywood Quartet and that of ourselves in the same area. All this background work is fine and dandy, but it does somewhat presuppose that you have a vocalist who is naturally diverse and can carry the burden of a homage to Sinatra. We went up and down and over and out. This singer, that singer – pop, jazz, classical, male, female, maybe one of each? – till one day, the perfect person surfaced.

Sir Willard White is a rare commodity. A supremely gifted and versatile artist with tremendous communication skills, he only has to walk on to a stage to command the attention of an audience. His speaking voice has the power to melt the coldest of hearts, and when he sings... well, that is a privilege to behold. When Willard agreed to join us for our homage we were blessed, and the whole vision came sharply into focus. We discussed at length the structure of the programme and the precise nature of the repertoire therein. We instantly had a 'special relationship' and I guess, for the most part, the programme reflected that, inasmuch as there was a very definite UK/US thing going on. We juxtaposed Britten and Copland, us playing 'Hoedown' and the 'Poeme', Willard joining us for some of their magical folk songs. Even Barber's glorious 'Dover Beach' had an obvious English slant with Matthew Arnold's haunting text. It would have been rude – nay, unforgivable – not to include Gershwin, but we also peppered this already tantalising feast with the likes of Schubert, Massenet and, not forgetting the purpose of the whole thing, 'Close to You' and a selection of other Sinatra classics.

Working with vocalists is always an education and a revelation. These are people who are trained to communicate the meaning of a piece of music to their public; they sing. Singing is what we're all trying to do, surely – sing through our chosen instrument. Granted, the technical demands can often make one lose one's way, but it is not enough to just play the notes reasonably well in vaguely the right order. We are interpreters of great theatrical masterpieces. We have to look way beyond the notes, find the characters, the dialogues, inhabit those characters and deliver those lines, those thoughts, those emotions. Yes, they have a storyline in front of them that gives them a head start, but singers are consequently way ahead of most instrumentalists and we need to get up to speed.

'In Memoriam Isidora'

Of all the clarinettists we've played with over the years, Joan Enric Lluna is one with whom we've enjoyed a more in-depth relationship. Together we have commissioned many pieces, two of which I should like to touch upon now.

'In Memoriam' by Paul Barker is an extraordinary work. Carrying the subtitle 'for those who fall in times of war', it was dedicated to the Sarajevo String Quartet, two of whom lost their lives in that bloody conflict. This exemplary group performed 206 concerts in the city during the siege. Exhibiting bravery and resilience in equal measure, they continued to play for fellow citizens through the tragedy of losing one member after the other.

Never have I known a piece illicit such emotion from an audience every time. It's a standard four-movement structure but, in line with Paul's conviction that 'music and theatre are inseparable', it is staged and played from memory. The staging, conceptualised by our dear friend – the irrepressible, irresistible and irreplaceable playwright and altogether adorable man, Stephen Clark (1961–2016) – is simple but effective. Two specially commissioned tapestries act as a backdrop, a solitary chair occupies centre-stage. Four music stands are used as props (for example, in the harrowing second movement entitled 'Soliloquy; Song of the Anchorite', where we enclose Joan with the stands, recalling the blood-curdling medieval practice of nuns from a particular Holy Order choosing to be walled in to a tiny cell, usually in their local church, which they then never leave).

The third movement is a Chorale that fuses the image of a vast cathedral-like space with the human body on a cross, leaving the outer movements, which tell the tragic story of the four musicians from Sarajevo.

We performed this piece all over the world and had many wonderful experiences with it, including an appearance at the Galway Festival, which was remarkable in two ways. The concert took place in the cathedral and in between the rehearsal and concert, someone came along and stole the huge backdrops... yes, in the cathedral... yes, in God-fearing Galway City. This heathen act left us not only having to cobble together a makeshift replacement in the short time left to us, but also having to re-commission two new tapestries at great expense. Then, in the concert itself, an inordinate amount of extremely impressive moths appeared out of thin air and danced around the lights, some choosing to sacrifice themselves to the irresistible flame. These dramatic masochistic acts were a bit more along the lines of what we were expecting from the good folk of Eire's west coast, and certainly added a heightened sense of reality to our proceedings on stage.

The other Brodsky/Lluna commission I wanted to mention is by the Serbian composer Isidora Zebeljan. It's always a joy and an inspiration to meet a formidable musician on your travels and Isidora is certainly that. When we arrived in Belgrade for the premiere of her compact, one-movement work 'Song of the Traveller in the Night', we were still struggling to understand the piece fully. In the rehearsal we were getting bogged down in the rhythmic complexities of the music, which were holding us back from giving a fully committed performance. Immediately seeing the problem, Isidora jumped up, went to the piano and played, from memory, the whole of this massively complicated fifteen-minute quintet faultlessly – dancing and singing as she played. It was a thrilling experience that totally brought the work to life and embodied everything I've always thought and tried to impart about music; that ultimately, it is song and dance. That piece has never posed us any problems since. The clue is in the verb; we don't work or grind music, we play it.

On that note, this unique human provided us with another unforgettable musical experience. After a concert of her music in Valencia, she inspired not only us, the performers, but the entire audience to arise and dance around the auditorium together – the assembled mass laughing, singing and dancing to 'modern music'. We have gone on to commission Isidora many times and have made a CD of her inspirational music.

Macao is a mind-bending place that has to be seen to be believed. Nestled off the coast of Hong Kong, it's like a Vegas of the East. One of the most densely populated and wealthiest places on Earth, it presents the eye with a dizzying plethora of scenes and styles. From your Venetian Palace of a hotel, you can look out of one window and be treated to a glittering high-rise skyline to rival Manhattan, whilst a cursory glance out the other window will make you think you are in Disneyland, as the seafront offers up fastidious copies of Ancient Greece next to Ancient Rome, alongside Ancient Egypt.

As if the place wasn't surreal enough already, the gambling gods arranged for us to arrive on the day the Olympic Flame was to pass through town on its journey from Athens to Beijing. Understandably, there was widespread chaos and it was almost impossible to focus on one's usual preparations for the concert when all our minds were elsewhere. Sure enough, halfway through our rehearsal, a friendly stage manager came running on stage, gesticulating madly, and we were escorted to a perfect vantage point above the road just a minute before the iconic flame passed not twenty feet beneath us. One couldn't help feeling that, like the Parthenon across the way, this wasn't the real thing at all but something Macao felt like organising that day, just because it could.

The day then settled into a more recognisable event with people quickly getting back into their routines. The next morning, as we arrived at the port for the shuttle back to Hong Kong, I was stopped in my tracks by an innocuous little sign that read, 'Petrus/Chateau d'Yquem/Rothschild for sale'. I decided this must be referring to something like that bath foam you get in champagne bottles; washing-up liquid in a pretend d'Yquem bottle, perhaps. Curiosity got the better of me, however, and I ventured into this tiny clinker-built cabin only to find row upon row of the most extraordinary vintage wines, interspersed with top quality Cuban cigars, all lined up and exposed to the ninety-degree heat and 100% humidity. These goods were not being offered at knockdown prices, let me tell you; a couple of thousand dollars wouldn't get you very far in that stifling hut. Any all-night reveller whose luck had been in the night before on the blackjack table was certainly playing Russian roulette with this lot. Your '69 Petrus might come in handy with your cod 'n' chips of a Friday night.

'Irina'

One of the mountains Daniel had to climb in double quick time was the Shostakovich Cycle. This magnificent musical journey had for many years now been a constant in our diaries, but for a newcomer, especially given that we were about to perform the cycle over a weekend, this was no mean feat. Within a year of Daniel joining us, we had performed them no fewer than three times, in Glasgow, Boda and Bologna. In Glasgow, we had played them in the stupendous City Halls, surely one of the great venues in the UK, if not the world. This heralded our arrival at the then-Royal Scottish Academy of Music and Drama, where we had started a residency that continues to this day.

The Norwegian outing was as part of the Boda Festival, the five concerts taking place in five different churches on five isolated spits of Arctic land. We arrived the night before the first concert and were invited to dinner by the festival director at his home overlooking the sea. Morten was such a generous soul and we immediately felt among friends neath that captivating, milky night sun. At one point he asked us how we were getting from concert to concert over the weekend. When we explained that, as far as we were aware, we were jumping on a small bus that would ferry us from one venue to another, he exclaimed, "Oh no, this is crazy. That will take forever. You would have to go all the way back to the mainland, round the fjord and out the next peninsula. No, no. You must come with me, on my boat."

This was a life-saving gesture. Doing a Shostakovich Cycle in such a short space of time is emotionally and physically exhausting, and those two-hour bus journeys between concerts would probably have done us in. This way, we would finish one concert, put all our stuff on the bus and tootle down to the jetty, where Morten and his craft would be waiting. Half an hour and a relaxing cruise later, we would arrive at the next idyllic venue ready to do battle. It made an already memorable experience all the more unforgettable.

As usual, we had Holly and Celia with us on our Arctic sojourn, and so we decided to stay on an extra day to do something special with them. Morten heard about this and during the 'end-of-cycle' party, came up to me and said, "Ok, Paul, I have everything organised for tomorrow. My driver will pick you up at the hotel at 11am."

It was a Miyake moment and we accepted his offer, whatever it was, without hesitation.

True to his word, the driver arrived bang on time, ferried us to our now-familiar yacht and we set sail westward. Our first stop was a place called Bird Island. As we pulled into the most romantic, deserted pier imaginable, Morten said, "Right, you lot – walk down this path about half a mile to the beach. Walk along the beach to the right, all the way to the end, where you can sit in wonder for a while. Then make your way back through the little village and you'll arrive via this other path here in time for lunch."

There wasn't another being on that island and for the next couple of hours we found ourselves transported, suspended in a heavenly time warp. One's sense of gravity disappeared and we simply floated about the place as if in a dream. An immaculate grassy path beckoned us through a meadow of awe-inspiring fauna to the perfect crescent beach, a carefully constructed mixture of boulders and sand languishing at the foot of sea cliffs, just imposing enough to add a sense of drama to the scene without overpowering it. The village was an adorable collection of higgledy-piggledy Wonderland houses, placed on a softly undulating, grassy knoll by some carefree Alice character. The only hint of reality in this mirage was the very real chains with which these abodes were tied to the earth, a whispered reminder that this Elysium might not always enjoy calm, sunny days like this one.

The sight of Morten in the distance, a solitary figure putting the finishing touches to our lunch, brought Mummy and Daddy to tears. Who was this warm heart who had so openly taken us under his wing and shown us such kindness? For what it's worth, Morten was a hugely successful businessman who owned half the town, but you would never have known it. The root of all evil had not poisoned this creature.

After a lunch of fishcakes and salad, washed down with an intoxicating glass of Margaux, we set sail from this haven and headed for Svartisen. The feeling of being at one with nature is salutary and one that we should all experience at least once in our lives. Being on an isolated Icelandic beach or by a remote, raging river in the Kola Peninsula can be at once intimidating and intoxicating. (You don't have to go so far afield, obviously; one can achieve this buzz in Donegal or Yorkshire, though for maximum effect, it does require minimal human content.) Turning off the engine in the face of that almighty glacier and hearing it creak and groan like some gigantic beast frozen in time was both thrilling and terrifying. The towering cliffs and the unwanted knowledge of the depth of that black water beneath didn't do much to placate things. The saving grace was the multitude of wildlife filling one's senses – seals bobbing around fascinated by these weird humans in their midst, Atlantic Salmon leaping into the air, bubbling with excitement at being nearly home, gannets dive-bombing unsuspecting sandeels, whales kicking back and letting off steam. It was a humbling place to be.

Before leaving Boda, Morten gave us a wonderfully atmospheric, framed photo of the Northern Lights, taken from his balcony where we had dined together just a week before. We haven't been back to Boda and have not seen Morten again, but if by any chance you're reading this, Morten – I cannot thank you enough for all those special memories.

Next up was Bologna. The red city of Northern Italy has been a regular and much-loved destination of the Brodsky Quartet over the last forty years, almost becoming our home back in the '80s, when we were in serious negotiations to move residencies from the second oldest university in England to the second oldest university in the world. This move didn't work out in the end, but Musica Insieme, the intrepid local music society under the expert guidance of our dear friends Alessandra, Bruno and Fulvia, took us under their wing and invited us on countless occasions to that glorious town with its magnificent porticoes, churches and market; not forgetting Cesari's, where a simple bowl of Tagliatelle al Truffo and a glass of Sangiovese brings any concert day to a perfect close.

Of all the happy days we spent there, one stands out as being particularly momentous. We were doing the complete Shostakovich, not over a weekend but over the whole 2009 season, and true to form, Bruno and his team had come up with the inspired idea of inviting strategic people to give talks in the intervals of the concerts. The Italian ambassador to Russia at the time of Shostakovich's death came; Italy's leading expert on Russian music put in an appearance; but by far the most remarkable presence was that of Irina, Shostakovich's widow. Still very much alive and well and looking radiant, she travelled all the way from Moscow for the third concert of the series. Whilst all five programmes are enthralling in their own right, that third one carried an added poignancy because it consisted of No.7, written in memory of his first wife, No.8, his very own epitaph, and No.9, dedicated to Irina herself. It was almost unbearably emotional playing these three works with this woman sitting right there in the front row.

It was also pretty amazing to find oneself sitting next to her at dinner later. We spoke mostly in French, her English not being good and my Russian non-existent, which was fine up to a point, but there came a moment when I suddenly thought to myself, *Hang on, here I am sitting next to the woman who shared her life with one of my idols, a man whose music we have been studying and playing and recording and bringing to the world for forty years. I may never meet her again.*

Throwing caution to the wind and ignoring any perceived etiquette, I enlisted the help of her translator, turned to her and said, "Irina, I'm so sorry. I realise you must be sick and tired of strangers asking you random questions about your dearly departed husband, but under the circumstances, would you mind terribly if I asked you just one thing about him?"

"No, of course I don't mind at all. What is it you want to know?" she replied.

"Well, I want to know what 'ba-ba-ba' means. What was the significance of this rhythm, which seemed to plague his thoughts?" I asked.

Judging by the surprised look on her face, I think she must have been expecting me to ask if Dmitri really was a football fanatic, or if he really could play just about any piece of music on the piano at the drop of a hat, from the 'St Matthew Passion' to the 'Rite of Spring'.

She took a moment to compose herself, then, looking me straight in the eye, spat out the words, "Ni-cog-da…"

I looked round open-mouthed at her interpreter.

"Never again," she translated.

"Oh my," I muttered, "that's amazing!"

"Bo-gee-moi…" came the next offering.

"Almighty God," said the interpreter.

My mind was reeling. *I have to remember all this.* It was like stumbling upon the Holy Grail.

"And one mustn't forget, 'ba-ba-ba---baaa'," she added, with fiery eyes.

Beethoven, of course.

"So, are you implying that it's not the gunfire, the bombs dropping, the knock on the door in the middle of the night?" I asked rather pathetically.

"It's all these things, Paul," she said. "We all had our bags packed. We were all terrified of the late night 'rat-tat-tat'. We all lived through the horrors of war."

She paused for a moment and then put her hand on my shoulder and whispered, "It's just too personal."

With that remark, we let it drop. She could not have answered my question more eloquently or informatively. I often think to myself, *Imagine if she had said, 'Aw that, yeah, that's the old knock on the door, mate, didn't you know?' Or 'It refers to 'mecinta', of course, his nickname as a boy.'*

Instead, she infused that already potent rhythm with infinitely more purport, without in any way explaining it away. I remain forever in her debt.

In addition to the vast number of repertoire pieces Daniel had to get to know, he, like us, loved to explore and collaborate musically. Luckily, we certainly hadn't slowed down in that area. Aside from our, shall we say, predictable classical friends, we were regularly getting up close and personal with all manner of unmentionables, the sort of distasteful pairings not seen since Bartok worked with Goodman or Menuhin with Grappelli.

Our ongoing work with the Malian composer and kora virtuoso, Tunde Jegede, reached a formidable climax with a huge, outdoor, televised concert in Paris, in which we and the likes of Toumani Diabate and Kasse Mady performed Tunde's epic, 'Fleuve Niger'.

We continued our explorations with the Argentinian singer and baroque flautist Diana Baroni, commissioning a flute quintet from the great Gerardo Gandini, king of Argentinian music and colleague of Piazzolla.

On that note, we toured with a bit of a phenomenon, the charismatic bandoneon player Ryota Kumatsu, who writes beautiful tangos and, as we found out, is like a pop star in his native Japan.

Happily, Elvis remained a fixture in our lives and in '09 we did some UK dates together. The tour was what you might term 'a game of two halves' inasmuch as it was a bit dodgy to begin with, but glorious at the end. I hasten to add that this is a purely personal reflection of events and not a comment on the performance side of things.

Our opening gig at the illustrious Basingstoke Anvil nearly ended in disaster when, miraculously, Elvis moved briefly from his central position to do our Supremes moment with myself and Ian just as one of the enormous stage lights exploded and crashed to the ground, right where he'd been standing. The next night in Glasgow, a paralytic Gorbal had to be physically restrained and removed because he hadn't clocked from the crystal-clear poster that EC was appearing with the Brodsky Quartet and not the Imposters.

By the time we finished the trip, at The Barbican in London, things had calmed down a bit. It happened to be our Holly's birthday and – as she was soon to be performing an arrangement of 'She' I'd made for flute quintet at her cousin Laura's upcoming wedding in Ireland – I persuaded Daniel and Ian to arrive ten minutes early to do a quick run-through with her during the soundcheck that afternoon. We were just getting to the second verse when one of the stalls doors swung open and in walked the man responsible for making this classic the most popular wedding song in the world today. With customary good nature and panache, Elvis burst into song and in no time, our wee Holly was dueting on the Barbican stage, in a rendition of 'She' with Elvis Costello. It was a thrilling moment, a bit like putting two past Bayern in injury time at the Nou Camp.

Did you know that Shostakovich was crazy about football and an avid Zenit Leningrad fan? He was actually a fully qualified referee and even wrote a ballet based on the game entitled 'The Golden Age'. I only mention this exhilarating fact because I want to share with you a cracking story the composer Gerard McBurney told me. Back in the '90s, news got out that a personal diary belonging to Shostakovich had been unearthed. As you might imagine, this caused great excitement, particularly among musicologists like himself. Upon hearing that this precious document had fallen into the hands of an old friend of his in Moscow, Gerard could contain himself no longer and made a call.

"I suspect you're phoning about the diary?" asked Sergei, knowing full well that this was not a casual call.

"Well, I can hardly pretend otherwise, Sergei, now, can I? So it's true, it exists…you've seen it?" enquired Gerard.

"Oh yes, it's true alright. Not only that, I've actually got it right here. Would you like me to read you an excerpt?" offered Sergei.

"Gosh, that would be so great. I mean, I don't want to put you out or anything but…"

"Hang on a minute," said Sergei as he leafed through the artefact for an appropriate example. "Ok, here's a typical entry."

Clutching pen and paper, Gerard was literally shaking with anticipation.

"It dates from 1974 and says, 'The power and pin-point accuracy of the left-footed, 60-yard, cross-field pass from Zinchenko in the 64th minute reminded me of Rivelino in the 1970 world cup. And that is high praise indeed.'"

Silence from Gerard.

"Shall I go on, Gerard? There's more, much more. I can give you all the results from any season with precise details of who scored, how Zenit's warm-up routine differs from that of Spartak, and…"

"No, no, no, Sergei. Thank you very much but I think I've heard enough," muttered a disconsolate Mr McBurney.

Returning momentarily to those extraordinary moments in Barcelona, when the entire Munich team were already tingling with the fever of success – when the engraver was busy perfecting the 'y' in Bayern and we sent in the SAS, George Best was not alone in hitting the bar and I fully admit I had lost interest, thoroughly depressed by the inevitability of it all. Only the United team remained in the moment. They were not writing the next day's headlines. This is an enormously important lesson for all us performers. As you're coming down the home straight, just as you're thinking to yourself, *My word, we were good tonight*, that's when you need to redouble your efforts; that's where disaster lurks and where all your hard work falls apart. Sheringham and Solskjaer, both seasoned pros, remained calm and focused, and those few moments of clarity rewrote the history books. Never take your eye off the ball. Play to the whistle; it's not over till the fat lady sings.

'Non rispetti'

Concert-giving is an occupation fraught with danger. It's not so much that you're endangering yourself physically, unless you happen to be playing in Basingstoke, of course; it's the amount of other things that can go wrong: flights missed, suitcases lost, bad hotels where the rooms aren't ready or are so noisy that you can't rest, insufficient lighting, air conditioners, programmes different to what you were expecting, strings snapping, inadequate backstage areas, temperamental instruments, broken instruments... the list goes on. In the fine tradition of the London bus, things can trundle along for ages without a hitch and then suddenly, you get a wave of irritations. It's at times such as these that you need experience and a cool head.

We were playing at the Teatro Massimo in Palermo. On hearing that Daniel's flight was severely delayed, we three decided to go to the venue anyway to make sure everything was ready to go when the time came. Eventually Daniel arrived, just in time to do a quick soundcheck before the audience were let in and we returned to the backstage area to get changed. We were somewhat perplexed when the stage manager gave us a fifteen-minute call at 7pm; it stated quite clearly on our itinerary '7.30pm concert'. Indeed, we reckoned we had misunderstood him and continued our preparations accordingly. In the event, none of this would have mattered. It was when we heard Ian repeatedly playing the opening bars of Beethoven's Op.95 Quartet that our problems really began in earnest. We let it go for a while before deciding to double-check.

"It is Op.135 tonight, isn't it?" Daniel directed the question at me.

"Yep. 135," I replied, with half an eye on Mr Belton.

The instant look of horror on his face told us all we needed to know. Daniel comes into his own in this kind of situation. With consummate calmness and lucidity he tracked down the sheet music we needed. But these impressive old theatres that you find dotted all over this part of the world are often cavernous and dilapidated; finding the music was one thing, but how were we going to get it printed in the next few minutes? Our friendly backstage man was invaluable. He whisked Daniel off to some faraway office, where Daniel somehow managed to coerce the dinosaur of a printer to speak to his ultra-modern mobile device. Upon their return, we all set about making the sheets into a little book from which Ian could work. Still convinced it was a 7.30pm start, we were fairly cool at this juncture, but the promoter, who had put in an appearance, was becoming extremely agitated. Not only that, we were becoming aware of some disgruntled noises coming from the auditorium.

"I really must ask you to make your way to the stage now, please. You're very late," he demanded.

"But it's only just gone 7.30pm," we rallied.

"Yes, but the concert was meant to start at 7.15pm. We've been trying to tell you that," said the increasingly fractious promoter.

"Oh my goodness. We are terribly sorry for the misunderstanding," we said, making our way side-stage, where the rumpus had now grown into a noisy demonstration of disquiet, accompanied by a slow handclap. We nervously took to the stage, Ian clutching his freshly printed Beethoven scroll, and faced the mob. Twelve hundred people hissing and jeering can be quite intimidating, let me tell you, and as we took our places, one gentleman on the front row remained standing, shouting, "*Non rispetti il tuo pubblico. Non rispetti il tuo pubblico!*"

We waited patiently for the din to die down and tentatively made a start. We didn't even have a raucous opener to hide behind yet somehow, with just Webern's 'Langsamer Satz' as ammunition, we managed to get them on our side. Later in the concert we explained our apparent rudeness and the evening ended happily for all concerned. These days, any time we have a Beethoven on the programme, one of us will always give a lighthearted rendition of that opening flourish to Op.95.

Over the years we've played in some odd places. From caves in Madeira, to purpose-built stages at the top of a ski slope in Vermont; a natural amphitheatre on an island in Norway with the ocean between us and the audience, who all arrived by boat, to a midnight concert on the 9th green of a golf course in Majorca. Equally, we have been fortunate enough to take to the stages of some of the world's most celebrated halls. From the Concertgebouw to Las Bellas Artes, the Palau de la Musica to the Sydney Opera House. All are memorable in their own way, whether it be the squashed mosquitoes of Majorca, which still decorate my copy of Pawel Szymanski's magnificent 'Five Pieces', or the persistent breeze due to the vastness of the Sydney Opera House stage, which causes havoc with your pages.

Inevitably, if you live much of your life travelling, you somehow invite coincidence. Like the morning we arrived in Sydney from London for example. We were in town for a few concerts in the festival and staying in an apartment with the kids. We'd just got off that long flight and were starving but couldn't face shopping for food yet. Spotting a breakfast place across the street, we left our luggage unpacked and made a beeline for that lifesaving café. Even in my laggy state, I could hardly help noticing that our waitress had a familiar accent.

"What part are you from, then?" I asked her, making sure she'd put in our order first.

"Oh, I'm from Ireland," she said.

"Naw, I know that. I mean, where exactly are you from?"

"Donegal."

"I know that too," said I, egging her on and annoying my girls no end. "But where in Donegal?"

"It's just a wee tiny town. You'll never know it," she said. Funny how people get embarrassed about saying the name of a place they're sure the other person won't even know.

"Try me," I chanced, as my final gambit.

"Carndonagh," she muttered.

"Carn!" we four choroused.

This was a place we knew extremely well. We had been grappling with the problem of finding a babysitter for this trip without much luck. Here was the answer to our prayers. This young lady, who was doing some work experience on the other side of the world, grew up next door to my sister and went to school with my nieces and nephews. A delightful trooper, she ended up looking after Holly and Celia for much of the next week.

Recently we brought all the Shostakovich Quartets to Perth WA, the first time the cycle had been played there. I'm proud to say that this is something we've done on many occasions, and continue to do – introduce this extraordinary music to new audiences across the world. After the final concert, the festival director and stalwart supporter of the quartet, Yarmila Alfonzetti, came to the dressing room excitedly reporting that the Russian Theatre Company, who were there to do a play about Shostakovich, had arrived in town and insisted on coming straight from the airport in order not to miss us. They were outside, waiting to say hello. A more cynical person would suggest that it was as a result of their long journey that these grown men and women were so overcome with emotion; that same person might quip that it was the lack of a common language that rendered the ensuing embraces overly long and silent. I prefer to put it down to the power of music and, in particular, live music. (Someone said to me the other day after a concert, "There were times when you all just disappeared and all that was left was the music." There is no greater compliment.)

These beautiful Russians were not homesick – they'd only just left Moscow earlier that day – nor were they lost for words. Art knows no boundaries and Shostakovich's music can speak to us all equally powerfully. They were overwhelmed by what they'd just heard. With the aid of a celebratory drink, tears turned to laughter and tongues began to loosen. When the theatre director learned that we knew Irina Shostakovich, he spontaneously phoned her. The incongruity of it all. There we were, having just completed a series of all the Shostakovich Quartets, sipping margaritas in the heat of a sub-tropical night, surrounded by giant palms and dripping bougainvilleas, chatting to Mrs Shostakovich, who was taking tea in her apartment in a freezing, snow-covered Moscow.

Sadly, we never got to see the play; by then we were in Albany, the oldest colonial settlement in WA. Once a famous whaling station, it now makes more money from whale *watching* than it ever did from slaughtering them – there's a lesson to be learnt there. On arrival, our host kindly took us to see West Cape Howe, the southernmost tip of WA, before dropping us at our hotel. I only mention this because not forty-eight hours later, we would be standing on Cape Byron, the easternmost point of the continent.

As a performer, you learn to block out the audience to a certain extent. Years of walking on and seeing some critic or string player gawking back at you, thereby ruining your evening, means it's safer not to look. Rather see those gathered as a friendly mass of people who have bothered to leave home and paid to come and listen to you. Usually this trick is easy to pull off – unless, as happened in Albany that evening, you're faced with something out of the ordinary. As we took to the stage to perform our 'Rhythm and Texture' programme, one could hardly help but notice a long line of fairies just a couple of rows back, all sitting to attention and eagerly awaiting our first notes. It's true that that programme has some magical music in it but we hadn't even started to play, and yet appeared to have conjured up a mirage of pink and white fluffiness. None of the other members of the public seemed in the slightest bit perturbed by their presence, and certainly these creatures could not have been better behaved, exhibiting impeccable concert etiquette throughout the show. As the concert went on, this vision of candyfloss began to blur and melt into the background till, by the time we threw off the final flourish of Ravel's masterpiece, we had forgotten about them altogether. It was then, however, that they started to materialise again in a hurry. As one they got to their feet and began stamping and whistling, clapping madly and hollering, "*Bravi, bravi*. More, more, we want more!"

Never ones to shirk our responsibilities in this respect, we duly obliged and played an extended encore set till I reckon even our make-believe friends were satisfied. Afterwards, the dressing room banter held hilarity and intrigue in equal measure and it wasn't until we vacated the hall that the mystery finally unfolded. As we came out of the artists' entrance there they all were, in their tutus, dripping with face-paint and glittery fairy-dust, fired up to high doh, waving their wands and jumping up and down shouting.

"OMG, you guys were amazing. Can we have your autographs, please?"

"It was better than I could have imagined."

"Jacky, you're so beautiful."

"I've got all your CDs."

"Could you please sign my shoulder?"

"Oh, mine too!"

This was a popular request, and pretty soon we were autographing not just programmes and CDs but increasingly personal body parts.

"Ok, you lot. Is this some kinda dare or what? What exactly is going on here?" we asked.

"Oh no, it's not a dare," answered the girl with the most flamboyant attire, the one with the balloons and the tiara and the beer cans tied to her silver stilettos. "I'm getting married tomorrow and this is my hen night."

"Hang on a minute. This is your hen night, and you chose to come to a string quartet concert?" we enquired incredulously.

"Well, not just any old quartet concert. We've been wanting to hear the Brodsky Quartet for years and when we saw that you were coming to town and playing on this night, there was no decision to be made. This was meant to be. This was my hen night treat."

I'm sure you'll agree, things don't get much better than that. Those girls were inspirational, and to them I'd like to say, I hope the rest of the night went well, that married life is bliss, and that you haven't washed off those signatures.

* * *

Not the greatest instrument in the world, I persevered with the 'Britten Viola' for so long because of its wonderfully romantic history and because of the manner in which I came to have it in the first place. Now, however, a viola came my way that had the potential to be something so much better than Ben's that it would have been foolhardy to ignore it. The instrument needed radical and extensive work to get it to a usable state, for which I enlisted the help of the brilliant Iris Carr, the woman who looks after Charles Beare's private collection. I contacted the Britten Trust to inform them that I wanted to return Ben's viola and, amazingly, they said that they were about to contact me to ask if they could borrow it for a few months because there was to be a big Britten Exhibition in the Red House Studio and they wanted the viola to be the centrepiece. They also asked me if I would record Britten's 'Elegy' for solo viola to be used in the pre-recorded soundtrack to accompany the exhibition. It just so happened that Iris lived in Wickham Market, a stone's throw from Aldeburgh, so I could kill two birds with one stone. Hence, horribly early one morning, I took that familiar route north-east on the A12 to the Red House for what was to be an emotional ceremony. Firstly, I had to record the 'Elegy' in one take into an ancient handheld Walkman of some description, at 9am, having had no chance to warm up. About halfway through that ordeal, I began to realise why Ben had cleverly ditched the piece that he had tellingly referred to as 'a nasty little work for viola'.

This done, I had my photo taken at the piano where Britten and Shostakovich had famously sparred, me cradling the viola next to a bust of Ben and a portrait of Bridge, the four of us in a line. I must confess it was a proud moment, and one which encapsulated our last twenty-five years together. It only remained for me to place my old friend pride-of-place in the centre of the exhibition and head for Wickham Market, where a new relationship awaited me.

The great financial crash of '08 had a dramatic effect on us. Spain, Italy, Switzerland and Japan, where we had performed regularly for over twenty years, all but disappeared from our diaries overnight. Luckily, we found that they were replaced by Mexico, Sweden, Norway and Brazil as the world's economy shifted. One place that thankfully remained constant was Australia. This magnificent country continued to embrace us and, despite the geographical challenge, we adore going there.

We had built up a strong relationship with the composer and bassist Robert Davidson and his inspiring group Topology. They're based at the Powerhouse in Brisbane, a terrific arts centre, run back then by the pioneering Andrew Ross. We have done many concerts together over the years and it was through them that we met the hugely gifted composer/ cellist Iain Grandage, who wrote an excellent guitar quintet called 'Black Dogs' for us and Craig Ogden.

It was at Iain's instigation that I one day found myself taking a call from a guy named Eddie Perfect. Now, it turns out Eddie is a gorgeous, multi-talented actor/musician/comedian, but frankly, I would have taken a call from an estate agent with the name 'Eddie Perfect'. Eddie wanted to write a song cycle for himself and us to perform and the more we chatted and got to know one another, the more excited I became by this prospect. As luck would have it, Eddie was from Melbourne and we were soon to visit that great metropolis. We were going there to work with the Australian National Academy of Music, an educational institution for whom I had devised a way of presenting the Shostakovich Quartets in a side-by-side format. [Here's how it works: We play five of the works and the students take five (coached by us). Then, each one of us takes the quartet written specially for our instrument (Nos.11–14), along with three students. And finally, everyone comes together to play the string orchestra version of No.8.]

What a thrill this turned out to be. It was also perfect for our Eddie Project because, as we finished our Shostakovich extravaganza, so began the Melbourne Cabaret Festival, the ideal showcase for that song cycle.

Even long-distance, my instincts were spot on. When we finally met Eddie and turned up for that, often tense, first rehearsal, it was like old friends meeting up again. Though Eddie had written every note of every song in what was entitled 'Songs from the Middle', he had wisely brought in our mutual friend and genius arranger, Iain Grandage, to orchestrate the piece. Somewhere along the line we had all agreed that it would be a lovely addition to the proceedings if we invited some woodwind, brass and percussion students from ANAM to join us. Eddie would also play piano on many of the songs. What unbridled fun we all had working, playing and recording this beautiful song cycle. I'm happy to report, those amazing WAAPA boys, Eddie, Iain and Tim (as in Minchin), are currently busy taking over the world.

The '10s

'Rickenbackers to Strads'

It was 2010 and we were in Copenhagen, celebrating the end of a Scandinavian tour with a memorable dinner of herrings and beer. Daniel, who was busy putting the final touches to his summer festival in Holland, started talking about *The Juliet Letters* and how it would fit in perfectly with the theme of that year's festival. The ensuing banter went something like this:

Dan: "We could never afford Elvis, unfortunately."

Me: "We couldn't possibly play *The Juliet Letters* with anyone but him. It would feel weird."

Dan: "But we wouldn't need the whole cycle. In fact, a selection of the songs in a late-night gig would be ideal."

Me: "Well that, of course, we can do. Just need to find the right person."

Dan: "Why don't you do it?"

Me: "Me... Hahaha. What on earth do you mean? I don't sing."

Dan: "Yes you do. You've sung that Irish folk song several times."

Me: "That's just a wee folk song. That's different."

Dan: "You wouldn't be scared now, would you?" (The beer was kicking in...) "I dare you to sing the *The Juliet Letters* – in Stift – this summer."

Idiotic, drunken pause... *Wait, did he just call me chicken?* Never one to duck a dare, in that moment I became Marty from *Back to the Future*.

Me: "You're on, mate. No flippin' problem."

And sing them I did. Well, that's a matter of opinion, I guess, but the concert certainly happened. Joel Waterman from the Utrecht String Quartet played viola and I let rip. We didn't do the whole cycle, but a substantial chunk of it, and I take it as a compliment that Joel and his delightful colleagues asked me to do the concert again with his beautiful group the following spring at their festival in Utrecht. A thrill indeed.

That same summer, EC and Macca were headlining a festival in Hyde Park, and Jacky and I took the girls. Paul's presence meant that security was extra tight. The array of stars wandering around the backstage village was distracting. You'd be trying to have a conversation with someone when Dave Gilmour or Mick Jagger would brush past you. Crowded House were on the bill and Celia made a point of getting their autographs for a friend's dad who was a huge fan. This accomplished, she set off on her next mission – Stella McCartney had just arrived and before I could restrain her, Celia had scurried off and accosted her. Barely ten years old, she was right into fashion in those days and knew exactly who was in our midst. Though they seemed deep in conversation, I felt I'd better call time on Stella's goodwill. I sidled over and interrupted them.

"Hey Stella, how are you? Lovely to see you."

"Hi Paul. Are you responsible for this one?" she asked.

"Ah yes, I'm sorry. This is Celia, she's our youngest."

"Oh, don't be sorry. Celia and I are having a great time. She's amazing. It's fascinating, staring competition in the face," said Stella, only half-jokingly.

A couple of years later Celia badgered me to take her to see Stella's store on Bruton Street. Incredibly, as we perused the merchandise, who should come running over but the woman herself? This was indeed fortuitous because Stella spent most of her time in the Notting Hill store and had only put in an appearance that day in order to do some press. I stood aghast as Celia waxed lyrical about the latest collection, even going as far as to mention a particular dress that had caught her eye. Stella took us off in search of that dress but it was sold out. She then escorted Celia around the kids' section, making her feel like the most important person in the world. Before she was whisked off upstairs, she made us promise not to leave without saying goodbye.

Celia and I, who up until that moment had been eyed, quite rightly, as two misfits who were looking for Carnaby Street but had lost their way, were now the absolute centre of attention, waited on hand and foot. Which was all very well, except for the fact that I had to somehow make darn sure Celia didn't find anything she liked; we were already mortgaged up to the hilt. Luckily, the one T-shirt she really fancied, which in itself might have broken the bank, didn't come in her size, and we were heading for the relative safety of the Bruton Street pavement when Celia reminded me, "Dad, Stella said we weren't to leave without saying goodbye."

"I know, darling, but she's a busy girl. We'll see her another time," said I.

At this, Stella's PA arrived on the scene and asked if we would accompany her to the top floor. Stella had a break in interviews and wanted to say goodbye. Who were we to argue? We followed the lady upstairs and said our farewells, but before leaving, Stella took Celia aside and, handing her a most beautiful gift bag full of goodies, said, "This is for you, Celia. Keep in touch. I'll be watching out for you."

We had gone to the West End that day to do some window shopping, to have a laugh dipping in and out of these impossibly expensive stores, pretending we could afford to be there, but after this experience, Celia was absolutely dumbstruck. I could get no sense out of her and she was barely able to put one foot in front of the other. I suggested Liberty's or Selfridges, to no response. Even Dior and Chanel drew not a flicker from the wee mite.

"Can we just go home now, Dad?" she eventually mumbled, gazing into the distance.

You see, Stella had done that wondrous thing that so many people in her lofty position have forgotten how to do; she had made time to engage with this little girl whom she'd only met once before, but who quite clearly looked up to her. She took a moment and made Celia feel special. For the second time, a member of the McCartney family had shown a member of my family great warmth and kindness.

I pretty much had to carry Celia home, at which point she went to her room, unpacked her presents and daydreamed of a red-haired princess.

Back in Hyde Park, Stella excused herself as she wanted to go and say hello to her dad, who had just arrived in his dressing room. To this day, I have no idea how he got there unnoticed. We were standing right outside and there was only one way in, yet one minute he wasn't there, the next, he was. A lifetime of practise, I guess.

Showtime was approaching and the atmosphere was building. EC and Crowded House did two cracking slots and as the sun fell away to the west, it was time for the main act. I had never seen Paul live and the backstage passes afforded us access to the area just in front of the stage.

It was mega. He played an extended set, belting out one hit after another without even scratching the surface of his extraordinary back catalogue.

Given that her big sister would taunt her mercilessly, making out that she had spent much of her infancy in Paul's arms, Celia was desperate to at least meet the guy. Though we tried our best to make this happen, it's easier said than done. This night was to be her big opportunity, and we figured that backstage after the show was probably the best chance of forcing a quick hello. This plan was scuppered when, towards the end of Daddy's set, Stella said her goodbyes and explained that there was a family birthday and that Paul and co. were all going to split, pronto, after the show. This caused an air of panic in our little one and halfway through the encores, she grabbed Jacky by the hand and most determinedly dragged her backstage again, only to find that they were stopped short by security.

"I'm sorry, madam, this area is off limits now. The whole place has been cleared," said the burly bloke.

Aware of Celia's increasing hysteria, Jacky quickly responded with, "Oh, but sir, it can't be. You see, we are guests of Elvis, and our bags are in his room. We simply cannot leave without them; they have our car and house keys in them. Please, we'll be super quick."

Jacky can be very persuasive in these situations and with Celia doing her 'little girl lost' act, the poor guy was helpless to resist. Having got past him, with the very bag she was supposed to be going to fetch nonchalantly draped over her shoulder, the two renegades made their way to the back of the stage, where Paul had just finished his show and was being escorted, wrapped up in towels and a dressing gown, to his waiting transport.

Celia was getting frantic as his bodyguards propelled him past them.

"Mummy, Mummy, do something. He's getting away!" she cried.

With this, Jacky let out a roar. "Paul, Paul. It's Jacky. Jacky Thomas from the Brodsky Quartet."

Paul stopped in his tracks and turned to face the two girls. Ignoring his minder's pleas to keep moving, Paul ran over and embraced them, introducing himself to Celia. Even there, in the dark, having just done a mammoth show to goodness knows how many people, and surrounded by pandemonium, this gentleman made the time to grab a set list and sign it 'To Celia, with love' before disappearing into the night. Another fairytale ending, thanks to the McCartneys.

***

Almost certainly it's down to his background in optometry, but Peter Millican is a man with vision. By the time I met him, he had sold his retail empire and was busy creating beautiful buildings. Our meetings were always the same – a coffee without the coffee. Instead, we would find ourselves below ground, in hard hats, amongst JCBs and pile drivers, with multiple cranes dancing overhead. We were in the giant hole on York Way that would become Kings Place. Peter would stand there in the bowels of the Earth, somewhere between The Canal Museum and King's Cross Station, brimming with excitement and exclaim, "The stage will be right here."

Only a couple of years later, in 2008, that prediction came true. His stunning building, expertly brought to life by the incomparable Sir Jeremy Dixon (of Opera House, National Gallery – and so many others – fame), rose from the clay and paved the way for that massive regeneration scheme that has totally transformed this once-seedy corner of North London. Though we took part in the grand opening in October of that year, our commitment to the Cadogan Hall meant that our much-anticipated residency at Kings Place didn't come about until 2011.

This would become a pivotal year for us. Our move to this vibrant new enterprise, to the best chamber music hall in London, coincided with the arrival in our lives of the one and only Sarah Trelawny-Ford. The life of a musician can become obsessive; you spend your time looking through a microscope, honing techniques, deciphering composer's scribbles. If, on top of that, you're in a group, things can get really anal. A successful group can take over your life. This is where a manager can make all the difference. It was never going to be easy replacing that special set-up we had with Marjon at Delfina's. We were there every day; she was literally like a fifth member. With Sarah, though we are in constant contact through email etc, we only meet periodically and this element of distance allows her to cast a clear eye on things where our vision may get blurred. She has everything you could possibly wish for in a manager. Alongside her tremendous presence, she instinctively knows when to be strong and when to be cool. Loyal, supportive and full of good ideas, she is great fun yet sagacious, and I don't know what we'd do without her.

Also in this year, we guested on that stunning Peter Gabriel CD *Scratch My Back*, and we all took part in a splendid, Jacky-inspired realisation of Britten's masterpiece 'Noye's Fludde' at the Wimbledon International Festival, which, with Anthony Wilkinson at the helm, is quickly becoming one of the most important festivals in the country.

To the best of my knowledge there are two 'quartets of Strads' in existence. By that, I mean a set of instruments commissioned as such. One is in the Smithsonian in Washington DC, the other in the Palacio Real in Madrid. Every now and then, a quartet gets invited by the Palacio to give a concert on their instruments, and in 2011 it was our turn to be asked. We chose an all-British programme – Bridge's 'Three Idylls', Elgar, Britten No.2 – and arrived a day in advance of the concert in order to spend a bit of time with our new instruments. The security was already insane just getting to the room where they were housed, but once there, it became absolutely mad. The origins of this set are not entirely clear but it seems they may have been presented to King Felipe V during a visit to Cremona in 1702. What is clear is that it was originally a quintet of instruments, two violins, two violas and a cello, all heavily designed with pearl inlay and the like. The two violas were stolen during the time of the Napoleonic Wars, the one I was to play retrieved as recently as the 1950s when it turned up at Hills in London; the other is still at large.

The whole time we spent with the instruments, we were closely guarded by a man in a white coat and gloves. Jacky's cello had a protective cloth attached that was not allowed to be removed. All this hullabaloo was perfectly understandable, but it was when I was warming up with a few scales and our friend stopped me abruptly, cautioning me that I was not to touch the body of the viola with my left hand, that things became untenable. There was no way I could play the concert we were supposed to play the next day without my left hand touching the body of the instrument. A national incident was narrowly averted when we reached a slightly ludicrous compromise, which was that I would do my level best to avoid third position or above until concert time.

I must say that, even for musicians who are used to handling this calibre of instrument, spending time with this family at their extraordinary home was a salutary experience.

It was clear that Stradivari had gone out on a limb with this commission or gift or whatever it was; their unique decoration was clearly a sign of where he knew they were going. In terms of the instruments themselves, the two violins were like twins, though one did seem to have the edge. The viola was very average. On the small side, it had an uneven sound, with the top two strings far outweighing the bottom two. The cello was probably the pick of the bunch. What became more and more unsettling was the inescapable fact that you were holding not just another instrument, but a unique artefact from the most celebrated maker in history, and that your instrument was an integral part of this priceless whole. By concert time the next day, I was genuinely uncomfortable and afraid. This nervousness was not helped by the fact that they had built an extremely rickety and precarious stage that moved every time you did and was covered in antique rugs, which, though they looked lovely, were a nightmare to walk on due to their unevenness. At one point during the hair-raising scherzo of the Britten, my bow hit the side of the viola, which was about half the size I was used to. It sounded to me like the whole palace had collapsed and I was waiting for the thousand invited guests to jump up and start pointing their fingers at me, the man in the white coat to dash onto the stage, wrench the viola from under my chin and have me dragged away to some underground dungeon, *persona non grata*, the laughing stock of the entire musical world. One could argue that this might be the lesser of two evils – banishment, or having to play the last two movements of Britten 2 on an alien instrument.

None of this paranoia transpired. No one but I heard the knock on wood and the instrument, which had survived the ravages of Napoleon's army, was unscathed. We avoided tripping on the carpets or stumbling on the precipitous stairway that led from the stage to the Green Room; heck, we even returned and gave them an encore. On leaving the stage for the last time I could not wait to give back my bejewelled friend to its keeper, monumentally relieved that we had survived the ordeal.

One horrible postscript to this adventure: just a few months after our visit, during an organised photoshoot, the beautiful cello got knocked off the table where it had been placed, fell to the ground and was badly damaged. No doubt it will have been expertly restored, but it is a sickening thought and proof, were it needed, that it's not musicians who need constant vigilance in such circumstances, but everyone else.

'Rolling up to Kings Place'

2012... Forty years young. What to do?

It could only mean I had too much time on my hands. I seemed to just sit around dreaming up increasingly bizarre things for us to do. My poor colleagues could have been forgiven for calling in the white coats when I tried to explain my harebrained scheme for celebrating this milestone. I don't for one moment profess to be in any way mathematically proficient, but I do find numbers intriguing. My idea, which took many months to formulate and realise, was to construct a Wheel of Fortune, on which would be forty different quartets by forty different composers, divided into four sections, ten works in each section. Ten starters, ten substantial works that would comfortably end a first half, ten pieces written for us, and finally, ten beasts to conclude the programme. Four times per concert, a member of the audience would come to the stage, spin the Wheel, and wherever it landed, we would immediately play that piece. The whole escapade went under the blindingly obvious title of 'The Wheel of 4tunes'.

Though clearly a bit of fun (we could have had one hundred and forty pieces on that Wheel), it had a hidden agenda up its sleeve. Not only could we potentially sneak certain pieces onto programmes that one would never usually get past a conservative promoter, it also made us a much better quartet, because we couldn't just rely on being together as a result of rehearsing a work to death, we had to actually listen – really listen carefully – to what was happening right there and then, and react. We had to follow more, lead more, be more communicative. Technically, it was a challenge, and I can remember being pretty scared on that first spin of the Wheel up in the Great Hall of Lancaster University. The real difficulty is not having the lead time. If someone said to me, *Could you stand in for so-and-so tonight? The programme is Britten No.1, Bartok No.6, Schubert G Major,* I would have absolutely no hesitation in saying yes. It's when the Wheel lands on the Brahms A Minor or Verdi, and you have to play that piece right there and then – that's scary.

My reinvention of the wheel proved to be very popular and my design, carefully calculated so that the cumbersome contraption fitted snugly in our car boot, certainly paid off.

I found an unsuspecting metal worker just off the North Circular Road named Barry, who got right into the idea and somehow made sense of my decidedly amateur drawings, expertly bringing them to life. The Wheel travelled the length and breadth of the UK but when we were invited to bring the show to mainland Europe, the cost of shipping it became prohibitive and so we had to think again. Jacky characteristically rose to the challenge. She went and sourced an actual Wheel of Fortune-making factory right there in North London and, under her expert guidance, got them to construct a table-top model that even had our credentials on it. Still retaining all the drama of the original, her ingenious design was way more compact and lighter, making it much easier to transport. Before that Wheel could be made, however, we visited the Risor Festival in Norway. The theme of the festival that year was 'Chance'… well, hello!

Finding out late in the day that we couldn't get the Wheel to the festival and 'necessity being the mother…' and all that, I came up with a way round our problem. An umbrella, of course. You know what the weather's like up there in Scandinavia. I'd always wanted to go into James Smith and Sons, that little gem of a place in Covent Garden that specialises in such things, and this was my chance. I immediately came up against a problem, which was that umbrellas have eight segments. My numerical prowess quickly informed me that eight times four would leave us with thirty-two pieces, eight short. Annoyingly, I had already found the perfect umbrella, and besides, commissioning one was horribly pricey and would take too long. I decided to buy the eight-sided umbrella anyway and see what happened. I enlisted the help of our Holly; she was always up for stuff and had a real flair for graphics and the like. Together we designed and produced what would become known as the 'Holly Brolly'. Midway through the production, the solution to the maths problem hit me. We would incorporate a Joker into the Brolly. If someone landed on the Joker, they could stick or twist. Twisting would lead them to a set of eight playing-cards that contained the eight missing works, and they had to pick a card to reveal the chosen work. In many ways, I actually enjoyed the Holly Brolly more than the Wheel, and from then on we would often incorporate it into the Wheel concerts. I loved the theatricality of running through the audience spinning this gorgeous umbrella, choosing one's victim and getting them to shout 'Stop!'

It was remarkable how many people were convinced the whole thing was fixed. It was all they could fixate on. We often had people actually stealing onto the stage during the interval to inspect the merchandise and try to guess how we'd done it, even though we assured them it wasn't rigged; where's the fun in that? We soon decided to publish on our website what programmes the Wheel threw up as a form of assurance for these doubting Thomases, but their cynicism continued unabated. The Wheel kept us amused for the best part of two years and furnished us with a particularly memorable event.

We had just spun it in Haarlem and the promoter took us out for dinner after the show. We went to a swanky place downtown that had an unusually fancy underground car park right next to it. So impressive was the park that, though we naturally took our instruments with us, Jacky and I decided to leave our suitcases locked away out of sight in the boot whilst we had dinner. Fed and watered, we returned to the car an hour or so later to find mayhem. The pristine car park was a battlefield. A gang had entered the place in a van, ransacked no fewer than ten vehicles, one of which was ours, and made off with the loot. It was a professional job leaving broken windows, forced boots and doors, and alarms and flashing lights going off all over the place. The police were on the scene and we had to fill out endless forms detailing what we had lost. It was hard to explain to them the enormity of the loss we had incurred. Our suitcases had within them all the things you might imagine – laptop, clothes, shoes, wash-bags, etc. – but they also had our music, much of it forty years in our possession. We had lost our parts to many more than forty quartets (lots of the quartets were in books containing several pieces), and with the final show in Utrecht the next night, we had a major problem on our hands.

One quirky thing that was a real sign of the times was that Daniel, who had not come to dine with us the night before but had instead gone to family in Amsterdam, awoke the next morning to a deluge of emails, posts and tweets, all offering him various degrees of condolence in light of the terrible events that had befallen the group the night before. Poor Daniel contacted us in a panic, fearing that something awful had happened to one or more of us –a car crash perhaps. Luckily that was not the case. We had been up early in an effort to alert people to what had happened and by the time he had awoken only a couple of hours later, the news had spread around the musical world like wildfire.

People were incredibly supportive and helpful, offering to send us scores and parts. The same lovely promoters in Utrecht who had been so accommodating back in '03 were once again understanding and more than happy to accept a watered-down version of the evening we had planned. Though hardly the end of the world, it was extremely disruptive and sad to lose all those old parts that had come through so much with us.

"Surely once these blaggards have copied our fingerings and bowings, they will see fit to return our precious pages," I quipped to Jacky.

Two weeks later, back in London, it was teatime and we had literally just received the final parts in a PDF from some composer or other when the phone rang. It was Sergeant Van der Valk from the Dutch police, informing us that they had recovered both our suitcases and we could collect them at our convenience. They had been found on a canal towpath thirty miles from Haarlem, along with a few other discarded bags. The police reckoned that the gang had driven to this secluded spot, rifled through their newly gained possessions and, keeping what they wanted, had chucked the bags with their remaining contents over the bridge and into the canal below – except they managed to miss the canal and the bags landed safely on the towpath. All our clothes, and miraculously our parts, were inside, none the worse for wear.

We performed a Shostakovich Cycle that season in Uppsala, where, upon arrival, we were treated to a mini siege in the middle of the town, right outside the hall. I had initially thought that all the furore was as a result of the mad clamour for tickets to our concert that evening but it turned out that some guys had actually robbed a bank, been trapped inside by the security doors, and were now holding a hostage. I'm happy to report that the incident came to a peaceful conclusion and our weekend marathon was thankfully unaffected.

We also brought the cycle to Kings Place to signal the beginning of our eagerly awaited residency there and mark our 40th anniversary. We hadn't performed it in London since the South Bank in 1989. This event was a joy and passed without incident.

We recorded all John Joubert's quartets for Somm Records and embarked on our 40th birthday disc, entitled *Petit Fours*, a collection of our arrangements of some favourite tunes, which also doubled as our signature CD for the decade. Apart from the '70s, when we weren't yet recording, each decade has contained a stand-alone, personal disc – *Unlimited*, *Lament*, *Moodswings*, and finally *Petits Fours*. I say 'finally', but now that I've made myself aware of this fact, I'm starting to imagine what CD the '20s will hold.

Apart from being a momentous thing to do anytime, anywhere, bringing the Shostakovich back to London seemed like the perfect way to announce our arrival at Kings Place. It also paved the way to achieving one of our goals there – to focus on and celebrate the complete chamber works of lesser known or neglected composers. Next up would be Panufnik. We recorded and performed all his string chamber music to coincide with his centenary, commissioning a very personal homage from his daughter, Roxanna. One of the perks of such endeavours is that sometimes you get to meet and make friends with new people. The Panufnik family certainly ticked this box. Getting to know them alongside Andrej's music made the whole experience a treat indeed.

Then it was Zemlinsky's turn, surely one of the neglected greats. I had to stop the car once, having turned on Radio 3 and heard music so riveting, I could no longer safely operate machinery. It turned out to be Zemlinsky. We had been playing his quartets for many years before getting the chance to share them properly with audiences. Getting his name past promoters isn't easy.

The four works are tremendously varied. The first, which I always think of as Brahms' 4th Quartet, is a straightforward but brilliant piece in the old style, and is as inventive and thrilling as any romantic quartet I know. The second is perhaps one of the most extraordinary pieces ever written for string quartet. It's like a Mahler symphony and its forty-five minute single movement stretches the quartet to its absolute limit, both technically and emotionally. The third sounds a bit more like what you'd expect from a second Viennese composer, but it still retains that wonderful romanticism that Zemlinsky never really loses. It's a private and subtle piece, even in the ingenious scherzo, which pokes fun at Schonberg's new twelve-tone idea, an idea abhorrent to Zemlinsky. The fourth is another truly great quartet. Written in memory of his friend Berg, who had just died, it was inspired by the deceased's epic 'Lyric Suite', which was itself inspired by Zemlinsky's 'Lyric Symphony'. It has six movements made up of three sets of two, slow/fast, slow/fast, slow/fast.

Getting to finally record these masterworks was a personal triumph for me. The whole process was made all the more special when Anthony Beaumont, the Zemlinsky scholar, presented us with the score and parts of an early piece for quartet that had not previously been published. It turned out to be a thoroughly worthwhile work and we were proud to have given its first UK performance and first ever recording.

'Bout ye, hi.'

2013 saw my home town of Derry awarded the honour of City of Culture. When I reflected on that city of my birth, two images came to mind: trees (Doire means oak grove) and walls (the impressive and immaculately preserved city walls date from 1613). Given Ireland's troubled history with its neighbour, I found the image of a tree bringing down a wall irresistible. With the invaluable help of Ian Richie, the then-Director of the City of London Festival, we charted a path of walled cities from Derry to Jerusalem, threw together composers and writers of opposite persuasions and asked them each to write a song. We took as our inspiration Schubert's masterpiece 'Wintereisse', using a tiny two-note motif from 'Der Lindenbaum' as a hook. This was to be the last utterance of that unique genius who had, at a tragically young age, come up against a wall he could not breach. The ensuing song cycle 'Trees, Walls and Cities', the premiere of which saw no fewer than ten composers and several writers on that London stage, was a privilege to have been a part of, and I'd like to think that its many roots and branches helped unsettle a few barriers in some small way.

'With Love and Fury'

You know that curious phenomenon whereby you see or hear something for the first time and then it seems to crop up again and again? Well, during an Australian tour I had been noticing a poster for an Australian Chamber Orchestra programme built around Britten's magnificent 'Les Illuminations' and starring the woman whose enchanting profile had been so hauntingly captured on the flyer, one Katie Noonan. I had never heard of this woman but as we travelled around the country, inevitably tracing out the almost identical map the ACO would soon do, I began to enquire about her from the various promoters and our numerous Aussie friends. Turns out, I really should have heard of her. Katie was a prodigious talent, playing piano concertos at a tender age and showing a precociousness that, quite rightly, had many people excited. She then took a gloriously left turn, forming a hugely successful pop band called 'George' with her delightful brother Tyrone, before gradually working her way back into the classical world, this time as a vocalist. Such are her abilities that she seems to be able to straddle these various areas of music effortlessly – not an easy feat, and one which most certainly attracted me.

After our Brisbane show, a strikingly colourful person came up to me in the foyer of our hotel to offer her congratulations for what she described as a 'thrilling concert'. It was Katie. We had an immediate rapport and agreed to meet the next morning for coffee and a chat. That meeting reminded me so much of the life Jacky and I had recently left behind, because when Katie showed up at the café with her gorgeous man Zac and their two adorable kids, she was festooned with pushchairs, bottles, changing mats, nappies and changes of clothes. She had bits of breakfast down one arm, eyes in the back of her head, and nerves generally exposed.

We talked at length about music, baby food and life in general. It was like we were old friends. I love Australians! Despite our instant rapport, it took many years of throwing ideas back and forth across the world before we/she hit upon the perfect reason for us to make music together. 2016 was to be the centenary of the remarkable Australian 'force for good' that was Judith Wright. Inspired by the life and work of this iconic personage, we agreed to commission ten Australian composers to take one of her poems each, and together compose a song cycle for us to play. What inspiration and beauty those composers brought to the table for us to enjoy, what diverse and thrilling offerings they conjured up. Judith used to sign off her correspondence 'With Love and Fury', and this typically incisive comment became the title of the cycle and subsequent CD.

One of those composers was the multi-talented Andrew Ford. We first met Andy back in '98 when, as part of the ABC team, he accompanied us on our whistle-stop tour of the country performing all the Shostakovich live to radio. Andy introduced the concerts and we did talks and interviews from the various venues, airports, hotels and so on. Not only is Andy a world-renowned composer, he is a wonderful and prolific writer of books and, just by the way, has the most important classical music show on ABC. He has written many pieces for us over the years, the most recent of which was his Quartet No.7, entitled 'Eden Ablaze', a heartfelt reaction to the terrifying bushfires of 2020, during which time he came perilously close to losing his own home to the flames.

It was great travelling around with Katie because, with her diamond-encrusted Qantas card and infinite charm, she succeeded in getting us all into the First Class lounges. On a tour like this, the days tend to merge, as do the airports, hotels and concert halls. One can all too easily zone out. A cautionary tale, if I may:

On one of the days, I decided to forgo the pleasure of the lounge and made my way to the departure gate early in order to do some emails etc. Working right up to the last second, I did vaguely wonder why I hadn't seen any of my colleagues arrive for the flight, but then figured they were probably being super cool and kicking back in the lounge. As I wandered towards the gate, I realised that I had misread the gate number and that my flight was boarding at a gate in the furthermost, opposite end of the enormous terminal. I set off at a pace, running like a madman till I thought I might either be sick or pass out. I couldn›t miss this flight and screw up everyone's day, this being the only flight that would get me to Perth for that evening's show. Reaching the gate only as the aircraft was pushing back, I was, in between gasps, pleading with the ground staff to somehow please let me get on board. There was absolutely no way they were even considering this possibility, and I slumped into a plastic chair in this now-deserted corner of the building.

I started frantically phoning Jacky to explain what had happened, only to be answered by a remarkably chilled voice unable to comprehend what I was babbling on about.

"But we're just finishing our coffee here, our flight's not for another half hour," said Jacky calmly.

Monumentally relieved but totally bemused, I sat there desperately trying to comprehend what could have happened. I decided to have yet another look at the boarding pass in my jacket pocket, only to realise that I was looking at yesterday's document. A carbon copy of today's, of course, being an internal Qantas flight, but it was Sydney-Melbourne instead of Melbourne-Perth; that one was in my inside pocket.

My bit of advice: always discard used boarding cards immediately.

The intensity of focus required to bring some of the most inspired and taxing repertoire ever written to life leaves precious little time for anything else. On occasion one is lucky enough to meet a like-minded spirit from outside of your closed world who can match this devotion, and with whom you can create something new – that is very special. We had such an amazing time working with Katie, not just the rehearsing, the recording, the concerts, the travels, but most of all, the interaction, the humanity, the endless fun. We made friends for life, and though geography challenges us, we remain close and will hopefully create some more lovely sounds in the years ahead.

'Run and Hide'

One piece of advice I always give young groups starting out is to never build up to a 'big' date, and never underestimate a 'small' one. I realise that I'm repeating myself here, but it's such an important point that I feel justified in trying to ram it home. So often the apparently prestigious concert ends up being a huge anti-climax, whereas the inconsequential one, the one you can't even pronounce on your itinerary, proves to be the memorable one.

As we approached Maasmechelen, in between a Shostakovich Cycle in Holland and a Late Beethoven Cycle straight to radio in Bratislava, we felt like we were on some apocalyptic film set. In disbelief, we obeyed the Sat Nav as it directed us further and further into a deserted maze of tiny streets and suburban Belgian brick houses. As we pulled up outside our B&B, an overwhelming sense of dread filled our bones. How were we going to get through the next forty-eight hours? As we got our bags out of the boot of the car, we noticed something that didn't exactly bolster our confidence in the place. It was a sight none of us had ever seen before. There on the pavement, next to a stray dog who appeared every bit as lost as we felt, was a vending machine selling pre-packed pasta, risotto and curry dishes, ready for the microwave; this abomination in a country that boasts that you cannot get a bad meal within its borders! Leaving the wretched mutt to fend for itself, we hightailed it and braved the accommodation. It was from this precise moment that things took a dramatic turn for the better. The Basil B&B – yes, you guessed it – bore absolutely no resemblance to its namesake. Nor was its delightful owner, Sara, in any way reminiscent of the buffoon from Torquay. Indeed, I could not recommend the establishment more fervently. That evening we dined royally at the nearby Vuchterhoise Restaurant, run by an enchanting young couple busy braving the cut-throat world of gastronomy. The concert the next day, which was in the church opposite, was full to overflowing with an obviously knowledgeable audience, who gave us a raucous standing ovation, after which we all piled into the buzzing bistro not fifty metres from the stage door, where we sampled various local delicacies, both liquid and otherwise, long into the night.

Suddenly, we were thanking our lucky stars that we had not one but two concerts in Maasmechelen. After the second show, the adorable Eef (the director of the Cultural Centre which had invited us) and her charming husband Bart took us to the Michelin-star Italian restaurant, Cellini's, which just happened to be not fifty metres from the stage door in the other direction. There we were joined by two of their friends, Vezio and Martine. As we were paying the bill I made the fatal mistake of pointing out a bottle of my favourite Sassicaia lined up in the impressive bar.

"You like Sassicaia, Paul?" he enquired.

"Well, as a matter of fact I do. We go back a long way. Can't afford it of course but...."

"That's it," he interrupted. "We're going back to my place. We're going to drink some Sassicaia."

Vezio would not take no for an answer and in no time, we were all entering his extraordinary Italianate villa in this increasingly bewildering town. By this stage, Vezio had explained to me that Sassicaia was in fact the third best wine of Italy, superseded by Tignanello in second place, with Masseto taking the coveted crown. We proceeded to try all three before being served a glass of dusty nectar which turned out to be nothing less than the extremely rare wine produced each year using the DNA of a vine recovered from the ashes of Pompeii. I have to admit, this was a mind-bending experience; drinking wine made from a vine that had lain dormant beneath the ruins of a city for nearly 2000 years.

In the end, we were sad to leave this funny little mining town on the edge of Belgium. Maas loves us, we love them, and future plans to revisit abound.

Another example of this phenomenon was a rainy afternoon in Ottawa. It was to be the last date on a slightly-too-long Canadian tour as Jacky and I pulled up outside the hall. It was an unusually nasty day in August and the venue looked like the sort of place that was going to drag this already dismal day into a deep depression. Added to this, Holly and Celia were already up at the lake house we had rented with Joe, Nora and the family, and we just couldn't wait to swap our instruments for a paddle board and join them. As the rain thundered down on that backstreet, almost obliterating the crumby entrance that would take us to yet another rehearsal/concert routine, we have never felt so close to just taking off. Jacky and I both had to dig deep.

Just like in Belgium, however, from the moment that door opened, we were transported to a very different place. This inauspicious back entrance belied a magnificent converted church with a stupendous acoustic. The backstage area was generous and clean, the committee members, helpful and charming. The stage was grand and welcoming and the twelve hundred strong audience, who snaked around the building for two hours before the show, were borderline riotous. That concert, which had earlier seemed like a penance, turned out to be one of the most exciting and memorable of that or any other season. We are due to return soon and I can guarantee a very different mood as we pull up outside.

Returning to my current favourite place for a moment, Maasmechelen… We performed twenty-six different quartets that week, eight of them straight to radio. That's almost on a par with the craziness of twenty years earlier. As any player will tell you, the concerts are often the easy bit, the bit you've put in the hours to be able to do. It's all the other stuff that can make life difficult and test the nerves – disrupted travel, dodgy accommodation, horrible backstage areas, inadequate staging, lighting, disappearing music, the list is endless. Take that Beethoven Cycle (Ops.74–135) in Bratislava as an example. Having slept in a draught the night before, I got the most unpleasant neuralgia all over the left side of my head, which didn't ease for the whole time we were there. Jacky's first finger inexplicably split open right by the nail, making it very painful to use, and both our lovely violinists simultaneously developed quite severe tennis elbow in their right arms. The concerts were Thursday, Saturday and Sunday. On the Friday, we rehearsed nine till one, Daniel went to a holistic physio guru chap while Ian and I got lunch for everyone, and Jacky went into makeup in preparation for a photoshoot we had organised because a favourite photographer, who happens to live there, was free that afternoon. At 5pm we were taken to a live, televised Q&A session in a trendy café downtown, which ended with a performance and a CD signing. After this we returned to our rehearsal till 9pm.

The next morning, we were back rehearsing when Ian's 400-year-old Maggini made such a loud cracking sound that it stopped us in our tracks. In a state of shock, Ian examined the violin and rested it on his lap while we discussed what could possibly have made that horrendous noise, when the instrument let out another series of blood-curdling cracking sounds. We honestly thought it was going to explode in front of our very eyes. With us all in a state of panic, it then decided to go quiet. Ian checked it again and, though he reckoned the sound had deteriorated, could find nothing obviously wrong. Soon, I was also beginning to sense all was not well with my viola, but thinking paranoia had set in, I decided to ignore it until Daniel turned to me asking if I could possibly play up a bit as he was having trouble hearing me. Convinced that I was not holding back, I thought it time to give my instrument a quick check. In all my days, I have never seen an instrument as open as mine was. You could have posted a letter through the space between the ribs and the belly, which was worsening by the minute. I simply couldn't play concerts on it the way it was. There was no sound coming out and frankly, it could have collapsed at any moment. It was becoming obvious that it had, in fact, been my viola that had made those blood-curdling noises and not Ian's violin. Luckily, the promoter of this festival, the cellist Josef Luptak, said he knew someone who could help me out in time for the show. Whilst this was terrific news, it meant that our crucial rehearsal had to be abandoned, and I next laid hands on my viola fifteen minutes before they turned on the mics.

Next, Jacky started panicking that the neck of her cello was giving way because her strings were getting closer and closer to the fingerboard. It was, in fact, Josef who explained that in extreme cases of humidity, bridges can expand or contract sufficiently to make a palpable difference to the string height. Finally we tested the humidity level on the stage where we had been working. It was at a terrifyingly low – 20%. We all ran to our dressing rooms, ran a hot shower and stood next to it, instruments in hand, in an effort to save a catastrophe. Then promptly went on and played, 'The Harp', Der Grosse Fuge and Op.130.

Life on the road is brutal. Sure, we might often have a little too much wine after a concert, but how musicians mix drugs with sex and rock 'n' roll baffles me. I tell myself it's because they're still so young, otherwise I have to face up to the fact that I'm a hopeless lightweight – I mean, one toke on a zoot and I'm a kaput.

Usually, if you've paid to watch someone do something, they're at the top of their game. They are the top few percent of all the people who have chosen that path. You sit there watching someone lovingly caress a theme from their instrument and it's easy to forget not only the hours but the pain. A dancer's feet, a golfer's back, a boxer's brain. Musicians are plagued with injuries. Before we started standing up to play, Ian and I had terrible back and shoulder problems from trying to communicate whilst rooted to the spot. As our fiddlers found out in Bratislava, tennis elbow is a favourite, from all that bowing, and neck pain an inevitability from nursing that unforgiving shape in that wholly unnatural position. Though I've experienced all these ailments to varying degrees over the years, my nemesis turned out to be my left wrist. It was probably the change to a much bigger instrument – where fourth fingers became an almost impossible challenge and second position my new best friend – that put too much strain on that precise area.

The situation reached its crisis point on stage in Auckland Town Hall. We were playing Bartok No.5 and Beethoven Op.131 live onto radio and, though I managed to cope with the pain and discomfort throughout the Bartok, as I'd been doing for some years already, it was the miniscule distorted movement required to negotiate the top of that run in the cadencial section of the variation movement of the Beethoven that caused such a sharp stab of unpleasantness that it fairly stopped me in my tracks. Being a human of a certain age, you have to put up with aches and pains, but as an instrumentalist, having constant pain in your left wrist, resulting in a terrifying lack of power in your left hand, is a crippling scenario and one I now had to take very seriously.

You'll think it's a tall story, but at dinner that night after the concert, I found myself seated next to a rheumatologist. His depressing prognosis was that I would have to have surgery, something I wanted to avoid like the plague. The next night, we played in Palmerston North. I had left tickets for a long-lost cousin of one of my brothers-in-law. We met up afterwards and in the course of our conversation, I mentioned my wrist problem. What do you think he did for a living? He was a wrist specialist. I mean, even though I just did, you couldn't write it. He was tremendously helpful and organised for me to visit his clinic in Wellington a couple of days later. They did lots of tests and took several scans but none of them proved conclusive. They could find nothing wrong but my symptoms remained. I was once again resigned to living and working with this horribly debilitating problem.

Nearly a year later, I bumped into an old mate, the lovable Andy Parker. Andy was looking a bit the worse for wear and when I inquired after his health, he told me that he had been on a skiing holiday the week before, had an accident and ruptured his rotator-cuff. This is a serious injury that can take months to heal, so how was Andy sitting there next to me about to play the viola? Someone had put him in touch with a holistic kinesiologist by the name of Roy Wallis, who, with a wave of his magic wand, had somehow made it possible for Andy to work. No drugs were administered, I hasten to add. Within forty-eight hours I was in his treatment room on Harley Street. Literally within seconds, he, where all those scans had failed, found not one but two major problems in my wrist, and proceeded to put them right in about thirty seconds – along with a whole series of other unconnected but ongoing issues. They took a little longer.

"When can I see you again?" I asked impatiently at the end of our one-hour session.

"Well, it's probably a good idea to make an appointment for a couple of weeks from now just to check that everything has held, but half an hour will do. Off you go now, you're a new man," he said, matter-of-factly.

It was nothing short of miraculous. Though my wrist did put up a bit of a fight and still requires care and attention, the rest of my physical ailments disappeared and have not, to date, come back. Power had returned to my left wrist, I could make a fist for the first time in years. What a feeling! I could once again lift a saucepan with either hand and, though I still push open doors and get up from a chair using a closed fist and not an open palm, that's just a force of habit. Roy, you have indeed made a new man of me. I cannot thank you enough. You are a genius.

'Muziekgebouw naar Prinsengracht'

Whilst we didn't exactly milk the Shostakovich potential back in the '90s, those recordings did make a mark globally and the cycle did become part of our ongoing persona. Daniel seemed to innately share our deep love of these pieces and twenty-five years after the original recording, our readings of them had changed so enormously that it felt only right to consider recording them again.

The fifteen string quartets of Dmitri Shostakovich represent the most poignant journey in all of music. It's impossible to overstate the import of this phenomenal body of work. His wish to write twenty-four quartets, one in every key, was thwarted only by his own demise, yet when you stand back and consider the fifteen he completed as a whole, it certainly makes you wonder whether there isn't in fact a greater force at work in the world. After the scandal surrounding his 'Fourth Symphony' and the tragic damning of his beloved opera 'Lady Macbeth', Shostakovich knew he had to find a more covert way of airing his thoughts and conveying his emotions. It was to be the birth of his son, Maxim, that would light the touchpaper and spark off an extraordinary set of pieces that would continue to inspire him till his dying day. To have a running commentary of such magnitude by one of the greatest musical minds the world has ever produced is a priceless commodity and a precious resource. To begin, as he does, with a celebration of new life and end with arguably the most intimate reflection on life itself ever written, is already hugely dramatic, but to then consider what lies in between these two statements... Gifts for friends, diatribes for enemies, tirades against war and suffering, humorous jibes at this and that, love letters. A piece in memory of his beloved first wife Nina, who died unexpectedly, another heralding his new-found love and happiness with his third wife Irina (his second marriage was a bit of a disaster – she didn't get a quartet!); these two works flanking his very own epitaph, a deeply emotional and tortured piece written when the composer was at perhaps his lowest ebb and contemplating suicide. To then realise that these three works sit at the very heart of the overall output really does lend the whole thing a feeling of being somehow preordained.

This was the task we had set ourselves: to record our current interpretations of these profound documents. Back in '89 we were still discovering many of these pieces, we were taking a wave – almost, one would say, reacting to much of the music. I'm not undermining that fact in any way; indeed, I feel it's an enormously valuable viewpoint, but now, having taken that wave so many times over a twenty-five-year period, it felt more like we were at rest on a rocky outcrop or a deserted beach, surveying the scene and, for the last time, relaying our thoughts on it.

In the end, we decided that the best way of achieving truth was to record them as we had come to perform them, in five concerts over a weekend. Now we needed the perfect venue. We chose the Muziekgebouw in Amsterdam. This magnificent hall is a contemporary classic in the medieval capital city of a country that has given us so much over the years, just the right size for such a venture, the backstage facilities are excellent and it has a comfortable hotel actually attached to the building. We arrived on a Thursday, did some preparatory playthroughs, performed the five concerts over the weekend and returned on the Monday to patch any unacceptable noises. Alexander van Ingen patiently guided us through the process. It was without doubt the most challenging thing I had ever done. We would never record these pieces again and, after a lifetime of studying and performing them, knowing that each and every sound you made would be the one captured forever was terrifying, yet ultimately exhilarating. Upon completion of this painful process, one felt an enormous release. We'd communicated the works as naturally as possible; now we could relax and start enjoying them fully again.

This hugely important milestone in the history of the Brodsky Quartet could never have been realised without the enormous generosity of our dear friend Neil Rackham. Neil, you know who you are, and I hope you know how much we will always appreciate your invaluable contribution to the cause.

Perhaps as a consequence of choosing Amsterdam for this mammoth undertaking, we received the sort of invitation that only comes along once in a lifetime. We were asked to do the infamous Prinsengracht Konzert. Any enquiry that offers more than the usual concert experience, which shows real input from the promoter and requires your particular services in a specific way, is a breath of fresh air, something to rouse the senses and get excited about. Generally, as you now know, I'm wary of prestigious dates, usually preferring the vibe of the more modest affairs, but it was immediately obvious that Prinsengract would be an unforgettable experience. Daniel's reaction was heartwarming, and that alone made our not-inconsiderable input into this event more than worth it. Having been born and raised in Holland, Daniel had witnessed many of these spectacles over the years, both live and on the TV; he understood the significance the concert holds for not just the people of Amsterdam, but for the nation as a whole.

The idea was the brainchild of two entrepreneurs, Hans Duijf and Theo Inniger, the then-directors of the magnificent Pulitzer Hotel. It was to create an annual outdoor classical concert for the people – a concert everyone could enjoy. To this day, the event is centred around this hotel. A magnificent red carpet spews like lava from the lobby, out across the street and onto the huge, purpose-built staging, which has been erected over the Prinsengracht Canal. Each year a particular artist or orchestra (often the Concertgebouw itself) would be invited to curate the event, but never in its thirty-six-year history had a string quartet been asked to carry the show, and it was a challenge we accepted with alacrity.

Entertaining twenty thousand people in the open air and many millions on live TV for over an hour is no mean feat. It was imperative to get the programme just right, but with the experience of their wonderful team, Dorette Kuipers and Hans van der Boom, the presence of our dear friends and colleagues (Nino Gvetadze, Zoran Markovic and Marcello Nisinman), and months of fine-tuning, we finally got to a place where everyone was happy. The concert provided us all with so many memorable moments – just the momentum of the build-up was inspiring – but nothing could prepare us for the emotion of the day itself. Take the normally deadly-dull soundcheck, for example. These necessary evils can often be frustrating, but here, we arrived on stage to find that that whole section of canal had been emptied of boats, the great gates closed temporarily. Gradually, as the sounds of our rehearsal filtered out, crowds began to gather. Prinsengracht was already beginning to work its magic. Then, at midday, a horn sounded and both sets of gates opened, inviting a flotilla of craft to enter that section of canal. Slowly but surely, and with impressive patience and expertise, these beautiful people in their sailing vessels filled every square inch of that waterway. Though it would choose to rain on our parade come showtime, nothing could dampen the spirits of those gathered there. They nonchalantly put on their cagoules, opened their umbrellas and continued to soak up the atmosphere. Families and friends crowded out onto the balconies and hung out of the windows of the homes overlooking the scene. A couple proposed right in front of us, and a married couple and their wedding guests chose to spend the evening of their big day moored next to our stage. People laughed and cried and made merry, yet when called for, you could hear a pin drop. The concert finished with the traditional rendition of 'Aan de Amsterdamse grachten', which I had arranged for our forces. It's difficult to put into words the complex emotions and depth of feeling encapsulated in those few moments. Extreme happiness, fondness and wonderment, mixed with an overwhelming sadness and fear as you struggle with the inescapable realisation that we are ultimately alone. This afforded us a rare glimpse of humanity at its very best – sensitive, warm-hearted and inclusive. Not for the first time I felt so envious of, proud of and close to, the Dutch people. These are the moments I live for. Being able to do something, however small, that allows you to bring people together, and for you to feel included and actually a part of that process, is where it's at, not being stuck up on a stage, distanced and aloof, admired like some inanimate object. Music, the universal language, is all about communicating; it's a miraculous gift that can reach into our very souls and create mutual understanding in a primal and abstract way, without the need for clumsy words.

'The Big Bs'

Next, the quartet gods decided it was time for us to take on the ultimate challenge, that holy grail for all quartets: the Late Beethovens. Together we would step up to that deep, dark, truthful mirror of pieces I love too much to say, and be counted. These six offerings, arguably the most all-encompassing collection of random notes ever brought to order, have been close friends for as long as the quartet has existed. Indeed Op.130, the piece we have just this week recorded, was an ever-present, firm favourite on the rickety stands of those four, wide-eyed kids from Middlesbrough. Not yet teenagers but already fired up, captured and helpless in the grip of this thing called music. Little did the boy from Derry know, as he stood watching his city go up in flames, that a similar fire would soon be ignited in his belly.

I love the industrious people at Henle and Barenreiter. Their invaluable work has revolutionised our interpretations of classical music. We had each and every quartet they were preparing on order, impatiently awaiting their completion and subsequent arrival on our stands. I cannot begin to evaluate the importance of these new bibles. They wiped clean those grossly over-edited publications we had all worked with, argued over and taken as gospel for so many years, and replaced them with gloriously clear parts, containing only those marks made by the composers themselves. Just imagine if we had to use editions of Shakespeare in which pages are littered with changes invented by actors or directors – there would, quite rightly, be outrage. We realised very quickly that we had no option but to literally relearn the Beethoven quartets. To discover and gradually decipher his extraordinarily precise language was humbling and thrilling. With tenacious perseverance, it enabled us to bring his miraculous plays to life, encouraging meaningful conversation in performance instead of the all-too-common mundane imitation.

Despite the familiarity of these pieces and our hugely positive Muziekgebouw experience, we elected not to record them live. We tended not to perform them as a series because, unlike the Shostakovich, they had no feeling of a journey. These are stand-alone works, each one a unique, towering edifice with its own story to tell. Instead, we booked some days at Potton Hall in Suffolk, our studio of choice. Recording is a hair-raising business at the best of times, but when it's music like this, it really is exhausting on every level. We did three four-day stints, starting shortly after 9am and only stopping at 9.15pm so we could get to the local pub for dinner. Though we might take half an hour to breathe a little and wolf down some dodgy sandwich, it was mostly tea, coffee, biscuits and adrenalin that sustained us. This was our usual timetable for any recording, by the way, but the feeling of elation upon completion of *this* Herculean task was intense. One day we will endeavour to capture the mighty Razumovsky Op.59/1, at which point we will have commited the entire set to posterity.

The '20s

'Stop Press!!'

In my experience, a quartet's life, rather like one's own, seems to progress in ten-year cycles. The '70s saw the group in its infancy, studying and finding its feet. The '80s witnessed my arrival on the scene, a gradual leaving behind of education and competitions, the formation of an identity and making our way in the big bad world. In the '90s, we consolidated a place in the music world and really began to express ourselves. The arrival of Andrew heralded the millennium, and finally, Daniel's appearance, which would carry us through to our 50th anniversary and beyond. But wait, wouldn't that then make a nonsense of my conviction? Something would have to change.

Never one to disappoint, Daniel announced his intention to, albeit reluctantly, leave the group in 2018. Jacky and I were celebrating Celia's 20th birthday with a bit of a gathering in Ireland when we each received a personal email. Incredibly, unsure of whether or not the other one had also received the correspondence, we didn't even discuss the news till the next day; we just powered through, expertly concealing the devastating reality those words conveyed.

Here we three were yet again, faced with the same old life decision. Playing quartets was what we did, it was all we knew, but the upheaval, the soul-destroying search, the insurmountable mountain of work, the emotional rollercoaster, the overwhelming stress involved in finding a replacement was more than we could bear. We went through the motions of composing a list of potential candidates and discussed at length various unlikely plans of how we could maybe alter our schedule to suit one or two particular favourites in the running, but our spirits had taken a serious battering. Though financially we were none of us in a position to pack up, logically it was fast becoming a very real option. Scraping a living separately, versus the enormity of the problem we now faced together, was beginning to look like our preferred route.

There was no hint of bad feeling where Daniel was concerned. Our last concert together would be a melancholy affair, yet it carried with it a pleasing symmetry. Like our first outing twelve years earlier, it was an all-Elgar programme – on this occasion, to mark the 100th anniversary of the Quartet's, Quintet's and Violin Sonata's birth. The performance, which went out live on the BBC from the Malvern Concert Club (itself founded by Elgar), was an emotional rollercoaster and together we brought Daniel's innings to a close by sharing a small gift from us three to him. We played an arrangement I'd made specially of a lost piece by Elgar for violin and piano, aptly entitled 'Adieu'.

He had his own reasons for branching out and remained committed and helpful to the bitter end. He was shocked and saddened when faced with the news that we would rather pull the plug than have to go through that whole weary process again. Likewise, our agents were dumbfounded at the prospect and showed us great support. We also took tremendous comfort from the number of people who contacted us from all over the world, expressing interest in the vacancy, but we were struggling emotionally.

One day, after many months of contemplation, the three of us decided to have a quartet meeting; a heavy-duty heart-to-heart, a final conflab. The minutes of this momentous coming together, which would decide our futures, went something like this:

"I think we need someone our age," ventured Ian.

"Yyeess!!" we chorused.

"Someone who knows the repertoire," he added.

"Yyyeeesss!!!" we screamed.

"Bye."

Agreement upon those simple, seemingly obvious, facts changed everything. Our list went from endless to minimal in a flash, allowing hope to return.

Someone who ticked these boxes with a big red pen was Gina MacCormack. Gina had devoted most of her life to playing quartets but had recently been spending more time teaching. She was openly thrilled at being asked to come and have a play with us and after only a few hours, we didn't have to think twice about inviting her to join us permanently. Here was someone who not only knew huge chunks of our repertoire but, crucially, understood the life. Gina appeared out of thin air and sprinkled some fairy dust on our wilting enthusiasm. She is not only a formidable player but a delight to work with and a pleasure to be around. Somehow, out of the depths of depression has sprung the most fragrant of flowers. We are continuing our work and are happier than ever.

Though we did one or two things together in the first couple of months of 2019, Gina's real initiation into the group was a three-week tour of Australia and New Zealand. She had never been to this part of the world and consequently this added to the general euphoria we were all feeling. Sydney Opera House followed by the Melbourne Recital Hall is not a bad way to start, and the whole trip was an ideal way to get to know one another. By the time we got to Invercargill (there's a song in there), we were as happy and relaxed as we'd ever been. Gina has all the attributes so vital for this crazy life we lead – she has nerves of steel, is gregarious, enjoys food and wine, and loves to travel, which is just as well since we visited fourteen countries in her first year.

A concert in Ludlow gave Jacky and me a rare opportunity to visit our dear friends, the Viners, who live not twenty minutes south of there on the A44. As we pulled off the M5 on that Friday afternoon it started to rain. This rain intensified, becoming monsoon-like by the evening, and didn't let up for a moment till the next morning. The ensuing deluge left us absolutely unable to get to the venue that afternoon. Try though we might, and try we did, there was no way through. This situation was made all the more bizarre by the fact that our two colleagues, who had tootled up from London, arrived trouble-free in perfect time for our rehearsal. Where they had approached Ludlow from the north, our route arrived from the south and we were currently up to the door sills in a kilometre-long mini lake. Speaking to the promoters on the phone, they likewise couldn't get into town and were suggesting cancelling the show. It was 6.30pm by now and in fairness, only the very determined audience member would have ventured out in these conditions. Nevertheless, Jacky and I are not ones to give up easily and we certainly didn't feel good about Gina and Ian having potentially come all that way for nothing... but what to do? Upon extricating ourselves from the latest watery obstacle, we spotted a farm with a light on. The friendly gent who opened the door could not have expected to hear the unlikely yarn we had to spin but he didn't think twice about helping us overcome our predicament. By the time we had our instruments and cases out of the boot, he had fired up his monster Massey-Ferguson and pulled it up alongside our defeated chariot. With his expert help, we managed to negotiate those final couple of miles, Jacky and I perched high above the water line, clutching our precious cargo. It's true that not everyone who had intended to go that night did, but it was a healthy enough turn out. Incredibly, our friends arrived having made the same journey as us, dry as a bone and ignorant of what had gone on before, the waters on that stretch of road having already receded back to normal levels.

This in-built instinct of 'the show must go on', was tested again not one month later but in very different circumstances. We were in Mexico at the Morelia Festival. We've attended this magnificent event on a few occasions, but this year was special because the festival was to have its very own orchestra. A group of mostly post-graduate students would assemble from all over Mexico and some neighbouring countries with the specific purpose of studying three or four programmes and giving concerts during the festivities. Our involvement was mainly to coach the string sections and give masterclasses, but we also gave concerts and even played a concerto with the orchestra, written by our old mate Javier Alvarez. The whole experience was life-affirming.

On our only night off we all went to a concert by the local professional orchestra, the Micoachan Symphony, at which the granddaddy of Mexican music, Mario Lavista, would be presented with the prestigious Miguel Bernal Jimenez Award. This was a big deal and the large auditorium was filled to the rafters, all eagerly awaiting the varied programme, which would begin with a formal presentation of the award followed by a short piece of Mario's. A Mozart Piano Concerto would finish the first half and Dvorak's 7th Symphony would bring proceedings to a triumphant close before the celebrations began in earnest.

Jacky and I decided to have an early dinner and turned up to the concert at the last minute. Upon entering the crowded foyer, I spied the director of the festival coming down the stairs in earnest conversation with Mario and Javier (there to present the prize to his old teacher), both of whom appeared to be strangely despondent given what was about to unfold. I made my way over to Javier and asked him if everything was ok.

"Hardly," he replied in a gloomy voice. These people were clearly in a state of shock.

"We've just been told that the orchestra will not be playing Mario's piece. They're saying they didn't have enough time to learn the work; but to tell us this now, at the eleventh hour... How can we possibly proceed? Everyone is devastated and at a loss as to what to do."

Faced with this horrifying news and with the final members of the public taking their places, I had to think quickly. Was there anything we could do to save the day? Before I knew what I was saying, I blurted out.

"Ok, here's what we do. Postpone the presentation till after the interval, let the orchestra and soloist play the Mozart, and we will open the second half with Mario's quartet, 'Reflechos de la Noche'."

This threw my friends into a new state of shock. "Are you serious, Paul? Can you guys really do this?" they enquired incredulously.

I knew I could speak for Jacky and Ian – we had been through so much together over the years – but poor Gina, how might she react?

"Listen," I said, "let's just put this plan into action. Worst-case scenario, the evening stays as it is now, right?"

I ran into the auditorium as the conductor was taking to the stage, to find only Ian. I made some frantic gestures to get him out of there, explained the problem and then we set about trying to find Gina. After some toing and froing, it transpired that she hadn't been feeling the best and had decided to turn in for the night. I felt awful but we were desperate and the situation critical. Her phone was on silent but she had left her room phone plugged in (page 9 of the touring booklet... always unplug your hotel phone). I'm ashamed to say that we kept phoning till she picked up. We needn't have doubted her reaction – what a trooper. She jumped out of bed, into the shower and was ready to go in seconds flat. We had security escort us back through the crowded streets to the hall and then to a dressing room backstage. We arrived as the presentation was taking place and were only vaguely aware of the orchestra members' indifference to our arrival. We were too busy getting our stands, music and instruments together to take much notice of the goings-on around us.

The delayed ceremony was fittingly joyous and emotional but alongside all the words of love and praise, Javier left the public in no doubt as to what had happened in the moments before the concert and how he felt about this outrage, and the public voiced their disgust in an impressive display of Latin temperament. Jeers and boos filled the auditorium, interspersed with loud choruses of "Bravo, Mario!"

Once Javier and Mario had retaken their seats, we took to the stage amid a raucous scene. 'Reflechos de la Noche' is a quiet, evocative work in which one uses only harmonics to create the magical sounds of a tropical night. During our rendition, it was impossible not to sense the disquiet unfolding in the wings. Thankfully this disturbance was less audible to the audience, allowing the performance to take place, and we gratefully acknowledged our rapturous reception. As we left the stage for the last time, we were taken in hand by a bevvy of security guards and festival staff, all of whom were visibly tense and afraid.

"Come," they whispered conspiratorially, "we have to get you out of here right now."

We were struggling to get up to speed with the situation. Still in performance mode, we moved involuntarily, our feet barely touching the ground as these bodyguards ducked and dived through the mass of formally dressed musicians, literally carrying us to our instrument cases. Their whispers quickly increased in volume to shouts of, "Quickly now... we haven't time for that. Forget about your music, someone will bring the parts to your hotel. Let's just get you out of here... now!"

As they escorted us back through the betailed, begowned throng, along a corridor to the foyer and into the street, the lamentable scene was becoming riotous. The orchestral manager had taken the microphone and was trying to explain to the public why they had taken the ill-considered, last-minute decision not to play Mario's piece. This was met by deafening whistles and loud roars of derision. Absolute pandemonium set in when the orchestra took the huff and announced that they now weren't going to play the Dvorak either. There was a lot of finger pointing and many people angrily throwing programmes and small change onto the stage in protest as the audience began to spill out into the narrow streets, where they continued to sing our praises and defame the orchestra at the top of their voices.

Obviously we had no idea that our well-intentioned gesture would cause such resentment amongst our peers. We were merely trying to rescue an embarrassing situation for our old friends and, indeed, potentially get the orchestra out of the deep hole they'd dug for themselves. Sadly, we, along with Javier and goodness knows who else, had become villains in their eyes, but luckily, heroes in everyone else's. We escaped the fracas physically unhurt and fervently hope that, with time, our colleagues will calm down, see sense, and we can once again return to our beloved Morelia.

As I mentioned before, in 2000, we recorded the forgotten quartets of Chapi for an organisation called the Sociedad General de Autores y Editores, based in Madrid. We went on to record the chamber music of Remacha and three of the fourteen quartets by one Conrado del Campo y Zabaleta (1878–1953). Del Campo, as he's known, was a brilliant and prolific composer, and it is a crime that his music has been largely ignored since his death. After the tragically early death of the 'Spanish Mozart', Juan Crisostomo Jacobo de Arriaga y Balzola (1806–1826), plain old Arriaga to you and me, not a single string quartet was written in Spain until Del Campo came along. He recognised this deplorable state of affairs and used his not-inconsiderable influence to rally the troops, encouraging his contemporaries not to ignore chamber music. Leading by example, his ruse worked and Spanish composers have happily embraced the idiom ever since. Therefore, when SGAE contacted us again in 2019, asking us if we would consider giving the world premiere of Del Campo's Piano Quintet, we had no hesitation in saying yes. From experience, we guessed this would be a bit of a tour de force so we asked our pal and collaborator, the ivory titan that is Martin Roscoe, to join in the expedition. Nothing could have prepared us for this trip, however – the viola part alone ran to thirty pages and the eventual performance, to over an hour. There's never a break in the technically demanding score, but all is playable and superbly written for all the instruments. If this extraordinary music had Strauss or Mahler emblazoned upon it, it would have established itself in the repertoire and be resounding through the concert halls of the world. As it is, we gave its premiere in the magnificent Fundacion Juan March nearly seventy years after it was written.

January 2020 saw the release of our Late Beethoven box-set and the first of several series highlighting this most revered of all music, at Kings Place. In February we returned to the Royal Conservatoire of Scotland to take part in our first ever Beethoven 'Side by Side Project', which mirrored our Shostakovich Side by Side. Student groups play the early Op.18s, three students and one of us come together to play the middle period works, and we old fogies take care of the lates, culminating in us all getting together to play my arrangement of the Grosse Fuge for string orchestra. These are invariably emotional weeks for all concerned and this one was no exception. Helping youngsters get these complex works up to performance level both physically and mentally is taxing. Playing something like Op.130 in front of your students and peers is unnerving, but perhaps most challenging of all is the actual side-by-side element of the exercise. One feels nervous for them having to go through this testing ordeal but also, frankly, terrified that you yourself might screw up, even slightly. A lot rests on the commitment of the institution and thanks to the hard work and belief of all those at the RCS, we all had a thrilling experience.

The 12th March 2020 found the Brodsky Quartet in fine form. We were returning to Utrecht, so not only would we get to see Gerritjan and Liesbeth Gijzel (long-suffering friends who always put us up when we're in Utrecht) but we would finally get to play in the new Tivoli hall. The old Muzieckcentrum had been like a second home to us, we'd played there so many times back in the '90s and '00s, but it had been demolished in '11 to make way for the new, all-bells-and-whistles Tivoli. Today was to be our debut appearance. Given our history with Utrecht, the more superstitious among you may well suggest that we should have seen it coming – bad things always come in threes.

But we were buzzing and such thoughts never entered our minds as we enjoyed a light lunch in the impressive open-plan foyer café before our rehearsal. Remember, this is where we were back in '03 when I received news of my mother's passing. This is also the same promoter who had been so understanding on the night of the famous Wheel disaster. Therefore, we probably should have realised that when Peter Tra and his assistant approached our table, it wasn't only to greet us with hugs and smiles. They had come directly from watching the Prime Minister give a press conference on live TV in which he announced that the entire country was going into an immediate lockdown.

Covid-19 had hit the Netherlands.

This evil virus had been in the news for the last six weeks and we were expecting some measures to be introduced at some stage (Jacky had spent the last forty-eight hours desperately ensuring that Celia got back from her backpacking trip to Thailand a full month shy of her planned return) but it was deeply shocking when, in that moment, it became real. We flailed around like headless chickens trying to get ourselves home that day, but soon realised that wasn't going to be possible as every flight was already not just full but shamelessly overbooked. Initially grappling with feelings of frustration, we suggested streaming the concert (a fairly radical concept back then) but the management said that the restrictions would have made this impossible. Helpless under the circumstances, they began emptying the building and we gradually expanded into the new day before us. Luckily, we were given permission to remain on site because our hosts were not at home, so we lingered a while over lunch and took photos on the empty stage, all set up for our presence. We lounged around in the spacious new Green Room, collectively trying to piece together what our immediate and long-term futures might look like. We could never have imagined the sci-fi world that would engulf us all within days. As we eventually left the eerily quiet building to walk towards our lodgings, a familiar face passed us in the doorway. It was the owner of the local record store, armed with boxes of our CDs for sale at the concert. His puzzled, despondent visage as we explained what was happening told of a new reality that was slowly but surely unfolding.

The next day we returned home via Stansted, dropped off our things and almost immediately went to pick up Celia at Heathrow. From there we hooked up with Holly, and the four of us went to see Elvis play to a sold-out Hammersmith Apollo. There was such an extraordinary atmosphere in that concert, a real feeling of love between audience and performers, a palpable, euphoric awareness that the world, as we'd known it, was about to change. We were sailing in uncharted waters.

Within forty-eight hours, most of our eighty or so remaining engagements for 2020 had disappeared from our diaries. The Spurs v Man U game that I'd been so looking forward to had been cancelled, along with all sporting events in the foreseeable future. A week later, we in the UK were in total lockdown.

* * *

What a surreal feeling...being forced into the slow lane of this crazy motorway we're all on. To relinquish control and become passive with impunity. To embrace a pace that allows contemplation and consideration, to re-enter your own space. Like this story, normal life is suspended…

It's been five months. In shock from having nowhere to be, nothing to practise for, I haven't so much as opened my instrument case – the first time that's happened in fifty years. I'm finding the experience strangely empowering. Like any crisis in an intimate relationship, the dust needs to settle. I know I still love playing but I want to return to it on my own terms; only when I'm ready, not when needs must. For now, therefore, it's a welcome break… a huge release of pressure. I'm somehow busier than ever. How has that happened? Probably something to do with the fact that I have grasped this opportunity to realise a dream. I have finally, after many years, arranged the three Solo Violin Sonatas of Bach for string quartet. What a marathon… what a joy. Getting inside this extraordinary music is a lifetime highlight.

Feeling lost… quiet and confused… fearful… waves of panic… overwhelming bouts of inadequacy…

Endless requests to get involved in isolated Zoom thingys… perish the thought. An initial crazed avalanche of 'memes' has run its course and now all but fizzled out…

One or two desperate dates resurfacing in the autumn. This will mean having to start limbering up in September ahead of rehearsals throughout October, before these confused promoters realise it's not going to be possible after all, cancel and render our two months of slog useless, OR the concerts go ahead but become two or three performances on the day instead of the planned one. So, wait a minute, who's paying the price there now? We'll have to be on high alert for about six hours instead of the usual two… feeling old, suddenly.

The UK is blacklisting other countries so that people arriving from those places have to quarantine for fourteen days. Spain, France, Holland and Belgium are all on that list. We're due to visit all four of these countries in the autumn. It's all collapsing again. We could be practising for a month and rehearsing for another month to do what will amount to a one-off in London, just at a time when the heavily predicted 'second wave' will be kicking in, leaving potential audience members so afraid of going outside their doors, never mind into a crowded environment, that we'll be playing to ourselves and the two promoters, who will at that stage be not only trying to keep the place afloat, but will also be ushering, doing the lights, bringing us drinks… stage managers who manage the building.

Oh dear, I got pretty down just then. Two weeks ago I lost the plot a bit... what's the point? and all that kinda shit. One does, however, feel suspended in time, which has a tendency to leave you numb, unable to track down and release those sunny endorphins that miraculously put a spring in your step.

Having yesterday felt as though I might never re-energise, today has greeted me with a surge. Thanks to the resilience of Helen Wallace and Rosie Chapman, Kings Place have managed to rearrange the remaining two concerts of our Beethoven Cycle, allowing us to complete it within his 250th anniversary year.

Also, out of the blue, NME has voted my arrangement of Bjork's 'Hyperballad' 'the best remix of all time'. Virus... what virus??!!

Postscript

For all its nastiness, Covid-19 is but a wimp compared to fate, which was about to deal us a cruel blow. No sooner had we returned from that wondrous first trip together than Gina received the shocking news that her husband Leif had been diagnosed with motor neurone disease. True to form, she quietly soldiered on through this horrifying reality, performing her own life's many tasks and only sharing the blow with friends and colleagues at a much later date.

On 2nd February 2021, Gina took the decision to leave the Quartet so she could properly care for Leif. Despite the devastating impact of Covid on our working lives, the two short years Gina spent with us were extremely happy ones, and they have left us with many fond memories of a blossoming relationship sadly cut short.

Dear Gina, we thank you for those memories and send you much love.

It seems like this damned virus is still at large. Am I dreaming? Is this nightmare real? Life no longer unfolds on solid ground. There is no more need for chemicals; life is a constant trip, forming and dissolving at will in the ether.

Out of the ashes of Gina's reluctant departure came an angel by the name of Krysia Osostowicz. Krysia is a firebrand fiddle-player with the warmest of hearts and the sunniest disposition imaginable. Though clearly heaven-sent, Krysia's was not a name out of nowhere. Both Jacky and Ian had known her from National Youth Orchestra days, and though I didn't know her personally, I was well aware of her formidable reputation, which speaks for itself. Fuelled by her tremendously intoxicating zest for *life, we find ourselves able to look forward and once again get excited about where the next turn might take us.*

Welcome, Krysia. Thank you for coming into our lives and keeping the dream alive.

'Legacy'

Playing in a string quartet is not a wise career path for those seeking financial security. Promoters seem to ask themselves, *Shall we have a piano recital or a string quartet? An evening of lieder or a piano trio?* Whatever the answer, the fee remains the same. It's easy to forget that we are four and that a one-off concert somewhere in Europe, for example, takes two, sometimes three days to realise. Then there are the crippling expenses to factor in (travel, food, accommodation, stage clothes, managers), not to mention the hours of practice, both alone and together.

"Ah, it's the repertoire. You get to play some of the greatest music ever written."

This is the stock phrase used by musicians to explain away the mystery as to why anyone in their right mind would do such a job. There's no denying that the quartet literature is second to none, but you can find a few friends, a nice bottle of wine and play these magnificent works any time you want. The performance angle is a massive part of the appeal, but then this lure is not without its perils.

Often, for the group to survive financially, you're forced to take every offer that comes in, but this leads to low morale and eventual burnout. Maintaining a level of self-respect inevitably means much less work, therefore less income, forcing one to look elsewhere for some extra cash. This tends to be hugely destabilising within the group, some people being more successful at these activities than others, leading to availability issues.

Whilst there is a potent argument for expanding your musical horizons, you do have to be insanely committed and put in the gruelling hours; there are no shortcuts, but equally, take care not to squeeze the life out of it.

Another downside to trying to be more considered with your workload is staying in shape. The older you get, the more spaces you have between concerts, the more you face the unenviable task of keeping your playing at the required level.

Over the years, I have gleaned tremendous satisfaction from the creative potential the Quartet has afforded me – dreaming up programmes and projects, doing arrangements, interacting with other musicians and often business people – but increasingly, at this stage of the game, it's the legacy that matters. Playing your best, inspiring the next generation, discovering lost masterpieces, shedding new light on the old favourites. Alongside our copious commissions, I am extremely proud of how we've unearthed top-notch works like Respighi's incredible 'Quartetto Dorico', relentlessly pushed discarded pieces like Elgar's Quartet and his extraordinary Piano Quintet, championed genius works such as the Zemlinsky Quartets, Kreisler, Korngold and Webern – and that's before you get on to Schulhof, Chapi and Del Campo. It's an extensive list.

As the Brodsky Quartet closes in on its fiftieth year, I am happy to report that I feel as motivated today as on that first visit to Manchester. For better or for worse, ideas as to how to augment and present this great repertoire we so cherish keep coming. Though financially the rewards continue to be poor, spending your life studying some of the highest forms of art can only be enriching for the soul. I can honestly say that I still love and cherish my beautiful colleagues and I hope that, in sickness and in health, we may remain together, if not unto death, at least to the point where we all agree to bow out gracefully.

Little bothers me anymore other than bad intonation or duff playing, and I feel blessed that I still relish the daily struggle to keep these evils at bay.

The Brodsky Quartet has given me a hugely fulfilling life, extreme highs and devastating lows. It has also, just by the way, given me the love of my life, Jacky. I hope that some of the lessons I have learnt in dealing with relationships at such close quarters have made me a worthy player in my other quartet, that most beautiful and precious little group that Jacky and I have created together.

Thank you both for coming into our lives, you teach us so much every day, and you have enriched our lives more than you could ever know. Here's to you, Holly and Celia.

'Acknowledgements'

My heartfelt thanks go to all our followers. Without you, no amount of dedication could have seen us survive.

A huge thank you, again, to the lovely Matador team for helping me get this thing off my back.

Much love and gratitude go out to our starship trooper and irreplaceable 'fifth member' Sarah Trelawny Ford. Thank you for expertly plotting our course.

I am, as ever, indebted to Holly at hollycassidycreativemedia.co.uk for masterfully taking my vision of the front cover and making it real.

Last but not least, I would like to acknowledge the mighty composers – those colossal beings who, over the centuries, have magically conjured up the soundtrack to our existence. Imagine a world without music. Avanti!

Matador

For exclusive discounts on Matador titles,
sign up to our occasional newsletter at
troubador.co.uk/bookshop

Also by Paul Cassidy

A comic book character is born, the youngest of sixteen, into a war torn country. Facing extreme brutality at school and on the streets, not to mention the oppression of the Catholic Church, he finds music. Armed with a violin and a burning passion, he escapes the madness and sets off to pursue his dreams.

"Get Beethoven!" is the inspirational story of Paul Cassidy's life. Overcoming adversity in his younger years, Paul recounts tragedy, joy, horror and humour. Informative and entertaining, the book charts his journey up to joining the Brodsky Quartet in 1982.

For more information about Paul and a fun picture gallery to accompany both his books, visit:

www.paulcassidy.org